# Tailwater Trout
in the South

# Tailwater Trout in the South

### A Guide to Finding and Fishing the Region's Man-Made Trout Fisheries

## Jimmy Jacobs

### Second Edition

**Backcountry Guides**
**Woodstock, Vermont**

An Invitation to the Reader

With time, access points may change, and road numbers, signs, and landmarks referred to in this book may be altered. If you find that such changes have occurred near waters described in this book, please let the author and publisher know, so that corrections can be made in future editions. Other comments and suggestions are also welcome. Address all correspondence to:

Fishing Editor, Backcountry Guides, P.O. Box 748, Woodstock, Vermont 05091

Copyright © 1996, 2003 by Jimmy Jacobs
Second Edition

Library of Congress Cataloging-in-Publication Data
Jacobs, Jimmy.
Tailwater trout in the South : a guide to finding and fishing the region's man-made trout fisheries / Jimmy Jacobs.—2nd ed.
p. cm.
ISBN 0-88150-539-0
1. Trout fishing—Southern States—Guidebooks. 2. Southern States—Guidebooks. I. Title.
SH688.U6 J32 2003
799.1'757'0975—dc21

2002038336

Book design by Faith Hague
Cover photo by Polly Dean
Interior photos by the author unless otherwise noted.
Maps by XNR Productions and Jeff Goodwin, © 2003 The Countryman Press

Published by Backcountry Guides, a division of The Countryman Press, P.O. Box 748, Woodstock, VT 05091
Distributed by W.W. Norton & Company, Inc., 500 Fifth Avenue, New York, NY 10110

10 9 8 7 6 5 4 3 2 1
Printed in the United States of America

# Acknowledgments

Special thanks go out to all of the members of Trout Unlimited and the Federation of Fly Fishers who provided information, guidance, and support as I put this book together. Without their help, such a wide-ranging project could not have been possible.

# Contents

# INTRODUCTION

# Tailwaters Today

M uch has changed on the tailwater rivers and streams of the South since the first edition of this book appeared in 1996. Most surprising is that it was necessary to add several new rivers to the list, despite the fact that no new major reservoirs have been built in the region in the ensuing years.

The first of these streams is the Stones River below Percy Priest Lake in Tennessee, where wintertime stocking of trout near Nashville was introduced. Though the tailwater has existed for years, it has only recently become a trout fishery.

Also in the Volunteer State, the tailwaters of the Holston River downstream of Cherokee Lake and just north of Knoxville are now stocked with trout. There were already tailwater fisheries in this river system below South Holston Dam and Patrick Henry Dam, so this creates yet another trout fishing opportunity along the watershed in northeast Tennessee.

In southeast Tennessee, the Ocoee River has also been added. Rainbow trout are now being released downstream of the Parkview (Ocoee No. 3) Dam.

Another addition is the Hiwassee River in western North Carolina, downstream of Lake Chatuge. Although the state of North Carolina has never released trout in this stream, a thriving tailwater fishery exists today—probably the result of private landowners releasing fish on their property and trout moving down from feeder streams.

Finally, in southwest Arkansas, the Ouachita River below Remmel Dam at Lake Catherine is once again a tailwater trout fishery. This river received stockings of trout until the early 1990s, but those efforts were abandoned. Attempts to create a trout fishery, however, have now been revived.

The past seven years have also seen a multitude of changes in fishing regulations and stocking patterns throughout the region's tailwaters. In most instances these changes have been designed to improve the quantity and quality of trout fishing.

Development and road building have continued in some areas as well, often at a breakneck pace. Thus, new roads, altered routes, and renamed thoroughfares abound. These, along with the welcome addition of new parklands and access points on some rivers, are also covered in this edition.

## A LOOK BACK

When discussing trout fishing in the southeastern United States, the natural tendency is to think of the highlands of the Cumberland Plateau or the Blue Ridge and Appalachian Mountains. With regard to wild populations of trout, these are in fact the correct places to look.

The only species of trout native to the region is the brook trout, which is actually a member of the char family. Even in humanity's earliest encounters with the South's trout, brookies were found in a limited range in the mountainous areas of the Carolinas, Georgia, Tennessee, Virginia, and possibly eastern Kentucky. Pressure from human activities and competition from introduced trout species relentlessly pushed the native brookies farther into the high headwater streams. Today, rainbow and brown trout dominate the region's trout fishery.

A milestone in southern trout fishing took place in the 1930s, when the United States Army Corps of Engineers and the Tennessee Valley Authority (TVA) began erecting dams on rivers throughout the region traditionally known as Dixie. The two stated purposes of these efforts were to produce power at hydroelectric facilities at these dams and to control floods on downstream areas. Another driving force of that period was the creation of jobs during the depths of the Great Depression.

Even prior to this great dam-building drive, private power companies had been damming the region's rivers since the early part of the 20th century. Georgia's Tallulah River, for example, had been stifled by a string of dams as early as the 1920s. Eventually, the dam-building frenzy produced

*Earthen or concrete dams are key to creating tailwater trout fisheries in the South.*

reservoirs whose mission statements targeted water-supply storage or even recreational uses.

Although none of the dam construction was begun with the idea of providing more trout fishing in the South, sporting and, in some cases, economic boons to the area have resulted from the creation of exceptional fishing resources. The waters impounded in the new lakes were the first to have an impact on southern fishing, as great largemouth bass fisheries developed in them. Fisheries managers were much slower to recognize the possibilities offered by the tailwaters below the dams. When it was realized, beginning in the 1940s, that the cold waters released through tailraces of these dams could support trout, a new era of angling dawned in the southeastern states.

Today the range of trout in Dixie has—thanks to tailwaters—expanded to include northern Alabama and portions of Arkansas, as well as western Kentucky and Tennessee. More than three dozen tailwaters are recognized by the various states in the region as trout fisheries. They run the gamut from large brawling flows to modest streams. More important, they provide some of the best trout fishing in the South and constitute the waters of this region most likely to give up a trophy-sized trout.

# ANATOMY OF A TAILWATER

To take full advantage of the exceptional trout fishing found in the tailwater rivers of the South, it is necessary to have an understanding of these flows. Knowing the characteristics common to such rivers provides the first hints as to how to fish them. Although at first glance the entire river may look very similar, distinct portions can be identified. Each of these stretches presents different challenges and opportunities to the trout angler.

While some of the tailwater streams of the Southeast do not fit the following description exactly, most will share the elements described. Due, however, to some individual eccentricities, a few of the rivers will lack a portion of the standard run. These exceptions are noted later, when discussing the various streams.

To qualify as a tailwater fishery, the river must, of course, have a reservoir located on it. This impoundment, for our purposes, must create the trout fishery, or at least greatly improve it. This latter qualification is added for waters such as the Cheoah River in North Carolina. The dam at Santeetlah Lake releases virtually no water to the river downstream, but instead diverts the flow through a pipeline to a powerhouse at Cheoah Lake on the Little Tennessee River. Below Santeetlah Dam the Cheoah's flow is provided by feeder streams only, as are the trout, which move down into what is left of the river.

Also, some impoundments in the region do not create tailwater trout fisheries because they dump directly into other lakes. The best example of this is the Little Tennessee River along its course through North Carolina and Tennessee. The river runs through Fontana, Cheoah, Calderwood, Chilhowee, and Tellico Lakes. The first four of these reservoirs support trout, but they do not fit the standard tailwater description because they have no riverine flow.

Now that we have established what a tailwater trout fishery is not, it is time to describe what does make up such a resource. The first essential is a dam constructed to impound the river and regulate the downstream flow. In most cases this will be a huge earth-and-concrete structure that also has a hydroelectric powerhouse for the generation of electricity. Water released from the lake turns the generators within this complex and then flows immediately into a tailrace below the dam. This flow varies from gentle to nonexistent during nongeneration hours to a raging torrent at peak releases. The tailrace often has a concrete-and-rock riprap along its shore, along with a deep hole under the water and immediately below the dam. This hole is created by the violent surges of water through the dam. Often a 100-foot or longer safety zone is imposed directly downstream of the dam, in which boats and wading are forbidden.

The next characteristic section of a tailwater, a portion of river that may be quite short or many miles long, is heavily influenced by the water released during power-generation surges. During generation hours, this part of the river is subjected to huge volumes of water that scour the bottom and sometimes erode steep banks. This portion of a tailwater can be dangerous, as the turbulent water can sweep away a wade-angler or overturn an anchored boat. It is also fairly infertile trout habitat: The scouring of the bottom destroys virtually all aquatic weeds and insect life as well as other food sources on which trout depend. Great caution is needed when fishing on or in the water of this predominantly put-and-take trout fishery.

Next, the standard tailwater goes through several miles of intermediate water. Here the scouring effects of the river surges have lessened. Some insects and aquatic weeds begin to appear, allowing a portion of the trout population to carry over from year to year. Through this part of the river, which will encompass several miles of water, one is likely to see larger fish appearing. Brush heaps, snags, and blown-down trees in the water along the shore are less likely to be swept away by the river's force, providing more cover in which the fish can hide.

The third characteristic area of the tailwater could be called the prime fishing portion. Here the water level still fluctuates with the release schedule of the upstream dam, but the effects have lessened to the point that insects and cover structure are basically unaffected. Trout have a much more constant food supply and plenty of places to hide, so here one will find better, more dependable fishing—particularly around shallow riffle or shoal areas. These areas serve as nurseries for the aquatic insects and crustaceans that make up the lower rungs of the food chain, and provide easy and enjoyable angling. Since this prime fishing area is generally several miles removed from the dam site, it becomes possible—by timing the downstream flow of the released water—to predict times of low water and plan angling excursions to utilize the prime fishing hours.

The final portion of the tailwater is the marginal trout fishing area. This is typically found far downstream, with water temperatures during summer months that make trout survival a dicey proposition. This area may begin anywhere from only a mile or two downriver from the dam on some tailwaters to as much as 60 or 70 miles distant on others.

Through this portion of the flow, insect life is usually present in great abundance, forage fish are readily available, and fishy-looking cover is widespread. Trout, however, are scarce, sharing the habitat with warm-water species such as smallmouth or largemouth bass and bream. As a rule, trout found in this marginal habitat tend to be large specimens—with a decided tendency to be brown trout. These European immigrants do better in turbid, marginal flows than other trout, plus they have an advantage when it comes to competing with warm-water species. Larger brown trout are basically carnivores, so they handle the competition by simply eating their rivals! As a result of this diet, the few trout present grow large quickly and come to dominate their home waters.

## CREATING A FISHERY

As mentioned earlier, tailwater streams provide some of the most outstanding trout fishing opportunities in the South. There are several reasons why these rivers have proven so productive for cold-water anglers. The first has to do with water temperatures.

The reservoirs created by the dams are often deep, ranging from as little as 60 to 80 feet in depth to as many as several hundred. The water released through the turbines of the powerhouses is drawn from near the bottom of the lakes and is quite cold. This fact explains the very existence of trout in most of the tailwater streams in the South. They were at best marginal trout water before the dams; more often, they were turbid, warm-water flows.

Below the dams, though, not only is the temperature ideal for trout (between 45 and 60 degrees), but the water is of a constant temperature year-round. This means that the fish are not only present but they are also enjoying a 12-month growing period, regardless of the air temperatures of the region. Growth rates of ½ inch a month are common, and in some rivers they have been documented at more than 1 inch a month! Such phenomenal growth produces large fish in a hurry. Thus, these tailwaters have a well-earned reputation for yielding large fish as well as large numbers of trout.

Two other facets of these water releases are the dissolved oxygen and the nutrients that the flow carries out of the lakes and into the river downstream. Both are conducive to aquatic weeds, insects, and crustaceans. As a result, the rivers produce great quantities of food for trout downstream of the areas swept clean by the surging water. In some cases, stunned baitfish sucked

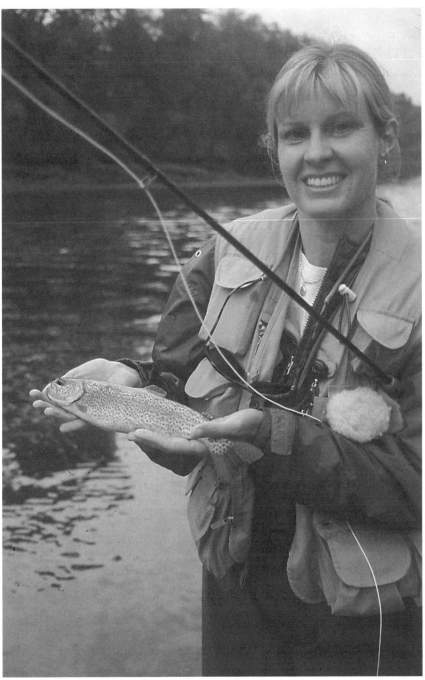

*Polly Dean shows off an average-sized rainbow trout from the
Cumberland River tailwater in Kentucky.*

through the turbines add to the food base near the tailrace. This large supply of biomass is the reason that tailwater fisheries are able to support enormous numbers of fish while producing some truly impressive lunker trout at the same time.

While tailwaters seem to provide excellent habitat for trout, this is not to say that no problems occur. At certain times of year the levels of dissolved oxygen in the depths of the reservoirs can fall so low that the water will not support life. When this water is drawn through the dam and released to the river below, fish kills can take place. This is a particular concern during late summer to early fall and—as noted in the river descriptions—has occurred on several streams with disturbing regularity.

A related problem that also affects the fisheries at times is high water temperatures, especially in times of drought. The period when electric power demand is at its lowest in most southern states is early fall, when the air-conditioning season ends. This, however, is also the period when rainfall is at its scarcest. This means that powerhouses do not need to release as much water, and often there is simply less water to be released. In years of drought, the water levels in some reservoirs have fallen to the point that downstream releases were so infrequent and small that the total trout fishery was placed in peril.

Fortunately, more attention is now being paid to the quality of water introduced into these trout rivers. In particular, the TVA, beginning with a 5-year, $55 million program in 1991, has corrected many of these problems. In some cases weir dams are installed just downstream of the main dams. These weirs create artificial waterfalls to oxygenate the water, lessening the danger of fish kills farther downstream. Another method being used at some dams is the placement of tower intakes, which draw water not just from the bottom of the lake where oxygen levels may be low, but also in part from several other levels. Thus, even if one stratum of water is depleted of oxygen, others will provide a minimum supply for the trout in the tailwater. Finally, the Corps of Engineers, the TVA, and private power companies are making greater efforts (often due to pressure from the angling community) to maintain minimum flows of water through the dams year-round.

Given the large size of most tailwater rivers and the abundant food they carry, the final ingredient making them fisheries is, of course, the fish. It is an unfortunate fact that southern tailwaters generally support almost no natural reproduction of trout. The scouring effect of water releases is not conducive to fish-spawning areas. Additionally, most of the feeder streams are low-altitude, warm-water flows that offer the trout no opportunities for spawning either. While some rivers show indications of very minor spawning activity, even there it is insufficient to support a fishery.

As a result, virtually all trout in tailwater rivers of the South are stocked. While many are caught quickly by anglers in the tradition of put-and-take streams, a couple of circumstances set these rivers apart from standard hatchery-supported waters. To begin with, the size of the rivers and the volume of stocking virtually guarantee that a significant portion of the fish will avoid immediately ending up in a creel. These carryover trout gain weight and inches at phenomenal rates, providing the base for trophy fisheries.

Also, the management scheme employed on some of the rivers is one of put-grow-and-take. The trout are stocked as fingerlings, so that they reach maturity in the rivers. In many cases these fish act like wild, stream-bred trout and are less susceptible to anglers. This is especially true of brown trout.

Tailwater stockings range from a few thousand fish released seasonally on some minor flows of the region to hundreds of thousands of trout planted year-round on the major rivers. The stockings usually consist of rainbow trout, with some browns added. From time to time, brook trout and—in the case of Arkansas' tailwaters-even cutthroat trout are stocked.

As a result of the excellent conditions of the rivers and the often massive infusions of fish, the tailwater rivers of the Southeast are now established as the premier trout waters in nearly every state in the region. Indeed, as we shall see in the descriptions of individual rivers, they also lay claim to being some of the most productive trophy trout waters in the world.

In the following chapters each of the streams recognized as a tailwater trout fishery in Alabama, Arkansas, Georgia, Kentucky, Missouri, North Carolina, South Carolina, Tennessee, and Virginia is discussed. Some of these waters do not fully fit the above description for a number of reasons. Some do not always have hydroelectric facilities, but rather originate in flood-control dams. Others are small flows below the dams, instead of large rivers. But all have waters drawn from the depths of a reservoir, are stocked with trout at some period of the year, and are managed as trout fisheries by the state authorities.

One final note is worth mentioning. With regard to the information provided in the following chapters, I do not claim to be an expert on fishing all, or even any, of the tailwaters discussed. Nor is this book intended to be the ultimate word on how to extract trout from them. Complete volumes could be written on the peculiarities and joys of wetting a hook in several of the rivers. Obviously, no one angler could produce a book that definitively speaks to the subject of how to fish all these tailwaters from his or her own experiences. Such knowledge would require several lifetimes.

What this book is designed to do is provide a brief overview of each tailwater. Much of the information was gleaned from fisheries biologists, state publications, and picking the brains of anglers, along with some firsthand fishing experiences by the author. The other aim of this book is to provide some information on where the public access areas are located and what rules and regulations apply to specific rivers. Be aware, however, that regulations can and will change in all of the states. Get a copy of the most current state fishing regulations before heading to any of the rivers, and read them with an eye toward recent rule changes.

# MAPS

Even the best fishing is useless to the sportsman unable to locate the river or its access points. The key is having some good maps. If you opt for relying on official road maps published by the states covered or upon United States Geological Survey (USGS) 7.5-minute quadrangle maps you face several challenges. In the case of the road maps, major federal and state highways are shown, but secondary roads are often lacking. Not a great deal of attention is paid to the exact locations of waterways, either. After all, these are road maps.

The USGS maps are great at showing the topography of an area, but they can be as much as 15 to 20 years old. This makes them useless for finding many of the newer secondary roads needed to reach access points on various rivers.

Fortunately, the availability of good standardized maps has greatly improved in the years since the first edition of this book appeared. The very best of these for showing tailwaters and access points are in the Atlas & Gazetteers published by the DeLorme Mapping Company of Yarmouth, Maine. These multipage map books show secondary and dirt roads, usually providing street or road names. In the case of forest service roads and trails, numbers are also provided. Additionally, many unincorporated communities and place names along the rivers are included. Enough detail can be found in these maps to make it easy to locate the streams covered in this book. Gazetteers are now published for all states included in this volume. The page number from the appropriate DeLorme gazetteer is listed beneath the name of each river in this book.

The gazetteers for individual states are available in chain discount stores or many sporting good and tackle shops throughout each state. They can also be obtained directly by contacting the DeLorme Mapping Company, P.O. Box 298, Yarmouth, ME 04096 or calling 207-846-7000. You can also visit their web site at www.delorme.com for more information.

In all but one case, these gazetteers are all that you need to find your way to the South's tailwater rivers. That exception is found on Georgia's Chattahoochee River. Its tailwaters flow through the suburbs and urban sprawl of metropolitan Atlanta, and the sheer number of roads located in a finite area makes using the gazetteer very difficult, especially as the river nears that major city. There is simply not enough room on the page for the amount of detail required to find all the access points in sections of the Chattahoochee River National Recreation Area located along the stream.

The National Park Service provides a solution to this problem in the form of a free brochure containing a detailed map of the Chattahoochee and all its public access points along the tailwater from Lake Sidney Lanier downstream to the end of trout water in Atlanta. This publication can be requested by contacting the Chattahoochee River National Recreation Area, 1978 Island Ford Parkway, Dunwoody, GA 30350 or by calling 770-399-8070.

The maps accompanying each chapter in this book show roads, towns, and landmarks that should aid in locating access points on the various tailwaters. They are most helpful when used in conjunction with the maps suggested above.

All the road names, numbers, and other landmarks used here were current when this book went to press. Be aware, however, that town, county, and state authorities often rearrange these. In particular, state departments of transportation are seemingly forever at work on the road systems. This often entails placing, replacing or removing—and at times neglecting to install—street, road, or highway signs at intersections. At other times road widening ends up removing some prominent landmark or sign that is mentioned in the directions to the river. Such instances are unavoidable, since the only thing that can be counted on is that things will change.

# CHAPTER 1

# Tailwater Tactics

It takes but a couple of fishing trips to a tailwater river to discover that the trout angling on these flows is quite different from that found on small mountain streams. Being an accomplished trout stalker on mountain brooks does not ensure success when the action moves to one of these magnum-sized, trout-rich habitats. There is a transition period involved for most anglers in which they must unlearn some old lessons while absorbing some new ones.

As a result, some trout enthusiasts never develop a taste for tailwaters, despite the numbers and size of the fish available. It is not unusual to run into anglers who spend inordinate amounts of time chasing highland trout, but shun the tailwaters. On the other hand, someone who learns trout fishing on large tailwater rivers is just as likely to express disdain for those "little fish" found in mountain habitats.

With tailwater fishing—as with fishing in any southern stream—a variety of tackle is found in the hands of the angling public, and the easiest way to define the various types of anglers is by their terminal tackle. The percentage of fly-fishers is usually a bit higher on tailwaters, due to the open fishing conditions. The overhanging foliage found on mountain brooks is not a problem here. Though some bushes line the rivers, there are also vast expanses of open water over which to let out some line. These are streams that beg for the graceful poetry of classic fly-casting.

Still, bait-fishers or anglers armed with spinning gear and small artificial lures heavily outnumber the fly-casters. In the case of the bait-anglers, the

South's tradition of "meat-fishing" is usually the driving force. Catching the state limit of trout, to be cleaned and served at suppertime, is what brings them to the river. This is not to say that fly-fishers or spinning-lure fanciers do not also take home some fish for the skillet. A number of them, however, simply fish for the fun of the sport, releasing most or all of their catches. Such altruism is rarely found in bait-fishers.

There is also a "hybrid" or crossover category of anglers on the tailwater rivers of Dixie. The big water and the possibility of big fish attract a number of folks who could be called "converted" bass anglers. The "converted" part of the description is used with tongue in cheek, however, since these anglers are unlikely to give up their pursuit of the South's favorite fish, the large-mouth bass. It is just that the chance of hooking into a huge trout is enough to make them backslide a bit and spend some time on a tailwater. These anglers are unlikely to use fly-rods or even light or ultralight spinning tackle. Instead, expect to see them fishing from boats (the standard bass boat if boat ramps and water levels permit) and using bait-casting equipment with natural baits—often minnows, where these are legal—or perhaps a jerkbait or crankbait, as for bass.

Crossover anglers usually concentrate their fishing directly below the dams and tailraces of the larger rivers, in order to take advantage of the dependable "hatches" of baitfish sucked through the turbines of the dam during power generation. These stunned shad and other forage fish litter the surface, weakly twitching, providing the larger trout with a dependable and abundant food source. Anglers who present live minnows or minnow-imitating lures at these times can fool some magnum-sized rainbows and browns.

# GEARING UP

## Fly-Fishing

As mentioned, the number of fly-fishers is higher on tailwaters than on most other southern streams. The open water is part of the appeal to these folks, but since the release of the movie version of Norman Maclean's *A River Runs Through It*, the urge to fly-cast has stricken even more people, especially novice anglers. Since many of the tailwaters are quite close to the metropolitan areas where most of these new fly-casters live, the rivers attract inordinate numbers of them. Of course, the excellent quality of the fly-fishing in the tailwater streams might have something to do with the phenomenon as well.

The gear used by fly-casters is more important to success on tailwaters than it is on smaller streams. On a mountain creek, an angler simply needs a rod he or she can handle, a floating line, and a reel of any description to store the line. On a large tailwater, however, a number of situations arise that call for specific reels, lines, or rods.

In the case of rods, longer and heavier-weight models are preferable. These open waters can make punching a cast into the wind a necessity. Another consideration is that weighted streamers, which are often productive flies, are difficult to cast with light, short rods. Six- to 7-weight rods that are 8 to 9 feet long are ideal for tailwater angling.

In the arena of fly-lines, tailwaters contain deep runs and river bends where it is necessary to get a streamer or nymph down deep to where the fish are holding. This may call for sinking or sink-tip lines—which are virtually never needed on smaller mountain waters. Some nylon backing for the fly-line is also advisable, since hooking a truly big trout in water where it has plenty of room to run is possible.

For the same reason, it is important to have a fly-reel with a good drag system. When that trout-of-a-lifetime takes your fly, you need a reel that helps rather than hinders the fight. The reel should have enough line capacity for 100 yards of backing, since a large fish can find open water into which it can make 50- or 100-yard runs.

Undoubtedly the biggest difference between fly-casting on a southern mountain stream and the same sport on a tailwater is the selection of flies. Mountain-stream fish are opportunistic in their feeding habits because of their infertile habitat. They eat whatever is available, in most cases, and they eat it whenever possible. Matching the hatch is irrelevant when pursuing trout in this environment.

The reverse is ordinarily true on the tailwaters of the South. Many of these are big, fertile waters. Fish grow large here because they have plenty to eat and their menu has plenty of variety. As a result they can be picky eaters, sometimes keying on a few insects, or even a single variety. The fly-caster who does not present a proper imitation of that food item is likely to come away without having fooled many fish.

While each river has its idiosyncrasies, there are several classes of trout foods common to most of them. The insect and invertebrate life that is important in the individual rivers is mentioned in later sections. Here the emphasis is on covering the broad classes of trout foods common to many of the rivers. These are covered in lay terms rather than in a form designed to send entomologists into fits of ecstasy. Providing enough information about the insects to aid fishing success is the main concern.

Among the most important and widespread insect forms in southern waters are the caddisflies of the order Trichoptera. These critters come in a wide variety of sizes and colors across the Southeast, with the common trademark of the order being the way the insects' wings lie on their backs—swept to the rear when folded.

The nymphs (actually the larval stage of the insect's life cycle, but ordinarily referred to as "nymphs" by anglers) of the caddisfly are case-builders that actually mold homes for themselves by gluing together tiny pebbles, sticks, or other materials to create a tube in which to live. Although trout will eat these worms, case and all, they are not usually imitated by southern flycasters, since the cases are often stuck to rocks along the bottom. When you hear an old-time angler in the South speak of using "stickbait" for trout, he is referring to baiting up with these tiny larvae or the entire nymph cases.

Caddis nymphs are vulnerable to predation when they begin moving to the surface of the water to hatch into the adult version of the bug. Trout feed on the nymphs swimming to the surface, on the emergers shucking their shells as they float in the surface film, and on the adults trying to take off from the surface.

A number of nymph-pattern flies will take trout from tailwater streams when the fish are feeding on caddis. In this type of fishing, exactly matching the food source seems to be unimportant. Just getting close in size ordinarily does the trick. Gold-Ribbed Hare's Ears or Tellico Nymphs in sizes 12 to 20 have produced fish from nearly all of the South's tailwaters when the fish were keying on immature caddis.

Once the caddis reach the surface, both the size and the color of the flies become more important. Often trout will ignore any size or color fly that does not match the size or color of what they are feeding on at the moment. Elk Hair Caddis and Chuck Caddis patterns tied in a number of sizes and colors are good choices for this fishing.

The second broad category of aquatic insects of importance is mayflies of the order Ephemeroptera. Suffice it to say that these bugs, which have an adult life span of little more than a day, are about as widespread and abundant as caddisflies in the region. The easiest way to differentiate mayfly from caddis adults is to look at their wings. Mayflies have wings that stand upright, unlike the caddis's wings, which lie on its back.

While in the nymphal stage, mayflies come in four distinct varieties.

Some are free-ranging, swimming as they feed. Others are usually found crawling on the undersides of rocks on the streambed. Still others spend their time clinging to the tops of rocks on the river bottom. Finally, some are burrowers, making their nymphal home in the mud and silt of slow-water areas. Since they are not glued to the bottom like some caddis nymphs, they are more likely to be available to the fish while in this stage of their life cycle. This is especially true of the free-swimming and clinging varieties.

As with caddisflies, mayflies are vulnerable to trout when hatching. As nymphs swimming to the surface, as emergers, and as adults, they present appetizing targets. In size they also resemble the caddis, so hooks in the size 12 to 16 range are in order. Standard flies to match the mayfly nymphs are the popular Hare's Ear and the Pheasant Tail.

Adult mayflies come in a wide variety of colors, so matching the hue of the bugs the trout are feeding on is again important. Patterns that work well at times are the Light Cahill, the Adams (regular and female), and the Hendrickson.

Although tiny in size, midges (order Diptera) are a more important food source for trout in tailwaters than they are in smaller streams. These minute insects favor slow currents and slick surfaces, as opposed to rough-and-tumble shoal water. Trout often feed on them in spring through fall, as well as on warm winter days.

Describing the shape of midges is pretty much an exercise in futility, since they usually appear as just swarms of specks on or over the water. While true midges are of the family Chironomidae, most anglers refer to all extremely small flies as "midges." In fact, tiny dry flies that imitate mayflies, such as the Adams, Light Cahill, or Blue-Winged Olive in hook sizes 18 down to 22, are often the choice of anglers casting to midge hatches; the Griffith's Gnat and Olive Midge are also popular. Many times, more than one of these flies will catch fish during a single hatch, since fly color seems to mean less than size when it comes to midge fishing.

Next among insects important as trout food is the order Plecoptera—the stoneflies. While several hundred species of these bugs have been identified in southern tailwaters, their life cycle makes them a bit less vulnerable to the fish than the insects I mentioned above. But since they tend to be larger morsels, the trout are attracted to them when they are available.

During the nymphal stage, stoneflies are bottom-dwellers, crawling on and under the rocks on the streambed. Fish will grab them when they are on exposed surfaces or when they are dislodged and floating in the current.

Eventually the nymphs climb out onto rocks or sticks above the surface to hatch into adults. Their drying nymphal cases are often found sticking to rocks or driftwood along the shore during these periods. Because the nymphs do not swim to the surface, they are more difficult for trout to catch at this stage. Still, flies such as the Ted's Stonefly or Montana Nymph can attract the attention of feeding fish. Larger hooks in sizes 6 to 10 are called for when tying stonefly nymph patterns.

When adult stoneflies have hatched and are laying eggs on the water's surface, their large size will attract trout. The fish attack these insects with great gusto, often creating noisy, violent rises. These hatches usually occur in rocky shoal areas, since the stonefly inhabits areas of the stream that have moving currents and are well oxygenated.

The key to catching trout feeding on stonefly adults is to put a big fly on the water. Elk Hair Caddis and Royal Trudes are two choices; the size should be 6 to 12. Speaking frankly, however, such surface action for stoneflies is a rarely encountered novelty on southern tailwaters.

Terrestrial insects are another common item on the tailwater trout's menu. These are land-dwelling or flying insects that spend no part of their life cycle in the water. It is simply bad luck that finds them falling or being blown into the rivers. Once there, they become fair game for hungry trout.

Grasshoppers, beetles, and ants (both crawling and flying) comprise the bulk of this category. Hoppers can provoke splashy surface action during the summer, as can Japanese beetles on some waters. There are a number of popular grasshopper-pattern flies—any of which is a good choice when the fish are explosively rising to the critters—as well as Japanese beetle imitations. Size 10 or 12 is about right for either of these. Good all-around choices to imitate other types of beetles are the Humpy and Goofus Bug series of flies. These are tied in a variety of colors; sizes 12 to 14 are good.

However, the most dependable of the terrestrials is the common ant. It is almost impossible to find a trout that does not have ants in its stomach if these insects are present. Red and black are the standard colors and sizes 16 down to 22 are preferable.

Another category of trout appetizers found in tailwater streams is crustaceans. These include crayfish ("crawfish" or "crawdads" to southerners), cress bugs, scuds, sow bugs, and freshwater shrimp. Of these, the crawfish, scuds, and sow bugs are most important to tailwater anglers.

The scud is the most plentiful regionwide. These tiny, hard-shelled relatives of the shrimp often thrive in water that has some aquatic vegetation.

Where they are present, they are generally quite small. Dead-drifting flies in sizes 18 to 22 under a strike indicator is the standard tactic when trout are keying on scuds.

Sow bugs tend to be similar to scuds in the eastern part of the region, but larger and more important in the western. Anglers headed to the rivers of Arkansas are advised to stock their fly boxes with some sow bug imitators in sizes 12 to 16.

Although crawfish are eaten by trout, and spin-fishers take the fish on crawfish imitations, the critters go largely ignored by fly-casters. Working a weighted crawfish pattern along rocky bottoms will improve the chances of tangling with the larger trout present.

Another form of trout food worth mentioning with regard to fly-fishing is worms. In this case, "garden hackle" or common earthworms are not the topic. Rather, at certain times, inchworms fall into the rivers in large numbers and some flows are inhabited by aquatic red worms. A light green worm pattern in hook size 12 or 14 works well when inchworms are present, while San Juan Worms in the same size are good patterns to imitate the aquatic worms.

The last important denizens of the tailwaters that trout use for food are minnows. As explained earlier, besides healthy swimming minnows, the area just below the tailrace of the rivers is sometimes littered with injured ones that were sucked through the turbines. Casting streamers such as the Woolly Bugger, Muddler Minnow, or Matuka in sizes that approximate the baitfish's length can produce some big trout.

### Bait-Fishing

For the bait-fisher, the baits that prove productive on tailwaters are the same as those that serve in mountain streams across the region. Crickets, earthworms, and salmon eggs adorn the hooks of those inclined to use natural baits, while cheese concoctions and kernel corn are also popular. The bulk of tailwater bank-fishers use bait, but bait-anglers will also take to the water in boats. For whatever reason, bait-fishers rarely wade in tailwater rivers.

### Spin-Fishing

Spin-fishers who prefer to toss artificial lures at the trout often employ in-line spinners, such as those produced by Blue Fox, Mepps, Panther Martin, and Rooster Tail. These all have a spinning blade up front, followed by a weighted metal body, then by either a single or treble hook. The hook may or may not be covered by a hair skirt. In-line spinners come in a wide variety of color schemes and body shapes and have long been staples in the tackle boxes of southern anglers, regardless of the size or type of water they tackle. The lures range in weight from $\frac{1}{32}$ ounce up to 2 ounces. Tailwater anglers are more likely to use $\frac{1}{2}$ ounce or larger sizes, which are rarely employed by small-stream fishers in this region.

Two more types of artificial offerings that spin-fishers present to tailwater trout are the crankbaits and jerkbaits ordinarily used for bass fishing. The crankbaits may be ultralight versions—often as small as $\frac{1}{10}$ ounce—of the original lure patterns. On the other hand, some fishers cast the originals—bass-sized models of up to $\frac{1}{2}$ ounce. Either way, crankbaits imitate baitfish or crawfish, and are retrieved with a steady "cranking" of the reel handle.

Jerkbaits float on the water's surface and get their name from the fact that they are twitched or "jerked" to simulate injured baitfish struggling to swim. In tailwaters, jerkbaits have proven very effective when fished around shoreline logjams and brush piles or in the tailrace just below the turbine outlets. They usually account for the magnum-sized trout taken in the larger rivers.

Spin-fishers are just as likely to wade the river as to fish from a boat or float tube. It is not unusual to encounter such anglers casting from shore.

The rods and reels used to present baits or lures range from ultralight models on up to heavy bait-casting rigs. This variety results in part from the differences in weight of the lures being cast, but also from individual angler preferences. The only requirement is that the gear be suitable to get the chosen lure out to where the fish are.

# CHAPTER 2

# Tackling Tailwaters

Trout fishing traditionally has been thought of as a sport practiced afoot. In Europe, where it began, it was thought of as a shorebound endeavor as well. Even today, it is considered bad form to wade into the water on English chalk streams. While some angling from boats was practiced on lakes, flowing waters were the bank-fisher's territory.

As with many other customs, however, we Americans took a more tolerant view. From the first days of pursuing trout on this continent, anglers used whatever means were needed to get to the fish. Very early on, trout fishers were wading streams as well as fishing from the shore, and they took to the water to float-fish from boats when necessary.

This utilitarian approach to angling has carried over nicely to modern-day tailwater trout fishing in the Southeast. In fact, one is hard-pressed to make a definitive statement on which of the three methods—bank-fishing, wading, or floating—is most prevalent in the region. On an individual stream there may be a clear winner, but in total the distinction would be difficult.

## REACHING THE FISH

Fishing from shore has been popular since the gates were closed on the first hydroelectric dam in Dixie. This is particularly true among bait-fishers. Shore-fishing was a natural carryover from river-fishing for warm-water species or from pursuing trout in smaller streams of the mountains.

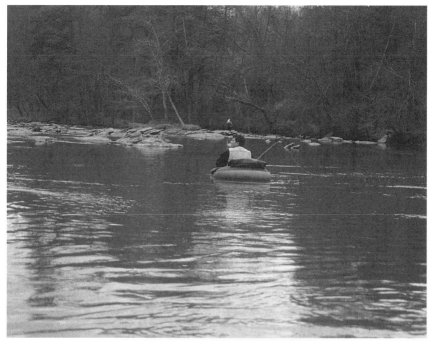

*Whether you call it a float ring, a belly boat, or a float tube, it is an ideal craft from which to fish southern tailwaters.*

Much of the early bank-fishing with bait was concentrated in the tail-race area, where concrete fishing platforms are located. Another factor was that trout were generally stocked at the foot of the dams. There was almost always roadside access to the water at these points, allowing the hatchery trucks to deposit their fish easily. Naturally, where the fish are known to be is where the anglers congregated.

Of course, in the ensuing years, anywhere that permitted shorebound anglers easy access to the tailwater became a popular fishing hole. Some spin-fishers tossing artificial lures from shore also practiced their art at these access points, but the need for mobility in order to cover more water limited this type of bank-fishing. Repetitive casting of a lure into a single area lacked appeal for these fishers, as well as rarely being very productive.

The next progression was taking to the water in boats. This step was taken by both bait-anglers and spin-fishers. The use of smaller, flat-bottomed johnboats came first, but as better access to the water in the form of gravel or paved boat ramps evolved, anglers used larger boats where practical. Again, this fishing was at first concentrated around the dam tailraces, giving the anglers better access to the water they were already fishing. Later, it developed into float-fishing from one access point to another.

Eventually, johnboats were joined on the tailwaters by canoes, V-hulled crafts, and inflatable rafts. Particularly in cases of rafts and canoes, anglers traveled farther and farther downstream. Both of these crafts made good vehicles for float-fishing from access point to access point.

More recently, float tubes have shown up in increasing numbers on the South's deeper tailwater rivers. These devices, which were originally adapted from automobile inner tubes, have now become quite sophisticated. Today's float tube comes complete with a fabric seat inside the tube, suspenders to raise it out of the water when wading shallow areas, a variety of zippered or Velcro-closure pockets, and fins that fit onto the feet for locomotion through the water. The modern float tube allows anglers, regardless of their preferred fishing method, to cover the whole river conveniently and with limited expense.

Another innovation seen more often on southern rivers is the use of McKenzie drift boats by some guide services. These river dories, pointed at one or both ends, have belatedly made their way from western and Pacific waters to our eastern tailwaters. Such crafts, in the hands of skilled oarsmen, are more maneuverable than johnboats and more stable than canoes, making them ideal for fishing. Since drift boats require one person always to be at the oars, they have always been more of a guide's boat. Now that tailwater fishing guides are more common on southern waters, the McKenzie boat has appeared as well.

The final method used in fishing tailwaters in the South is wading into shoals. While this has always been common for fishing smaller streams, it is relatively new to tailwaters. It is also limited on many such flows due to their lack of shallow shoals. On other streams, however—particularly at low water levels—virtually the whole river is conducive to this type of approach. In the case of several area rivers it is also possible to find some wadable areas even at higher water levels.

Wading has always been more popular with spin- and fly-casters than with bait-anglers. Still, one major drawback has been that shore access is needed to get into the water. Most tailwater rivers are considered navigable and are, therefore, open to unrestricted boating and floating. Land along the shore that is in private hands may be posted, however, preventing easy access. This is an all-too-common problem on these waters.

# TAILWATER SAFETY

The single greatest safety concern on tailwater rivers is the water surge that occurs during power generation at the dam. While this is the major distinguishing characteristic of this type of trout water, it is also the major threat to life and limb for the anglers utilizing these fisheries.

On some of the region's smaller tailwaters, such releases may raise the water only a couple of feet, while streams like Arkansas' White River, Kentucky's Cumberland, and Georgia's Chattahoochee can rise by as much as 6 to 8 feet very quickly. Even a 2-foot rise, however, is enough to be life-threatening.

On most tailwaters, fishing activity is virtually nil during high-water periods. These streams have a tendency to turn into violent torrents of muddy water, making angling difficult, if not impossible. As with any rule, however, there are exceptions. The White and Cumberland Rivers mentioned earlier, as well as the Nantahala in North Carolina, are noted for providing fishing opportunities at all water levels.

Probably the most dangerous aspect of water releases on tailwaters is their unpredictability. One of the major purposes of most reservoirs is the generation of electric power. During the spring and summer in the South-

*Many tailwater rivers are large enough that you can fish for trout by boat.*

east, a driving force of power demands is the use of air conditioners. The resulting peak demands tend to fall during the time of the year when interest in fishing these waters is also at its height.

Although efforts are made to establish water-release schedules and to make them public, if power demands require additional hours of generation, unscheduled water surges do occur. This, of course, creates very dangerous conditions for the unwary wader or boater downstream. All dams have published phone numbers that provide recordings of the scheduled power-generation hours. These also include a disclaimer stating that the plans are tentative, and unscheduled releases are possible.

Other safety precautions include powerhouse sirens, which are sounded several minutes prior to the opening of the turbine gates. These are usually powerful enough to be heard several hundred yards downstream. Needless to say, when they do sound, any sane bank- or wade-angler heads for the high-water mark. Boaters also need to get off the flow or be prepared for the rapidly rising water.

In some instances, low-power radio transmitters have been used at the dams to broadcast release schedules, including any sudden change of plans. Signs are posted along the river instructing visitors to tune their radios to a specific AM setting to hear the recorded messages. While these broadcasts can be received up to several miles down the river, few anglers tend to take a radio on the water with them. For this reason, such broadcasts have not been particularly effective.

Naturally, the area of most serious concern on any tailwater is the portion of the river immediately below the dam. From the tailrace to a couple hundred yards downstream, the surge is violent and immediate when water is released. Thus, some special rules apply to fishing these areas.

Wading or even fishing from shore is forbidden below the high-water mark within a safety zone immediately downstream of the dams on some streams. Also, boaters on the water in the tailrace area are mandated to wear Coast Guard–approved life jackets at all times. In some instances, such as on the Savannah River below Hartwell Lake on the Georgia–South Carolina border, the safety zone is completely closed to wading and boating.

The best rule of thumb for fishing tailrace areas on any river is to find out what regulations apply and follow all of them to the letter, while remaining aware of your surroundings. There is always the chance that you will not hear the siren announcing an imminent release. Anytime that you see other anglers scurrying for shore, it is wise to follow them. It could be that

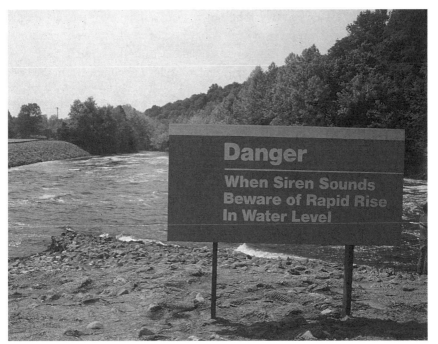

*Fast-rising water is a safety concern on all southern tailwaters.*

they are just in a hurry to get ashore for a snack or cold drink; but they may have heard something you did not. Tailrace areas are great places to err on the side of caution!

Due to the fact that most anglers are so aware of the potential for trouble near dams, these areas actually end up being responsible for fewer problems than portions of the river farther downstream. On most flows, it is the part of the stream a couple miles downriver that accounts for most rescue situations or drownings. In these areas, dam sirens are out of anglers' hearing range, so water releases can take them by surprise.

The best defense against trouble here is to always pay attention to the water level. Since a surge has to travel several miles from the dam, the water will not rise instantly. By mentally marking the water level on a rock, log, or other feature on shore and monitoring it constantly while fishing, it can be seen when the level begins to rise and anglers will have several minutes to get to shore. It is lack of attention or procrastination that leads to life-threatening situations.

It is impossible to put too much emphasis on the fact that anglers should obey all the posted or published safety rules applying to the various rivers.

These are not designed simply as nuisances or to rain on one's parade. People have lost their lives on tailwater rivers because of foolhardiness or just bad luck. The regulations were developed to make fishing these waters safe.

One other safety concern on tailwaters is water temperature. On the bulk

*Low water and morning mists make the Sipsey Fork of the Warrior River in Alabama an ideal stream for fly fishing.*

of these waters, year-round temperatures are in the 45- to 60-degree range. These levels are conducive to hypothermia for the individual exposed to them for very long. If an unexpected dunking occurs while boating or wading, get out of the water as quickly as possible and take appropriate measures to restore body heat immediately. One of the dangers of hypothermia is that a person suffering from it can become disoriented and is often incapable of helping him- or herself. Thus it is always wise to have a fishing buddy along to offer aid in the event of trouble.

Several manufacturers now produce fishing vests, wader suspenders, or belt packs that have built-in flotation devices. These use a carbon dioxide cartridge to inflate compartments when an activation ring is pulled. Although many such devices are not Coast Guard–approved as personal flotation devices, they do add a margin of safety for the wade-angler, and some models have now received Coast Guard approval. If you get caught in rising water, or simply wade into a deep hole, the price of this additional equipment may seem very reasonable.

# Alabama

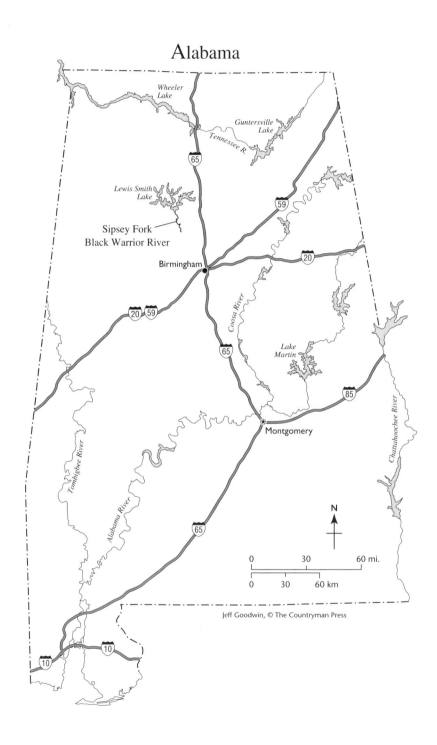

Wheeler Lake

Guntersville Lake

Tennessee R.

65

59

Lewis Smith Lake

20

Sipsey Fork
Black Warrior River

Birmingham

Coosa River

20  59

65

Lake Martin

85

Chattahoochee River

Montgomery

Tombigbee River

Alabama River

65

N

| 0 | | 30 | | 60 mi. |
| 0 | | 30 | 60 km | |

65

10

10

10

Jeff Goodwin, © The Countryman Press

# Chapter 3

# Alabama

When discussing trout water, there are few places in the United States less likely to pop into most folks' heads than the state of Alabama. Nestled between Mississippi on the west and Georgia to the east, this state stretches from the Gulf of Mexico to just north of the Tennessee River valley. The bulk of the land in the southern and central portions of Alabama is on the coastal plain. It then fades into the southernmost foothills of the Blue Ridge mountain chain in the northern edge of the state. Alabama is known as the Cotton State for its close association with that agricultural commodity, which was once king in Dixie. It is, however, not a plant that is synonymous with trout country.

Alabama had no natural trout populations within its borders when the first Europeans entered the area. Indeed, the highlands in the northeastern corner of the state are composed of sandstone ridges separated by limestone valleys, which make for poor cool-water habitat, particularly at the Cotton State's latitude.

Alabama's fisheries managers have experimented with introducing trout to the state—with mixed results. Some seasonal trout fishing exists in Madison County Lake, a state-operated pond north of Huntsville, as well as in the streams of Tannehill State Park near Birmingham. The former is a fall and winter fishery; Tannehill offers strictly spring put-and-take fishing.

On the other hand, attempts to establish brown trout in the streams of the Talladega National Forest in the northeast of the state proved unsuccessful. One oddity is that Alabama's state record for rainbow trout (there is no official record for any other species of trout) was caught in Weiss Lake, a Coosa River impoundment that straddles the Georgia border. The 7-pound, 2-ounce fish was caught by a crappie fisherman in 1991 and is reportedly the only trout ever taken from the lake. It undoubtedly found its way downstream from a stocking done on a fork of the Little River in northwestern Georgia.

On a more positive note, a successful and growing trout fishery has been established on the tailwaters of the Sipsey Fork of the Black Warrior River below Lewis Smith Lake in the hill country of northwestern Alabama. This is also the only tailwater trout stream found in the Cotton State.

There is no closed season for trout fishing in Alabama; the creel limit is five fish per day, regardless of species of trout. No minimum or maximum size limits apply to trout taken from tailwaters.

To fish for trout in Alabama requires only a regular resident or nonresident fishing license. These may be purchased over the telephone by calling 1-888-848-6887. A Visa or MasterCard is required for the transaction.

## SIPSEY FORK BLACK WARRIOR RIVER

### DeLorme 24

Located in the northwest portion of the state near the town of Jasper, the Sipsey Fork of the Black Warrior River is Alabama's only tailwater trout fishery. The tailwater begins at the base of the dam at 21,200-acre Lewis Smith Lake and flows in a southeasterly direction for about a dozen miles before dumping into the Mulberry Fork of the Black Warrior River. Along this course the river forms the border between Cullman and Walker Counties. The dam and powerhouse at the lake are operated by the Alabama Power Company.

With no real competition, the Sipsey tailwater is the Cotton State's premier trout water. For a number of years this would have been a misleading statement, indicating simply that the Sipsey was the only site of regular put-and-take stocking in Alabama. Fortunately, new meaning has been attached to the claim in recent years due to the efforts of the Birmingham Fly Fishing Club. By bringing pressure on Alabama Power to improve the fishery below Lewis Smith, as well as rolling up their collective sleeves and pitching in on manual labor, the local angling club has made this tailwater a promising resource.

Jeff Goodwin, © The Countryman Press

The Sipsey Fork begins as a warm-water flow. When it exits Lewis Smith Lake it is a 50- to 60-foot-wide river, carrying waters from the bottom of the reservoir that are well within the temperature range needed by trout. The first rainbows were stocked in the river back in the early 1960s, but the fishing was lackluster then. Any carryover of fish from year to year appeared to be minimal, and—particularly in the upper stretch of water near the dam—the river was quite infertile. Very little food was present for the fish, even if they did manage to avoid anglers' hooks. This lack of aquatic insect life continues to plague the area immediately below the dam. Turning over rocks on the streambed through here will reveal virtually no bug life.

From the dam downstream to the Birmingham Water Authority pumping station on the eastern shore, the river is very shallow, crystal clear, and extremely cold during low-water periods. This roughly ½-mile stretch is quite popular with anglers, since it is almost all wadable. Below this point the river broadens to about 70 or 80 feet, and becomes deeper as well. This lower portion appears more suited to floating in a canoe or float tube, but a gravel-and-mud shelf extends out from the accessible east bank. This shelf allows anglers to get out to the main channel during low water, providing limited access for wading much of this area. When water releases are taking place, the river is virtually unfishable.

Today the tailwaters of the Sipsey are stocked with 24,500 catchable-sized rainbow trout annually. These fish come from the U.S. Fish and Wildlife Service, since Alabama's Department of Conservation and Natural Resources has no trout-hatching or rearing facilities. The releases of fish take place at the foot of Smith Lake dam in increments of 3,500 each, occurring in January, March, April, May, July, September, and November each year.

In 1999, the Alabama Power Company did a tracking study by implanting radio transmitters in a limited number of released rainbows. Most were found to move slowly downstream, eventually reaching the lower half of the tailwater. A few fish have been caught in the Mulberry Fork of the Black Warrior, above where it is joined by the Sipsey, and rainbows have even been reported on rare occasions as far downstream as the Tuscaloosa area on the Black Warrior River. Still, the trout are most common in the Sipsey for about 6 miles downstream from the dam. Nearly all of the fish here are recent stockers of 8 to 12 inches, but a rare holdover fish can be found in the downstream areas that will go 20 inches.

The most dependable source of insect life for the trout continues to be the midge hatches that are common year-round on the deeper downstream areas of the river. When fishing these hatches, matching the size of the insects with very tiny flies seems to be more important than color on most days.

Nearer the dam, bead- or bullet-head Woolly Bugger patterns are reported to work well, with black or olive the favorite colors for stocked rainbows.

Access to the tailwater below Lewis Smith Lake begins with a catwalk above the tailrace at the foot of the dam. This concrete fishing platform can be reached on the west side of the dam via Smith Lake Dam Road. It is located high above the water level and is only practical for use by bait-fishers. Even if you could get down to the water here, it would be an extremely dangerous place to be during power generation.

The next downstream access is at the Birmingham Water Authority facility on the east shore. Cullman County Road 95 is a paved road that runs north along the east side of the stream. This road dead-ends at the pump station, where parking and easy entry to the river are available. Although a dirt path continues upstream of the pumping station as an extension of the road, it is easier during fishable water levels to simply walk upstream on the rocky shore. All of this water up to the tailrace is shallow enough for wading, but this is also the area of greatest concern during releases; the water level rises quickly. Listen for the warning siren when fishing here.

Along the 2 miles of road between the pumping station and AL 69 there are several other points of river access at dirt spurs off the paved road. All are obvious from the road and provide a couple of parking spots, plus a trail down to the water. This is along the portion of the stream where the shelf extends out from shore.

For boating access to the lower portion of the Sipsey tailwater, there is a public boat ramp off County Road 22 on the east side of the river to the northeast of the community of Sipsey. This is about 12 miles downriver from the Lewis Smith Dam and just above the point where the Sipsey joins the Mulberry Fork.

The Alabama Power Company provides a toll-free number that gives the tentative release schedules for all of its dams in the state, including the one at Smith Lake. One unique feature of the recordings is that they generally cover a 3-day period, rather than the single-day information given for many other tailwaters in the region. The number to call is 1-800-525-3711.

# Arkansas

Jeff Goodwin, © The Countryman Press

**1** Little Missouri River
**2** Little Red River
**3** North Fork River
**4** Oauchita River
**5** White River—Beaver Tailwater
**6** White River—Bull Shoals Tailwater

# CHAPTER 4

# Arkansas

Of all the states covered in this book, Arkansas is the best testament to the angling variety, quantity, and quality that can be achieved in tailwater trout fisheries. The Natural State historically had no native trout populations, yet today the Ozark Mountain region in the northwestern part of the state has arguably the best cold-water fisheries in the world. The two most recent all-tackle world-record brown trout were caught in Arkansas, and the number of magnum-sized trout taken from the state's rivers each year is astounding. Oddly enough, this situation came about more as an "apology" than as any planned program.

The story of trout fishing in Arkansas can properly be traced to 1898, when the first of several major floods struck the White River drainage. From then until 1927, the valuable farmlands along this river system were inundated a total of four times. The desire to control these natural disasters lay at the heart of the Flood Control Act of 1938, which was pushed through Congress by the Roosevelt administration. The fact that the resulting dam construction would employ a large number of Ozark folks during these Depression years was another selling point of the plan.

An unforeseen consequence of the dam-building projects, which began in earnest in 1941, was the eventual destruction of a world-class smallmouth bass fishery. The White River and its feeder streams had for years been noted for the quality of the fishing available for this species, drawing anglers from around the country. A tradition of float-fishing was long-established in the area, and some of the local families had been guiding anglers on the rivers for several decades.

Once the dams began to come on-line, the cold water released into the river system from the depths of the lakes made the habitat too cold for small-mouths; the fishery soon collapsed. Beginning in 1948, the Arkansas Game and Fish Commission (AGFC) released small numbers of brown trout into the tail-waters below Norfork Dam on the North Fork (or Norfork) River. This was followed by larger plantings of browns and rainbows in the Bull Shoals tailwater on the White River in 1952. Additionally, the AGFC transplanted aquatic veg-etation from Ozark springs into the Norfork River during the early 1950s.

All of these plantings proved very successful, prompting the U.S. Fish and Wildlife Service to get into the act in 1955. That year, Congress autho-rized the construction of the Norfork National Fish Hatchery as compensa-tion for the loss of the smallmouth bass fishery in the region. By the late 1950s, the White River system was already becoming renowned for pro-ducing trout weighing in double digits, and many of the smallmouth bass guides of the Ozarks switched over to guiding for these newcomers.

Today, the White River system in the Ozark Mountains provides the bulk of Arkansas' trout fishing. Beginning at the foot of the Beaver Dam, the White River's trout water runs through a short stretch of Missouri below Table Rock Lake before reentering Arkansas. It then passes through the dam at Bull Shoals Lake and continues southeasterly. Along this route it picks up the cold flows of two tributary rivers that have trout-bearing tailwaters: the North Fork and the Little Red River. All told, the White River system contains 159 miles of trout-supporting tailwaters. All but 22 of those miles are located in Arkansas.

While the White River basin gets most of the publicity, the Natural State has experimented with trout in other areas as well. A number of free-flowing streams, most notably the Spring River, have been stocked and are now quality trout waters. Also, several tailwater fisheries have been estab-lished in southwestern Arkansas. One is on the Little Missouri River below Lake Greeson and three more are located around the resort town of Hot Springs on the Ouachita River. These are downstream of Blakely Mountain Dam on Lake Ouachita; below Carpenter Dam on Lake Hamilton; and downstream of Remmel Dam on Lake Catherine. All are rather marginal trout fisheries, and the former two do not merit coverage because the down-stream lakes back up virtually to the foot of the dams. At best they can be described as providing seasonal lake-fishing opportunities.

Unlike the tailwaters of some of the other southern states, Arkansas' rivers tend to run clear and cold, whether or not the hydroelectric generators at the dams are in operation. As a result, local anglers have developed tactics for fishing these rivers at all water levels. These tactics are discussed in the river descriptions that follow.

The fish these anglers target are a bit different from those in other Dixie tailwaters as well. While browns and rainbows constitute the backbone of the trout fishing, brook trout are also stocked. Additionally, some of Arkansas' tailwaters have received plantings of cutthroat trout, which have also thrived.

To fish for trout in Arkansas both a regular fishing license and a trout permit are required. The only exceptions to this rule are for persons under 16 years of age or holders of lifetime fishing licenses. Anglers under 16 do not need either the license or the trout permit, while lifetime license holders are not required to have a trout permit.

The trout permit is required in order to keep trout caught from any waters in the Natural State, but is mandatory simply to fish in the tailwaters of the White River below Beaver or Bull Shoals Dams, as well as in the tailwaters of the Norfork and Little Red Rivers.

Fishing licenses and trout permits can be purchased from many sporting goods stores, discount chain stores, bait shops, or trout docks throughout Arkansas, as is normal in most states. Additionally, in Arkansas it is possible to purchase the license and permit by phone using Discover, MasterCard, or Visa. Have your credit card and driver's license numbers ready and simply call 1-800-364-GAME (4263). Upon placing the order, a confirmation number is issued and fishing privileges begin immediately. The actual license and permit will arrive a few days later by mail. Licenses may also be ordered using the Internet. Visit the AGFC web site at www.agfc.com and follow the prompts for license purchases.

An individual can use no more than one rod to fish for trout in Arkansas, and it must be attended at all times. On stretches of water that have catch-and-release or seasonal catch-and-release regulations in effect, only artificial lures with single, barbless hooks may be used. The use of marshmallows, salmon eggs, or moldable substances for bait is specifically banned in these waters.

The creel limit for trout is six per day in any combination of brook, brown, cutthroat, or rainbow. No more than two of that number may be brown trout, brook trout, or cutthroats. There is no minimum size for rainbow trout, but browns and cutthroats must be 16 inches long to be harvested. The minimum size limit for brook trout is 14 inches. There are exceptions to these regulations in effect on some of the tailwaters; these are covered in the individual stream descriptions.

One other regulation unique to Arkansas merits mention. It is illegal to drive, harass, rally, or pursue trout with noise, objects, or boats, or by wading, to concentrate or congregate them. The wording of this rule was prompted by some anglers' discovery that large trout could be driven into pods in the clear tailwaters. These fish would become excited and were susceptible to either baited hooks or illegal snagging. The regulation was enacted to put an end to this practice and to make the policing of it easier on the rivers.

# LITTLE MISSOURI RIVER

## *DeLorme 47*

One factor that sets the Little Missouri River apart from most other tailwater trout fisheries in Arkansas is its location. Situated in the southwest corner of the state, this river is not part of the famed tailwater fisheries of the Ozark Mountain region on which Arkansas has built its reputation as a world-class trout fishing destination.

The Little Missouri River rises in the Ouachita National Forest. Descending from the Caddo Mountains in Montgomery County, the upper portion of the river above Lake Greeson is a small, free-flowing stream that is stocked with rainbow trout in the winter months, especially around the forest service's Albert Pike Campground. After the river crosses into Pike County, running into and emerging from Lake Greeson, it is a larger stream, but still rates as only moderate in size when compared to Arkansas' other tailwater rivers.

The Little Missouri tailwater is ordinarily stocked with trout only from January through early April each year. There is, however, usually one release of a couple of thousand fish immediately below the dam in early June. Due to its southerly location and the relatively small size of Lake Greeson, the releases of water from the Narrows Dam are not particularly cold during the summer months. Although there is some carryover of fish near the dam, farther downstream it is minimal.

The history of the Little Missouri tailwater closely parallels that of Ozark rivers in that it was a noted smallmouth bass stream prior to the building of the Narrows Dam in the early 1950s. When it was realized that the dam had adversely impacted that fishery, the AGFC first tried restocking smallmouths. This proved impractical because the water temperatures in winter and spring

Lake
Greeson

Riverside
Picnic
Area

Narrows Dam

River Ridge
Access

Hinds Bluff
Access

Old Factory Rd.

Mt. Moriah
Baptist Church

Green Thumb
Access

19

Weir No.3
Access

**Little Missouri River**

27

5

Murfreesboro

West 13th
Street Bridge

Crater of
Diamonds
State Park

301

27

**Little Missouri
River**

N

0        1        2 mi.

0      1      2 km

Jeff Goodwin, © The Countryman Press

*The Riverside Picnic Area at the foot of the Narrows Dam offers some shoreline fishing possibilities even during periods of high water.*

were too low to support these fish. Next, year-round stocking of rainbow trout was attempted. This also did not work out, because summer and fall water temperatures could soar to over 75 degrees when no generation was taking place at the Narrows Dam. Finally, the present program of a winter-through-spring trout fishery was accepted as the only practical alternative.

In 1992, the U.S. Army Corps of Engineers and the AGFC cooperated on a plan that made structural changes in the Narrows Dam to improve the amount of dissolved oxygen in the water released into the river. Additionally, boulders and several rock weirs were placed in the riverbed to create more turbulence, which also aids in improving the dissolved oxygen levels.

All of the trout stocked in the Little Missouri below the Narrows Dam are rainbows. Fish of 10 to 12 inches in length are planted at five locations along the tailwater. The sites are at the foot of the Narrows Dam at Riverside Picnic Area, in the River Ridge area a couple of miles downstream, at Hinds Bluff; near Weir No. 2 at Green Thumb Access, and at Weir No. 3 at the County Road (CR) crossing near the town of Murfreesboro.

From January through mid-March an average of about 10,000 rainbows are released every two weeks. The final two stockings in late March and early April consist of roughly 3,300 fish each. As mentioned earlier, in the first part of June, 2,000 rainbows are planted just below the dam. All of the trout released in March through June are 12 inches long. In total, the Little Missouri is stocked with just short of 60,000 fish annually, of which 35 percent are the larger 12-inch trout.

To catch numbers of trout, the best months are February to April. For larger fish in the 13-plus-inch range, concentrate on the area immediately downstream of the Narrows Dam in June through October.

On this tailwater, most of the angling pressure comes from bait-fishers using corn and wax worms. In-line spinners and small spoons are the choices of spin-casters, but heavier marabou jigs or small diving crankbaits are called for during higher water levels.

Fly-fishers are most often found on the river during low water levels; at these times, much of the river is wadable. There are a couple of insect hatches that are of particular interest to fly-casters here. From late February through May good numbers of March Browns come off the water. In late summer through October, hatches of Light Cahills provoke some very good dry-fly action.

Many of the anglers taking advantage of the trout fishing on the Little Missouri are from southwest Arkansas, but this fishery also draws folks from northwestern Louisiana and northeastern Texas.

There is public access to the Little Missouri at the foot of the Narrows Dam at Lake Greeson, about 6 miles north of the town of Murfreesboro on AR 19. The Riverside Picnic Area has ¼ mile of the eastern shore within its boundaries. This park has picnic tables, a playground, and rest rooms. Although there is no boat ramp, the sloping grassy bank does permit the launching of canoes. A bridge on AR 19 crosses the river just below the power plant at the dam, but there is no fishing access here.

The river is roughly 150 feet wide through the park. There are both concrete and wooden piers that permit handicapped anglers to fish this portion of the river. Just upstream of the piers is a shelf running out from shore that permits some wading, even during high water.

From the foot of the Narrows Dam for 100 yards downstream, no fishing is permitted in the river. From the point that fishing is allowed downstream to the upper end of Riverside Park pool the Little Missouri is open as a catch-and-release area. Only artificial lures with single, barbless hooks may be used, and all trout caught must be immediately returned to the river. Next, from the upstream end of the Riverside pool down to the gas line that crosses the river just above the River Ridge Access, the stream is open under seasonal catch-and-release rules. From May 1 to October 15, only single hook, barbless artificial lures may be used and all trout must be immediately released. From October 16 to April 30, regular trout rules and creel limits apply.

The next downstream access is located 1½ miles below Greeson Lake at the River Ridge Access. This site is just off AR 19 and provides a gravel parking lot with a canoe launch. There is also a small shoal just downstream of the access point.

Farther down the river at 2½ miles, the Hinds Bluff Access is also situated on AR 19. This site has a gravel parking area, canoe launch, and walk-in access to the water. There is a deep run immediately in front of the access area and a long, wadable shoal downstream.

At 5 miles south of the dam is an access point that, while still open to the public, is in rather a neglected state. It is located at the end of Old Factory Road to the west of AR 19. This is the first gravel road running off the highway to the south of the Mt. Moriah Baptist Church. An old overgrown county-owned picnic ground called Green Thumb Access is at streamside. This area is also known as the Weir No. 2 Access. There is a ¼ mile of access, along with a rough canoe launch site.

Another approach to the water, known as the Weir No. 3 Access is available at just over 6 miles downstream of the Narrows Dam and upstream of the CR 5 bridge over the Little Missouri. To reach this access, take AR 27 west from Murfreesboro, then turn north onto CR 5.

The final point of access is located at the Low Water Bridge on West 13th Street, 1½ miles west of Murfreesboro on AR 27. This site marks the downstream limit of practical trout water, since the restriction on the use of more than one rod that must be attended ends here. This regulation applies to all trout water in Arkansas.

Both shores of the river can be reached at this point, which is sometimes referred to as the Old Factory Site. The parking area is on the eastern shore and a canoe-launch is provided. The river upstream of the bridge features a long, deep pool, then narrows considerably into a shoal under the highway crossing.

The powerhouse at the Narrows Dam is operated on a "power on demand" basis, so there is no telephone number available to anglers for regular water release schedules.

# LITTLE RED RIVER

## DeLorme 34

If you want to start an argument among anglers in Arkansas these days, just try gaining a consensus on which is the best tailwater trout fishery in the Natural State. It is fairly easy to find supporters for three heavyweight

Little Red River

Greers Ferry Lake

Big Creek

Canoe Creek

Greers Ferry National Fish Hatchery

JFK Park

Cow Shoals Access

Barnett Access

Wilburn

Vogel Avenue

Lobo Landing Access

Libby Shoals Access

Dripping Springs Access

Second Avenue

Pangburn Bridge Access

Pangburn

Ramsey Access

Dewey Bridge

Little Red River

N

3 mi.
1.5
0

3 km
1.5
0

25
210
110
110
110
337
337
16
110
124
305

Jeff Goodwin, © The Countryman Press

contenders in this field. All can make some strong arguments in favor of their pet waters, whether they choose the Little Red, Norfork, or White River below Bull Shoals Dam. All three rivers can lay claim to producing vast numbers of trout for anglers, plus some truly gargantuan catches.

Though reputations can change quickly on all of these fantastic Arkansas waters, at the moment it would be hard to produce better credentials than those owned by the Little Red River below 31,500-acre Greers Ferry Lake. Located in Cleburne and White Counties, the Little Red is a feeder stream of the White River, but these two formidable trout streams do not join their flows until they merge at the eastern edge of White County, long after both have ceased to carry water cold enough to support trout.

Although a shorter, smaller, and less heavily stocked river than the White, the Little Red makes up in quality what it gives away in quantity. Receiving almost 437,000 stocked rainbow trout each year along its 32-mile course from Greers Ferry Dam to the Dewey Bridge on AR 305, it obviously contains plenty of fish. It is the presence, however, of a wild, reproducing population of brown trout and an abundance of aquatic plant life that gives the Little Red its edge. Not only does the river yield wild browns, but they run very large. The best evidence of this is Rip Collins's May 1992 catch of the present world-record brown from this river. His fish tipped the scales at 40 pounds, 4 ounces, swiping the record previously held by a Norfork River trout.

Collins's behemoth is not the only brute that has been wrestled from the flow of the Little Red tailwater. Back in 1988, Melvin Hallmark hauled a 27-pound, 8-ounce brown from the river just below Greers Ferry Dam. Additionally, in August 1993, Dee Warren took a 28-pound, 14-ounce brown from the Little Red, while Ricky Hunt got in the act a week later with a 24-pound, 10-ounce catch.

An indication that the Little Red has lost none of its trophy potential was a huge brown trout found dead on the river in 1998. The fish's carcass was pulled from the river near the Swinging Bridge Trout Dock. The brown was 38 inches long, sported a 28-inch girth, and although it had already begun to decompose, still tipped the scales at more than 38 pounds!

While these gigantic fish are the main evidence for giving the Little Red the nod as the best tailwater fishery in the state, it is the presence of abundant moss beds that make the reputation possible. Soon after rainbow trout were first stocked in this tailwater in 1966—two years after the completion of the Greers Ferry Dam—a program of sprigging aquatic mosses was begun in the river. Both the newly introduced fish and the plant life did well. Soon, tiny crustaceans called sow bugs were infesting these new moss beds. These aquatic relatives of the land-bound "roly-poly" bugs most of us remember finding under rocks and playing with as children are present in astounding numbers in the Little Red. One study at John F. Kennedy Park at the foot of Greers Ferry Dam found 500 of these critters for each square foot of area checked.

While the sow bug is found in all of the Arkansas tailwaters, it is most abundant and important in the Little Red. A major reason for this is the river's lack of sculpins and crayfish. These two forms of aquatic life are food staples of the big trout in the White and Norfork Rivers, yet absent from the Little Red. This void in the food chain is filled by the sow bug. While the sow bug is unable to swim and spends its life crawling and scavenging along the bottom, it is easily swept loose and into the river's flow by changing water levels or simply by strong, localized currents. At these times, the ¼-inch morsels become the targets of every trout in the river, regardless of the fish's size. The result is that almost every fly-caster on every Natural State tailwater has some sow bug imitations in his or her fly box.

There is another interesting facet to the Little Red's saga: The presence of brown trout in this tailwater is an unusual tale in itself. Neither the AGFC nor the U.S. Fish and Wildlife Service has ever stocked any of these European immigrants into the flow. Rather, the browns got into the Little Red beginning in the mid-1970s due to the efforts of a couple of local fly-fishing clubs. Those introductions were done with the blessing of the AGFC.

In 1975, the Arkansas Fly Fishers of Little Rock placed Vibert boxes containing 10,000 eggs in Cow Shoals. These fertilized eggs were protected until they hatched, thus releasing brown trout fry to the river. In 1979 the club teamed up with the Mid-South Fly Fishers club of Memphis, Tennessee, to plant an additional 5,000 Montana fingerling browns in the Little Red.

The infant brown trout fishery took hold quickly, and no stockings of browns have taken place in the Little Red River since 1983. The population of these wily fish has continued to grow in the ensuing years, with the trout steadily increasing the number of shoals that they use for spawning. Heavy spawning runs are recorded as beginning in mid-October each year, with peak activity occurring during the first half of November. In 1988 the two fly-fishing clubs mentioned above raised the money to purchase land adjacent to Cow Shoals on the Little Red. They then donated this property to the AGFC for use as a low-impact, walk-in access point, thus providing protection to this valuable spawning area.

Beginning in 1990, special size and creel limits for brown trout were enacted on all Arkansas tailwaters. They were patterned after rules that had been in effect on the Beaver tailwater of the White River since 1988, and were designed to enhance the brown trout fishery. The creel limit was reduced from six browns per day to only two. Additionally, only brown trout of 16 inches or longer were legal to harvest.

The results of these regulations again provided proof that catch-and-release angling is a good fisheries management tool, but one that cannot successfully be applied indiscriminately. Within a couple of years the large population of browns in the Little Red became unbalanced. Samplings of the fish found that some areas of this tailwater had densities of up to 12,000 brown trout per mile, and average populations of over 6,700 per mile! Of these, the vast majority were under 16 inches, indicating that most browns were being harvested soon after reaching minimum size. On the other hand, angler surveys revealed that even prior to the change of regulations, 88 percent of brown trout being caught were released. Meanwhile, the numbers of subminimum trout were exploding.

These conditions actually came as no surprise to AGFC biologists. When the regulations had been extended to all Arkansas tailwaters in 1990, they had recommended that the Little Red be exempted. Due to the problem of enforcement, however, the rules were applied to this river as well. Now—since January 1995—the Little Red River tailwater has its own set of special regulations governing brown trout. The daily creel limit has been increased to 4 fish, only 1 of which may be larger than 21 inches. There is also a slot limit in effect, requiring anglers to release all brown trout between 16 and 21 inches. It is hoped that this new approach will get the population back in balance.

It is obvious that despite the imbalance, large trout have been in the Little Red all along. This was highlighted by Rip Collins's world-record brown taken in May 1992. Collins, a longtime Little Red River angler from the nearby town of Heber Springs, ordinarily fished the river with fly tackle, but on that fateful day was using ultralight spinning gear. He was fishing with angling buddy Van Cooper of Forrest City, who was having a better day than Collins: The tally showed Cooper with four trout to Collins's none.

Then, about a mile upriver from the Barnett Access near the Swinging Bridge Resort, Collins switched lures, tying on a $\frac{1}{32}$-ounce olive marabou jig. Three casts later he hung something he described as feeling "like a log." When the log began to run, the world-record battle was on. Collins finally brought the fish to the boat, but neither man had thought to bring a landing net along. They flagged down a passing boat, but the anglers only had a small, trout-sized net. The next boat flagged did have a boat net, and the monster trout was brought aboard.

Collins managed to keep the record trout alive in a cage in the river until it could be taken by a U.S. Fish and Wildlife Service hatchery truck to be weighed on a certified scale. His plan was to release the fish back into the river after documenting it. Unfortunately, the 40¼-inch female, with a girth of 28½ inches, died before the release could be made. Collins's catch has since been recognized as the all-tackle world record by the National Fresh Water Fishing Hall of Fame and the International Game Fish Association.

Despite all the attention garnered by the brown trout fishery on the Little Red, the fact remains that the bulk of the action is provided by rainbow trout, which are heavily stocked here. Each year, more than a quarter-million rainbows are released in the tailwater, which has a constant year-round temperature of 40 to 55 degrees. While most of these fish are in the 9- to 12-inch range, carryover rainbows of 5 to 12 pounds are common. Growth rates for the released rainbows of up to 1 inch per month have been documented on this tailwater, so a day of fishing will generally yield at least a couple of fish in the 1- to 3-pound range. Back in 1968 a 15-pound, 8-ounce Little Red River rainbow taken by David Kitchens of Conway held the Arkansas state record for the species for a period of more than two years. There is negligible rainbow trout reproduction in the Little Red, and no minimum size limit for harvest of the species.

Another facet of the stocking program is the annual release of roughly 50,000 cutthroat trout into the flow. This program began in 1990 with the introduction of 25,000 of the 6-inch fish and has grown to its present level. Only 2 cutthroats may be creeled per day, with a minimum 16-inch size limit.

Some brook trout are released into the Little Red each year. Like the other species, these fish have exhibited outstanding growth rates in this stream. In fact, the Little Red is second only to the Norfork River as the best producer of these trout in the state and for a short time laid claim to the Arkansas state record for brookies. In the summer of 1999, guide Donald Burns of Heber Springs held that mark for a 4-pound, 6-ounce brook trout caught on a live minnow from the dock at Lindsey's Rainbow Resort in Heber Springs. That fish was 18 inches long and had a girth of 13 inches. A larger brook trout was later taken from the Norfork River.

With abundant fish, the Little Red River attracts its share of Arkansas' anglers. You will rarely have a stretch entirely to yourself when fishing here, and the stream can become downright crowded on long holiday weekends. Still, with more than 30 miles of water, fishing is easily had on the tailwater, and under usual conditions there is enough elbow room for a quality experience.

The factor governing fishing conditions on the Little Red—as on any tailwater—is the volume of water being released into the river. There are two power generators at Greers Ferry Dam. When one of these is in use, the level of the river will rise 4 feet above the minimum flow, but when both are on-line the level rises from 8 to 9½ feet. During the spring and summer months, the turbines ordinarily are quiet up until about noon.

Conditions on the Little Red tailwaters are a bit different from those on the White and Norfork Rivers. This stream is, as mentioned earlier, smaller; it tends to run less clear, especially at high water levels; and, due to its more abundant vegetation, drift-fishing is less popular and a bit more difficult on the Little Red. Whereas bait-anglers tend to drift the larger rivers, fishing upstream behind the boat, on this tailwater anchoring and fishing to specific bits of in-stream cover—such as weed beds, deep holes, or downed trees—is more common. Be aware, however, that when two generators are running, anchoring in the current can be dangerous. The force of the moving water is sufficient to swamp most boats, which puts the dunked anglers at risk of hypothermia during any season of the year. Some fatalities have been recorded on the Little Red due to just this kind of situation. Despite the drawbacks of the vegetation, drift-fishing during high water is still the most practical and safest alternative.

On the other hand, during low-water periods the Little Red becomes a series of long pools separated by shallow, swift runs. Expect to find a lot of the trout concentrated near the heads of the pools where the shoals empty into deeper water. It is easy to wade many of the riffles and some of the pools during low water. The shallower waters, naturally, are particularly popular with fly-casters.

Aficionados of the long rod find the Little Red River gives up its trout to dry flies, streamers, or nymphs, depending on the season of the year and the conditions of the water. In the spring, up through the month of June, caddisfly hatches will occur on the river, since the Little Red contains both case-building and burrowing varieties of these aquatic insects. Elk Hair Caddis in standard tan hues and size 16 are popular imitations for this fishing. Local casters add some life to these flies at times, rather than simply dead-drifting them on the current. Indeed, twitching or skittering the fly on the water can be effective in provoking strikes, since this imitates the action of actual adult bugs on the surface.

Beginning in June and becoming more prevalent into July and August, hatches of midge-sized blue-winged olives are frequently seen on the Little Red. The fly-fishing during this time can be tough, however. All types of food are most abundant at this season, giving the trout plenty of choices. Also, fishing pressure will be at its peak, making the fish a bit more skittish. Finally, when no water is being released from Greers Ferry, the water temperature can get warm enough to make the trout sluggish.

In the summer, midge-imitating flies fished in the surface film on extremely fine tippets (7X to 8X) are often needed to fool the trout. Hook sizes of 18 to 24 dressed in gray or olive will usually do the trick. Look for trout that are steadily rising and actually breaking the water's surface. These are usually fish taking emergers from the film, rather than adult bugs on the surface. A common mistake novice midge fishers make is to set the hook too quickly when fishing to this type of action. The tiny flies are usually quite difficult to see when floating either on the surface or in the film, so when a rise occurs in the vicinity of where you think your fly is, wait an extended count—to give the trout a chance to turn with the fly—before striking. If the hook is set as soon as the fish breaks the water, it will either just barely strike the trout in the lip or miss it altogether.

For subsurface fishing, local anglers turn to such patterns as the Squirrel Tail, Pheasant Tail, or Tellico Nymph fished beneath a strike indicator. The most common fly, however, is a sow bug imitation. Some local experts suggest that up to 90 percent of the trout's staple diet year-round on the Little Red is made up of these crustaceans. Again, suspending a size 12 to 18 sow bug pattern beneath a strike indicator and fishing it around rocks or moss is a surefire tactic.

When the waters are on the rise in the Little Red, streamer fishing is another option. Big patterns such as the Zonker or Woolly Bugger in hook sizes up to 4 are excellent choices for taking larger brown trout. White or olive are favored colors for the flies, as is either of these hues in combination with yellow. The technique most often employed is to drift the river, casting to rocks, timber, or backwater eddies along the shore. The key is to make those casts extremely close to the bank, where the trout tend to hold. The fishing for browns is at its best during the fall and winter months.

One final fly-casting tip merits mentioning: When the brown trout are making their autumn spawning runs into the various shoals on the Little

Red, an egg pattern can be deadly. Rainbow trout congregate at the foot of the shoals to feed on any brown trout eggs that drift downstream and will readily take imitations.

Anglers who prefer to tackle the Little Red with spinning gear use a number of lures successfully. Mepps, Rooster Tail, Cordell, and Panther Martin in-line spinners in small sizes all attract the rainbow trout in this tailwater. The Little Cleo Spoon, the Rebel Wee Crawdad crankbait, and the No. 7 Rapala top-water minnow imitation are also favorites of many Little Red anglers.

Probably the most often used spinning lures on this river are marabou jigs in sizes ranging from $\frac{1}{16}$ ounce down to micro sizes of $\frac{1}{32}$ to $\frac{1}{64}$ ounce; at times, local anglers add a wax worm to the tip of the hook on these jigs to further entice the fish. (The wax worm is the larval form of the bee moth, which lays its eggs in beehives. When the eggs hatch, the larvae feed on the wax found there. The worms are off-white in color, about $\frac{1}{4}$ inch long, and dry to the touch. They are sold at some of the trout docks along the Little Red River tailwater.) The marabou jigs are fished either on the bottom or suspended 3 to 4 feet beneath a float, although most of the largest trout taken on these lures come from bottom-fishing. Black, brown, green, yellow, and orange are all colors that produce fish on the jigs, but black and brown are the two most often used by local anglers. It is worth noting, though, that Rip Collins was using a $\frac{1}{32}$-ounce version in olive when he boated the world-record brown.

The jigs are generally cast to the edges of weed beds or submerged structure in the river during periods of low water. If the stream is running high, drifting near the shore and casting onto the submerged weed beds is a favored tactic. Rainbow trout tend to hold close to the bank at these times to escape the heavy current.

One other spin-fishing technique is employed on the Little Red during high water levels. Some anglers use rigs with line of up to 14-pound test and cast big jerkbait-type bass lures. These are fished on the surface around shoreline structure in a series of jerks in the fashion used on lakes for largemouth bass. This method targets large brown trout, which show less caution when feeding during high water.

In the case of bait-fishers, corn, salmon eggs, earthworms, and wax worms are good choices. Ordinarily these are bumped along the bottom with the current, or slowly hopped along the streambed in eddy areas. Just as fly-casters use egg patterns to catch rainbows below shoals where brown trout are spawning in the fall, bait-fishers can effectively use the real salmon eggs at the same time and places. These are drifted downstream to the hungry trout waiting at the foot of the riffle areas.

Another technique employed by bait-anglers is to place a split shot or other tiny weight about 18 to 20 inches above the hook to get the rig down to the bottom. Then, a tiny marshmallow is threaded over the eye of the hook, with one of the standard baits added on the bend. The marshmallow adds enough buoyance to raise the baited hook just off the bottom and, hopefully, entice a strike from a trout.

Special creel and size limits apply on the Little Red River tailwaters in all sections that lie outside of the catch-and-release portions of the stream. The daily creel limit is 4 brown trout per day, but only one of those may be longer than 21 inches. Additionally, a slot limit is in effect that mandates the release of all browns from 16 to 21 inches long.

Public access to the Little Red River tailwater is provided at eight points, plus about a half-dozen trout docks along the flow. All of these are found from Greers Ferry Dam down to Dewey Bridge on AR 305. Between these access points, float-fishing is the only way to reach the water.

At the dam, John F. Kennedy Park provides access to the river on the east side. It is interesting to note that the park received its name in honor of President Kennedy, who made his last dedication ceremony appearance at the opening of Greers Ferry Dam in October 1963, just prior to his assassination in Dallas. This park contains a campground, parking area, and boat ramp, and is the site of the Greers Ferry National Fish Hatchery. Located just off AR 25, which crosses the dam, JFK Park is the only access point on the river controlled by the Army Corps of Engineers.

Just downstream of the dam the park contains some shoal water, then a deep-water bend at the boat ramp. The west bank of this bend has some large boulders that generally hold trout. A trail down the eastern shore leads to what is called the Power Line Pool (which obviously lies beneath a power line crossing the river). This is a favorite with fly-casters during low water. As mentioned earlier, the Little Red in JFK Park gave up a 27-pound, 8-ounce brown trout to Melvin Hallmark back in 1988.

The portion of the river in the park, from 100 feet downstream of Greers Ferry Dam to the last outlet pipe from the national fish hatchery, is open to fishing as a catch-and-release area. Only artificial lures with single barbless hooks are legal and all trout must be released back into the stream unharmed.

The next public access point is 5½ miles downstream at Cow Shoals, which was the first site on the Little Red River where brown trout were confirmed to have spawned. It quickly acquired a reputation as a good fly-fishing destination and continues to attract long-rodders. Fishing is possible here for 1½ to 2 hours after releases at Greers Ferry Dam; then the water begins to rise.

Cow Shoals is a walk-in area. As noted earlier, it was purchased by local fly-fishing clubs and donated to the AGFC. It is located at the end of AR 210 on the west side of the river and to the east of the AR 210/AR 110 junction. A parking area is provided. The last ½ mile of AR 210 as it nears the river is gravel. Foot access to the river is easy during low-water levels, as is wading, due to a ½-mile-long gravel bar located on the western shore.

Since 1995, seasonal catch-and-release regulations have been in effect from the head of Cow Shoals down to the mouth of Canoe Creek. From October 1 through December 31, only single barbless hooks with artificial lures may be used, and all fish must be immediately released unharmed. Night fishing is also prohibited in this area. The purpose of the rules is to protect the brown trout during their fall spawning run.

Farther downstream at the AR 110 bridge is the Barnett Access. This is another of the AGFC properties and is located on the southeastern side of the river. Upstream of the highway bridge is a deep pool with a boat ramp. Under and downstream of the bridge is Winkley Shoals, which provides good wading access, but attracts a lot of anglers on weekends. Collins's world-record brown trout was taken roughly a mile upstream of this point, and Ricky Hart caught his 24-pound, 10-ounce brown in this area as well.

Water releases from the dam take 3½ to 5 hours to reach the Barnett Access, which is 10 miles downstream of Greers Ferry Dam.

Another walk-in access point is located at Libby Shoals, on the south side of the river, off AR 337. Through here the tailwaters flow in the shadow of Libby Bluff, which lines the north shore and is a very scenic part of the Little Red's course. It is a steep walk down a flight of stairs from the gravel parking area, then about 50 more yards to the water's edge. Rising water takes 6 to 7 hours to reach this point 16 miles downriver of Greers Ferry Dam.

The next two downstream accesses are at Lobo Landing and Dripping Springs. These are 17 and 22 miles below the dam. Both have AGFC boat ramps and parking lots, but neither offers much in the way of wading access. Dunham Shoals and Mossy Shoals are located between these two landings, though. The waters from Dunham down to Mossy are designated for catch-and-release angling. Only artificial lures with single barbless hooks are legal, and all fish must be released. These restrictions are enforced at all times of

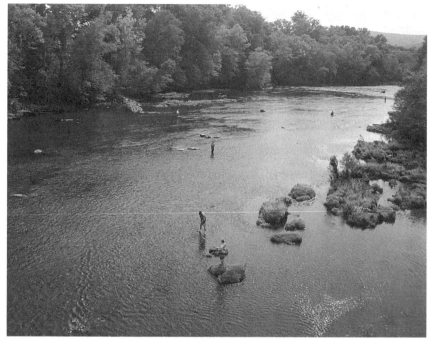

*The Barnett Access is a very popular angling site on
the Little Red River tailwater.*

the year. Float trips from Lobo Landing down to Dripping Springs are popular with fly-casters, who stop off in the shoals to wade.

To reach Lobo Landing, on the south side of the river, a 0.1-mile drive
on Vogel Avenue off AR 337 is required. Dripping Springs Access is at the
end of Second Avenue, which runs north off AR 16 in the town of Pangburn. There is a sign for the access point at the intersection in town; from
there, the point is 1.5 miles.

The Pangburn Access, where AR 110 again crosses the Little Red River
at 24 miles downstream of the dam, offers handicapped anglers an approach
to the water. An old bridge downstream of the present highway span has
been left standing, with only the middle segment removed. This creates
fishing piers on both shores, and parking areas are provided on either side of
the river as well. Additionally, Pangburn Shoals are located just downstream,
and can be reached from the south side of the tailwater.

Although the official end of trout water on the Little Red River is at the
Dewey Bridge on AR 305, the Ramsey Access is the last practical approach
to the water for anglers. Located 3 miles upstream of the Dewey Bridge and

32 miles from Greers Ferry Dam, Ramsey has a parking areas and boat ramp at the end of a paved road running north off AR 124. Although there is no sign identifying the road, there is a directional sign for the Ramsey Access at the intersection. A wadable shoal is just downstream of the boat ramp.

To obtain current information on water conditions on the Little Red River tailwater, call 501-362-5150 for a recorded message, courtesy of the Army Corps of Engineers.

# NORTH FORK RIVER

## *DeLorme 26*

Although the North Fork River is the shortest tailwater fishery in Arkansas that holds trout, it is also arguably the best trophy-trout water in the world. Better known by its shortened name, the Norfork River, this flow is only 4.8 miles in length. It originates at the foot of Norfork Dam in the north-central part of the state and runs to the southwest through Baxter County to empty into the White River. Norfork Dam impounds 22,000 acres of water in Norfork Lake, which extends across the state line into southern Missouri.

While often identified as the North Fork of the White River, or the Norfork, the officially correct name of this stream is simply the North Fork River. Part of the confusion over its moniker results from it flowing through Norfork Lake, which is actually named for the nearby town of Norfork. In the interest of brevity, "Norfork" is the term that will be used to discuss this flow.

While the Little Red River tailwater has recently attracted most of the attention for trophy-quality brown trout, and over the long haul the Bull Shoals tailwater on the White River has been Arkansas' most consistent producer of big trout, the Norfork has also yielded some very impressive fish. To date, this short tailwater has given up three of the last four Arkansas state-record brook trout. The most recent and current record-holder is a 4-pound, 12-ounce specimen taken by Greg Corkin of Norfork, Arkansas, on September 25, 2000. His fish measured 19.75 inches long with a girth of 13.5 inches.

These large brookies are actually the Natural State's most difficult to catch trophy trout, since only 40,000 of the 3 million fish stocked in Arkansas annually are brook trout. Yet, an electroshocking survey of the Norfork River in 2000 found that 38 percent of the trout present were brookies.

Additionally, a former Arkansas- and world-record brown trout was

North Fork River

Norfork National Fish Hatchery

Norfork Lake

Dry Run Creek

177

177

5

Quarry Park

North Fork River

5

River Ridge Access

River Ridge Road

Otter Creek

63

N

Norfork Access

White River

Norfork

5

0        0.5        1 mi.

0      0.5      1 km

Jeff Goodwin, © The Countryman Press

pulled from these waters by Mike "Huey" Manley of North Little Rock on August 7, 1988. That huge 41-inch trout tipped the scales at 38 pounds, 9 ounces and stood as a disputed world record for two years.

The controversy surrounding Manley's fish centered on the fact that his ultralight gear, which used 8-pound-test line, ended in a baited treble hook. While perfectly legal in Arkansas at the time, the use of treble hooks with bait is not recognized as a sportfishing technique by the International Game Fish Association; thus the IGFA never accepted his catch. On the other hand, the AGFC recognized it as the official state record, as did the National Fresh Water Fishing Hall of Fame. The Manley trout was finally displaced from both record books by Rip Collins's 40-pound, 4-ounce brown, taken from the Little Red River in 1992.

Manley's trout, however, still reigns as the Hall of Fame's 8-pound-test line-class rod and reel record. Another line-class world record on this list that came from the Norfork is held by Tony Salamon in the 6-pound-test category for a 30-pound, 8-ounce brown taken on August 31, 1986. In the 17-pound-test class, a 34-pound monster caught by David Wooten on August 13, 1988, stands as the benchmark for browns.

Often overlooked in this flurry of brown trout records are two former Arkansas record rainbow trout that the Norfork also produced. Back on June 14, 1970, Frank Mandernach of St. Louis, Missouri, boated a 16-pound, 2-ounce rainbow he caught while tossing a Mepps spinner. Just over two years later, on July 1, 1972, his record was broken by Raymond Sullivan of Des Moines, Iowa, with the 16-pound, 12-ounce fish he took from the Norfork. That catch stood as the state record for the next four years.

While it is abundantly clear that the Norfork River is capable of producing record fish, what makes it outstanding among tailwaters is the consistency with which it produces big fish within its very limited length. Brown trout of 4 to 6 pounds are common, and browns of 10 to 15 pounds are so often caught that they go almost unnoticed. In the earlier years of this tailwater, rainbows of 2 to 6 pounds were also the norm, but fishing pressure has greatly reduced this fishery. Cutthroat trout have been stocked in the Norfork since 1982 and thrive here. In fact, Arkansas' first state-record cutthroat came from the Norfork on March 13, 1985, when Thomas Else of St. Louis, Missouri, caught a 3-pounder. That fish has since been bested by several from the White River. Some brook trout continue to be planted in the Norfork River as well.

With such a varied and high-quality fishery, it is hardly surprising that the Norfork is a very popular fishing destination. One survey revealed that this 4.8-mile stretch of water was the site of 16 percent of all the trout fishing in Arkansas the previous year. The fishing on the Norfork tailwater can get crowded, particularly during low water, when neither of the dam's generators is active. This is especially true from spring through fall, when the bulk of the stocking takes place. Planted fish are released year-round, however, and anglers looking to beat the crowds will find February and March the times of lowest usage. Fishing pressure also is lower at other times of the year when one or both of the turbines at Norfork Dam are active.

The North Fork was the first of the streams in the White River system to be dammed by the Corps of Engineers. Norfork Dam was begun in 1941, and its two power generators came on-line in 1944. With the release of 600 fingerling rainbow trout in July 1948, the Norfork also became the first Arkansas tailwater to receive stocked trout.

As with other stockings in tailwaters of the Natural State, these were intended to compensate for the loss of smallmouth bass fishing in the river. The first trout released into the Norfork were an experiment—to see if the new tailwater would be able to support the cold-water species. Within a year of the first planting of 4- to 6-inch trout, rainbows of 2 to 3 pounds were being caught, and in the second year 4- to 6-pounders were showing up. The productivity of the river was astounding and the program a success by any standard.

An appeal to the U.S. Congress resulted in funds being allotted for the U.S. Fish and Wildlife Service to build a trout hatchery on the Norfork. In 1957 the Norfork National Fish Hatchery was opened on Dry Run Creek, a feeder of the river that enters it just below Norfork Dam. Just 5 years later this hatchery was supplying 1.8 million trout annually for planting in the Norfork and White Rivers.

In recent years the Norfork has received just short of 165,000 stocked trout per year. Roughly 60 percent of these are rainbows of 9 to 12 inches. Cutthroat and brook trout each make up about 15 percent of the released fish, while the remaining 10 percent are brown trout. The browns are stocked because the Norfork has very few spawning shoals in which the fish can reproduce. All of the brook, brown, and cutthroat trout are in the 6- to 8-inch range.

The environment into which these hatchery fish are released is referred to by some experts as the most productive trout stream in the world. Growth rates in the fish have been documented at as much as $7\frac{1}{2}$ inches per year—in some cases, $\frac{3}{4}$ inch a month. Add to this the fact that the growing season for trout on the Norfork is year-round, and the numbers of huge trout it has produced are easily explained.

The fluctuating water levels of the tailwater are not conducive to high populations of mayflies or stoneflies, but the fact that Norfork Dam has only two power generators mitigates the problem. Water surges are not as pronounced here as those found on the White River below Bull Shoals Dam, so aquatic vegetation has an easier time hanging onto the riverbed.

Of course, the sensational growth rates mentioned above need a tremendous forage base to sustain them. For a number of reasons, the Norfork has the most substantial and dependable such food chain in the White River system. To begin with, fish of up to 20 inches gorge themselves on the abundant freshwater shrimp, sow bugs, and scuds found in the flow. These tiny critters are quite at home in the Norfork's weed beds.

Once the trout, particularly the browns, get past the 20-inch plateau, they become quite carnivorous in their feeding habits. They can still find plenty to eat, though, thanks to the river's large population of sculpins. These small bottom-dwelling fish, which are sometimes referred to locally as mountain minnows, are a favored food of the browns. It is during the winter months, however—when cold weather causes shad die-offs in Norfork Lake—that the brown trout in the tailwater attain their greatest growth spurts of the year. The dead and dying shad are sucked through the turbines at the dam and the trout binge on the minnows. Additionally, many of the large number of small trout stocked into the river yearly end up being feed for the huge browns.

Because of the short length of trout water and the scarcity of spawning shoals on the Norfork, there is thought to be a close and unique connection between this tailwater and that below Bull Shoals Dam on the White River. Some of the association is obvious. By the time the two rivers join, the White has already flowed more than 60 miles as a cold-water trout river and is beginning to warm. The infusion of the Norfork's chilly waters renews the White, allowing it more than 40 more miles of life as a cold-water fishery.

Less obvious, but strongly suspected, is the movement of brown trout from one river to the other. Some big browns in both the Bull Shoals and Norfork tailwaters were tagged with radio transmitters during the 1992 spawning season; one result was the discovery that these fish traveled up to 24 miles in a day. Movements of 18 miles were recorded in several instances, and all of the tagged fish traveled at least 8 to 10 miles every 24 hours during the spawn. With the abundance of big browns in the Norfork, it is almost certain that some would have to move into the White to spawn. On the other hand, the survey also found that after spawning, all of the fish returned to virtually the same location where they had lived when first tagged.

The amount of water being released at Norfork Dam dictates the fishing conditions downstream. The least appealing conditions occur during high water when both generators are in use. At these times virtually the entire tailwater is unwadable, leaving float- or bank-fishing as the only options. Since almost all of the shoreline of the Norfork is privately owned, bank-fishing is limited. Fortunately, it is such a short river that float-fishing all of it in a single day is feasible during high water.

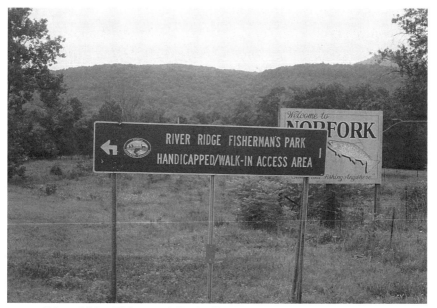

*River Ridge Fisherman's Park offers the best access for wade-fishing on the North Fork River.*

High water was traditionally thought to make fly-casting impossible on the Norfork, but some local anglers developed fishing patterns to beat the conditions. The key, they discovered, was to imitate bait-fishers. By using heavier gear (often in the 6- to 10-weight range) with sinking tip lines, egg patterns or San Juan Worms can be fished very near the bottom and catch fish even during the highest water flows. Zonkers, Squirrel-Tailed Nymphs, and streamers that mimic small trout or shad will also attract some fish. Fishing these imitations in eddies, backwaters, and calmer runs will produce the most action.

Another key to fishing high water is boat handling. Guides who take johnboats into this tailwater during maximum generation must run their outboard motors continuously to hold the boats into the current at either the head or foot of shoal areas. For the most part, anchoring is an iffy, and quite possibly dangerous, idea on high water. At one time anglers dragged heavy chains along the bottom to slow the drift of their boats, but this tactic has been outlawed on the Norfork because of the damage it did to the aquatic weed beds.

Anglers with spinning equipment during high water use all of the popular in-line spinners, plus Shad Raps, Countdown Rapalas, and Rebel Fastracs; they also use a host of other ultralight bass-type lures. Silver hues that imitate shad, or colors that mimic juvenile brown and rainbow trout, are popular.

When only one generator is in use at Norfork Dam, the tailwater develops a split personality. While floating is still practical, many areas become wadable as well. One good way to fish the stream at this time is to float from shoal to shoal, then get out to wade each shallow area.

It is during low water—when no power generation is taking place—that the Norfork is at its best. Virtually the entire flow is wadable; the river is so low that floating is practically impossible. Spin-fishers will continue to attack the fishing with the same methods they used during higher water, but for fly-casters the river becomes very different.

Almost all of the North Fork's insect hatches occur during low water, and the midge hatches of spring and summer can be abundant (although they are often overlooked by anglers). When a lot of gentle rises are taking place on the more placid water, tossing a size 20 to 22 midge pattern can produce some exciting fishing.

Although fish can be found throughout the river during low water, many will congregate in the remaining deeper pools. Fishing these locations with 5- to 6-weight fly-rods using Matukas in black or olive, Woolly Buggers, or Muddler Minnows usually provokes some strikes. Subsurface fishing with sow bug or scud imitations also works, as do Squirrel-Tailed Nymphs, Woolly Worms, or Gold-Ribbed Hare's Ears.

Beginning in 2003 the entire length of the Norfork tailwater to the downstream end of the island at Norfork is open to fishing under special regulations. Only artificial lures may be used that have either a single barbless hook or one barbless treble hook. The creel limit on rainbow trout is five fish, but only one of those may be longer than 21 inches. Also, all rainbow trout between 12 and 21 inches must be immediately released. For brook, brown, and cutthroat trout the minimum size limit is 21 inches, and the daily creel limit is one fish.

Along the Norfork's course, there are only three sites that offer public access to the fishing, but there are five privately operated trout docks. Still, considering there are less than 5 miles of water, access is good.

At the foot of Norfork Dam on the north side of the river is Quarry Park, which is managed by the Corps of Engineers. This access contains a paved boat ramp, parking lots, and a campground. Near the park is the Norfork National Fish Hatchery on Dry Run Creek. The creek itself is open to fishing only by anglers who are disabled or under 16 years of age. (Fishing piers over the water are provided for the handicapped anglers.) Only artificial lures with single barbless hooks are allowed, and all fish must be released.

It is also worth noting that Quarry Park is the best place on the Norfork to find brook trout. These fish appear to move up closer to the dam in search of the colder water emerging from the bottom of Norfork Lake.

Just below the boat ramp and the mouth of Dry Run is a small shoal that is quite a popular fishing destination. The 22,000 gallons of water emptying out of Dry Run and into this shoal every minute are high in dissolved oxygen and carry plenty of excess fish food from the hatchery. Such a combination attracts both trout and anglers to the shoal. Also benefiting from this situation is Long Hole, which is roughly ¼ mile downstream from the shoal and accessible to float fishermen. This spot is noted for giving up some of the Norfolk's bruiser brown trout.

Of course, when you are fishing so close to the dam, it is imperative to keep an ear peeled for the whistle that sounds when water releases are about to occur. Since there is plenty of time after the horn sounds to exit the river, it is not necessary to run for shore, but it is a good idea to immediately begin wading back to your access point.

In all, Quarry Park offers roughly ¾ mile of bank access to the North Fork. Foot trails run along the north shore from the boat ramp to the downstream areas. Quarry Park is just off AR 177 where it crosses Norfork Dam.

The River Ridge Access is managed by the AGFC and is the next point of public access to the North Fork. It is located at the end of River Ridge Road to the east of its junction with AR 5. A boat ramp, handicapped fishing pier, and walk-in area are provided here. At low water levels, a long gravel bar is exposed on the near shore.

The final access point to the North Fork is the Norfork Access just off AR 5 at the town of Norfork. This access is at the junction of the Norfork and White Rivers and features a parking area, a gravel bar (where boats can be launched), and bank access. These are located on the southeastern side of the river. The opposite shore—from the railroad bridge visible upstream, down to the junction of the rivers—is lined with downed trees and is noted for holding plenty of trout.

To obtain water-release information on the Norfork tailwaters, call the Corps of Engineers recorded message at 870-431-5311. This automated system is located at Bull Shoals Dam on the White River and provides schedules for both rivers.

# OUACHITA RIVER

### *DeLorme 48*

The tailwaters of the Ouachita (pronounced Wah-chita) River form another Arkansas trout fishery situated outside of the Ozark Mountain region and the White River watershed. This tailwater fishery is located downstream of the Arkansas Power and Light Company's (APL) Remmel Dam, which

Jeff Goodwin, © The Countryman Press

*Trout are once again being stocked below Remmel Dam on the Ouachita River tailwater in southwest Arkansas.*

backs up 11-mile-long, 1,940-acre Catherine Lake in the southwest quadrant of the state.

The Remmel Dam is actually one of three such structures that lie along the Ouachita in Hot Springs and Garland Counties, near the towns of Hot Springs and Malvern. The first of these is Blakely Mountain Dam on Lake Ouachita, which at 40,000 acres is the biggest of the reservoirs. The tailwaters below this dam are stocked with just over 30,000 trout annually, but empty directly into 7,200-acre Lake Hamilton, named for APL's second president C. Hamilton Moses. Thus, there is no true riverine tailwater fishery here.

At the other end of Lake Hamilton is the Carpenter Dam, named for peace officer Flave Carpenter, who discovered the dam site and recommended it to APL after tracking some outlaws into the area. The tailwaters of Carpenter Dam flow directly into the upper end of Lake Catherine. Roughly 35,000 trout are released into this lake each year, but again, the upper end of Catherine offers no river habitat.

The Arkansas Power and Light Company constructed Remmel Dam, at the lower end of Lake Catherine. The dam was named for U.S. Army Colonel H. L. Remmel, while the lake took its name from the daughter of

Harvey Couch, the founder of APL. The dam was completed and the impoundment flooded in 1924, but the trout fishery did not develop here until the 1980s. Since then, the fishery has had a checkered history and has not exhibited the angling results produced by rivers in the Ozarks. In fact, the stocking of trout was completely abandoned in the early 1990s, although efforts were restarted late in that decade.

Today, the Remmel tailwater can, at best, be described as a marginal trout fishery. The stocking pattern for this river consists of 2,500 rainbows trout released monthly in January and February, followed by a single release of 1,500 more fish in early April. All of these trout are 12 inches long at the time of planting.

The stockings take place immediately downstream of the dam and there is virtually no carryover of fish from year to year. It is rare for the fish to stray downstream from this stocking area. Access to the water is from gravel bars along the northwest shore at all water levels. It is possible to wade the flow through here on low water levels, but most fishing pressure is from bait-anglers on shore.

To reach the foot of the dam, take US 270 from the Malvern Exit on I-30, traveling west to the Jones Mill community. At that point, turn left onto Remmel Dam Road, which leads to gravel parking areas along the northwest shore of the river. Public access is possible along about ½ mile of the stream and includes an unimproved boat launch site.

## WHITE RIVER–BEAVER TAILWATER

### *DeLorme 23*

When tailwater trout fishing in the Ozarks is mentioned, most southern anglers immediately think of the White River below Bull Shoals Dam. That reaction is understandable in light of the river's 100-plus-mile length and the spectacular quality of the trout it produces. Competing for second billing with regard to trout fishing in the region are the Table Rock tailwaters of the White in Missouri and Arkansas' Little Red and Norfork Rivers. The tailwater below 28,000-acre Beaver Lake on the upper White River in northwestern Arkansas is relegated to the status of the "red-headed stepchild" of the White River system.

There are several reasons for the relative obscurity of this part of the White River. Located entirely in Carroll County between the towns of

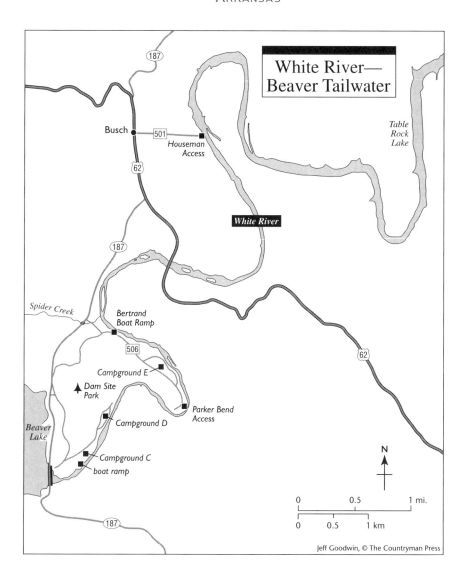

White River—
Beaver Tailwater

187

Busch

501

Houseman
Access

62

Table
Rock
Lake

White River

187

Spider Creek

Bertrand
Boat Ramp

506

Campground E

Dam Site
Park

N

Parker Bend
Access

Campground D

Beaver
Lake

Campground C

boat ramp

62

| 0 | 0.5 | 1 mi. |
| 0 | 0.5 | 1 km |

187

Jeff Goodwin, © The Countryman Press

Rogers and Eureka Springs and flowing northward to the Missouri border, the Beaver tailwater trout fishery is only about 8 miles long, depending on the water level in Table Rock Lake downstream. The stream is also narrow by Arkansas tailwater standards-only a "cast" wide at some places during low water. The trout fishery was created by the last of the dams built by the Corps of Engineers in the White River basin, completed in 1966. Being such a youngster in a region of spectacular trout tailwaters is not an ideal way to gain notoriety—even though the Beaver tailwater fishing would be considered terrific if it were located elsewhere. Although it does draw anglers from the northwestern corner of Arkansas, as well as from southwestern Missouri and adjoining portions of Kansas, the area below Beaver Lake still accounts for only 8 to 10 percent of all trout angling taking place in the state.

While this may give the impression that the Beaver tailwater is deserted, that is not a true picture of the situation. Since there are only three public access points between the dam and the end of stocked trout water at County Road (CR) 501, anglers will often be thick at these sites. On weekends, evenings, and holidays when the weather is fair, bank-anglers spread their lawn chairs and two legal fishing rods apiece all along the shores. At times it becomes difficult to wade some portions of the flow without getting tangled in these staked-out bait rigs.

The fishery in the Beaver tailwater is supported by the stocking of more than 200,000 trout per year. Most of these are catchable-sized rainbow, with releases taking place at all three access points on a monthly basis. The first planting of trout in this portion of the White River took place immediately after the dam was completed back in the 1960s. Brown trout have also been stocked in the river since 1985, when an initial release of 7,600 browns that were 7 inches long occurred. At present, about 10,000 brown trout are added to the fishery each year. Beginning in 1990, roughly 25,000 cutthroat trout have been released annually, and up to 6,000 brook trout are also stocked. The brookies, browns, and cutthroats are planted in the winter months and spread out along the course of the river, away from the access points.

Among Arkansas' tailwater trout rivers, the White below Beaver Lake was traditionally a classic put-and-take fishery. An electroshock survey conducted on the river in 1988 provided some interesting specifics. To begin with, AGFC biologists discovered a rainbow trout density of close to 1,200 fish per river mile, with over 40 percent of those 12 inches or larger. Of particular interest was the fact that the shocking had been carried out in September, after the tailwater had been subjected to heavy fishing pressure through the spring and summer. It was estimated at the time that the rainbow population fluctuates between 300 and 1,500 fish per mile at all times. A later check of the river in March 1991 found 429 rainbows per mile, even though no stocking had occurred since the previous September. Most of these fish were 12 to 14 inches long, but 2-pounders were present, as well as the rare rainbow of up to 8 pounds.

On the other hand, the brown trout population found in the 1988 survey indicated that up to 94 percent of these less heavily stocked fish were harvested within a year of stocking. The survey also revealed the fact that the browns that did avoid being caught grew at the astounding rate of 1 inch per month here. Even before the survey, such growth rates had been suspected. One tagged brown that was stocked in 1985 at 8 inches long was caught in August 1988 and tipped the scales at 10 pounds, 3 ounces. Its growth rate topped 3 pounds per year!

It was such unrealized trophy potential that led to the Beaver tailwater becoming Arkansas' "laboratory" for trout management. Beginning in 1988, a 2-fish creel limit with a 16-inch minimum size was established for brown trout on the White River between Beaver Dam and Table Rock Lake. Very quickly the population of browns in the tailwater rose from 40 or 50 per mile to 340. Within two years that figure reached 2,000 per mile.

The success of the brown trout regulations led to them being applied to other tailwaters in Arkansas; they became the state norm in January 1990. The excellent results of the brown trout rules led to a 2-fish, 16-inch minimum being applied to cutthroat trout as well. These fish had also shown a growth potential in the Beaver tailwater of 0.7 inch per year. Cutthroats are particularly popular because they do not become as carnivorous or as nocturnal as brown trout when they attain trophy size. It is possible to catch them on flies and baits regardless of the time of day or whether they have attained trophy proportions.

Through the 1990s, the waters below Beaver Dam continued to be a classroom for trout biologists. An electroshock survey in the fall of 1991 discovered that the brown trout population had plummeted to only 340 fish per mile. The two suspected causes of that collapse were the record rainfall in the spring of 1990 and an outbreak of disease among rainbow trout in federal hatcheries that year.

The record rains spawned flood conditions on the upper White River, prompting the Corps of Engineers to leave the Beaver Dam floodgates open for 10 straight days. Fifty thousand cubic feet of water per second (cfs) poured through the dam—where 10,000 cfs was the normal maximum—and a number of striped and hybrid bass in the 8- to 12-pound range were washed downstream into the tailwater.

These voracious feeders are quite fond of dining on trout. When 400 were subsequently removed back to the lake via electroshocking, stomach samples showed that about a third of them had been eating trout. In the ensuing years, some 20-pound stripers were taken by surprised anglers in the Beaver tailwater. Fortunately, since no hybrids or stripers are stocked down-

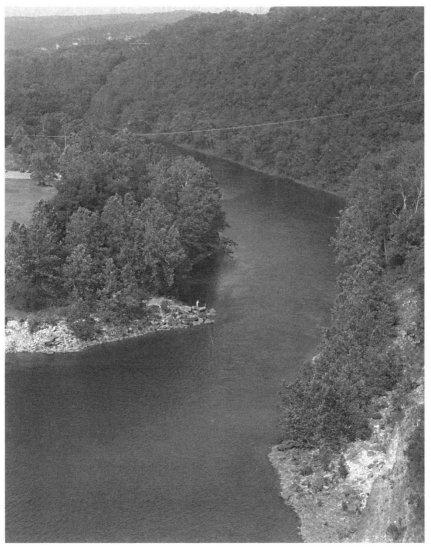

*The Beaver tailwater as seen from the top of Beaver Dam on the White River.*

stream in Table Rock Lake, these odd catches were just leftovers from the flooding; they likely spent most of their time in Table Rock and moved up into the tailwater only occasionally. Neither of these species spawns in the White River system.

The other possible cause of the decline in trout numbers was a 30 percent cutback in rainbow stocking in 1990 due to disease problems. It was feared that anglers who were used to taking their limit of six rainbows with relative ease became frustrated and began poaching undersized browns to fill their creels. Adding to that problem was an apparent unwillingness by local courts to take violations of the brown trout restrictions seriously.

The result of this situation was that local Trout Unlimited chapters began watching the judicial proceedings closely to highlight the problem. Meanwhile, AGFC officers worked to improve enforcement procedures. Those measures soon rectified the situation.

To counter some of the damage caused by the flooding and to learn more about how the trout habitat on the Beaver—and thus all tailwaters—functions, the AGFC began a $150,000 research and restoration project on the river in 1993. A consortium of public agencies and Trout Unlimited chapters repaired the flood damage with in-stream placement of boulders and log shelters to re-produce the deep holes and gravel bars that previously existed and benefited the trout. They also planted maple and sycamore trees along the shore and constructed steps on the walk-in trail at Parker Bend to curb bank erosion.

Probably the two streamer patterns most often used by fly-rodders on this portion of the White River are olive or black Woolly Buggers in sizes 4 to 12 and Muddler Minnows with olive or yellow marabou dressings. Pheasant Tail and Hare's Ear nymphs are also standards here, with egg patterns getting some use as well. As with all the other Ozark tailwaters, scud and sow bug imitations are usually found in anglers' fly boxes, too.

Although occasional mayfly hatches take place in the spring, most of the surface action for fly-fishers will involve casting to midge hatches that come off virtually year-round on the Beaver tailwater. Tiny flies in sizes 18 to 24 are needed for this fishing.

Anglers using spinning gear and artificial lures fish standard in-line spin-ners on this river, with gray and brown the most popular colors. On overcast days, however, fluorescent patterns in orange and chartreuse are better choices. Spoons, Countdown Rapalas, and ultralight crankbaits are also good choices. Lines 4-pound-test or lighter are recommended because of the very clear water below Beaver Dam.

Other popular lures on this tailwater include ultralight to microsized jigs. And we are talking about very small ones here! Sizes of $\frac{1}{32}$ ounce all the way down to $\frac{1}{256}$ ounce are used. These are fished under a tiny float, either with or without a small split shot beneath the float, on 2-pound-test line. In beige or brown, these can be deadly on the river's rainbow trout.

When bait-anglers tackle the trout in the Beaver tailwater, the choice of baits resembles those used on other Ozark rivers: salmon eggs, wax worms, night crawlers, marshmallows, cheese concoctions, crickets, and corn are all popular. Either live or dead shad work well when shad die-offs take place in Beaver Lake from January through April. For trophy browns, a lip-hooked sculpin fished in a shoal area after dark is another option. In fact, night-fishing for all sizes of trout seems to have a larger following below Beaver Dam than on other Arkansas trout rivers, with many anglers preferring to take to the water from midnight to dawn.

During high water, anglers most often target the backwaters and eddies created as either one or two turbines operate at the dam. Of course, float- and bank-fishing are the only options at these times, since wading is not practical on high water.

When the generators at Beaver Dam are silent, the river becomes a series of pools separated by wadable shoals. Floating in a canoe, which makes for a long day of fishing from the dam down to the end of practical trout water at the Houseman Access, is a favorite way for many anglers to tackle this water. Areas just above shoals or the holes washed out below the shoal waters are the best places to look for trout under these low-water conditions.

The Beaver tailwater is noted for having the most public access per stream mile of any of the rivers in the White system. This statement may seem a bit contradictory when matched up with the fact that there are only three access points along this portion of the White River. The Dam Site Park below Beaver Dam stretches for 3.2 miles downstream, contains two of these access areas, and takes in almost half of the stream's trout water on the north-western shore. Extending from the tailrace down to the junction with Spider Creek, this park has three campgrounds, two boat ramps, a walk-in area, a couple of shoals, several long gravel bars, and a catch-and-release angling area.

The catch-and-release regulations apply from ½ mile below Beaver Dam to a point 100 yards above the Parker Bend Walk-In Access. Through here only single, barbless-hook artificial lures are legal, and all fish must be re-leased. These rules apply year-round.

The gravel bar extending downstream from the boat ramp and the boul-ders along the opposite bank from the ramp are very popular angling desti-nations in this part of the park. Both bank- and wade-fishing can get crowded, in part because of the location of Campgrounds C and D along here. Cane Brake Hole, which lies next to Campground D, contains deep water that holds a lot of fish and is ideal for bait angling.

To attain access to this part of the park, travel ¼ mile north of Beaver Dam via AR 187 (which crosses the dam) and turn right into the paved entrance drive. As with most tailwater fisheries, a horn sounds at Beaver Dam to alert anglers to imminent releases of water.

Between the upper and lower portions of the Dam Site Park lies Crane Roost Bluff, where tall cliffs overlook a sharp bend in the river. Below this spot is Parker Bend Walk-In Access at the end of CR 506, to the east of AR 187. The shoals at this bend of the river in the shadows of Wallace Bluff are the most popular fishing sites for both wade- and bank-fishing on the Beaver tailwater. They are also noted for producing big brown trout. There is a fishing pier at this location.

The part of the river along CR 506 is also within the confines of the Dam Site Park and contains Campground E (Parker Bottom Campground), the Bertrand Boat Ramp, and some off-road parking, as well as the walk-in access. Wallace Bluff's sandstone ridge overlooks the river in the walk-in area, adding to the beauty of this portion of the tailwater.

The final 4 miles of trout water down to the Houseman Access can only be reached by boat and contain virtually no wadable water. The Houseman Access has a boat ramp and a parking area and is the last downstream site that is stocked with trout. To reach this access, take CR 501 east from US 62 at the crossroads of Busch. There is presently no sign at the intersection indicating that the access point is at the end of the road. It is ¾ mile from the intersection to the Houseman Access.

To receive information on water releases at the Beaver Dam, call 417-336-5083 for a recorded message. This service of the Army Corps of Engineers is provided from the Table Rock Dam farther down the White River in Missouri and also gives water level data for that dam.

## WHITE RIVER–BULL SHOALS TAILWATER

### DeLorme 25, 25, 34

If faced with the problem of coming up with a single word to describe the tailwater trout fishery on the White River below Bull Shoals Dam, one's uncontested choice would be "big." Everything about this resource is outsized. Bull Shoals Lake, from which the tailwater emerges, is the largest reservoir in the White River system, spreading to 45,440 acres at normal level. Bull Shoals Dam contains eight turbines in its powerhouse, and these generators are capable of changing the river from a trickle to a raging, big-water torrent in minutes.

# White River—Bull Shoals Tailwater

Bull Shoals Lake

Bull Shoals State Park

178

White Hole Access

Whiteville

126

9

178

5

412

62

7

Wildcat Shoals Access

1

315

Cotter Access

Cotter

Cotter Rim Shoals Access

Jenkins Cr.

58

4

126

57

Buford

126

Shipps Ferry Access

61

Cartney Access

72

126

Ranchette Access

101

Buffalo City Access

Buffalo City

Buffalo River

341

201

201

5

North Fork River

Norfork

Norfork Access

68

Red's Landing

5

White River

Chesmond Ferry Access

Calico Rock

Calico Rock Access

5

Optimus River Road

Optimus

5

Boswell

69

9

9

58

Boswell Shoals Access

Mt. Olive

Mt. Olive Access

Wild Haw Landing

Guion

9

58

Sylamore

Sylamore Access

9

87

9

14

14

St. James

Flippin

178

N

0        5        10 mi.

0    5    10 km

Jeff Goodwin, © The Countryman Press

Downriver from the dam, the tailwater continues to merit expansive adjectives. The stream's width is measured in hundreds of yards along its roughly 92-mile course as a trout resource. Its fishing rates with the best in the world as a result of massive stockings—more than a million trout per year. Additionally, the naturally reproducing brown trout found in the flow regularly reach weights measured in double digits; more monster trout of 30-plus pounds are produced here than in any other single stream in the world. Finally, the portion of the river from the dam down to the town of Cotter (self-proclaimed "Trout Capital of the World," but only officially recognized by the Arkansas General Assembly in 1993 as the "Trout Capital of the USA") boasts more than 200 fishing guides and better than two dozen trout docks or resorts.

The tailwater below Bull Shoals accounts for fully 36 percent of all trout fishing in Arkansas. Since it is estimated that each day of angling here generates $123 for the local economy, this river provides a hefty portion of the $150 million that trout fishing produces for the statewide economy. This is a stream that truly invites superlatives.

Beginning at the foot of Bull Shoals Dam near the Arkansas-Missouri border, this tailwater on the White River flows in a southeasterly direction. Fueled by the frigid waters from the 120-foot depths of the impoundment, the river contains excellent trout water for 44 miles down to its junction with the North Fork River at the town of Norfork. Here the infusion of the North Fork waters again lowers the river temperature, keeping it within the tolerance range for trout for an additional 48 miles down to the AR 58 bridge at the village of Guion.

Originating on the border of Marion and Baxter Counties, the White's tailwater cuts a swath down through the north-central portion of the state. Along this route toward the sea, the river forms the border of Stone and Izard Counties before changing to a warm-water flow. The river towns of Cotter, Buffalo City, Norfork, Calico Rock, Boswell, Mount Olive, Sylamore, and Guion are all situated on the White's trout-supporting tailwater. The White River's course is laden not only with trout, but with a heavy dose of history as well.

The Bull Shoals area was described as early as 1819 by Henry Rowe Schoolcraft, who was impressed by the power of the rapids situated on the present site of the dam. Beginning in the 1830s, the White was the scene of a thriving steamboat trade that carried agricultural and other products down to the Mississippi River. The need to ship iron and zinc ore mined along the Buffalo River (a tributary of the White whose mouth is located at Buffalo

City) prompted the construction of locks and dams along the river, starting in 1899. Only 3 of 10 planned locks were completed by 1905 when the St. Louis, Iron Mountain, and Southern Railroad linked the town of Cotter to Batesville downstream, effectively ending the building program and the riverboat era in the White River basin. In the ensuing years, the White River was used to float rafts of cedar trees out of the Ozark Mountains to be turned into pencils in a factory at Cotter. The stream's waters were also probed by local folks in search of freshwater mussels. These shellfish supplied a thriving button industry, and old-timers report seeing piles of shells as big as houses at buying stations near the old ferries. On rare occasions fine pearls were even found in those White River mussels.

The first bridge on the upper White was completed in 1930, replacing a number of the ferries. This highway bridge near Cotter, with its twin, rounded arches, is still in use on AR 315 and has been placed on the National Register of Historic Places.

Disastrous floods along the White River in 1898, 1915, 1916, and 1927 led to the Army Corps of Engineers' program of building dams on the river system. The Bull Shoals Dam was the second and largest of the projects, beginning power production in 1952 with four generators. An additional four turbines came on-line in 1963.

Once cold water began flowing in the Bull Shoals tailwaters and the smallmouth bass disappeared, the earlier experiment with trout on the North Fork River was extended to the White. That first year saw 16,156 rainbows and 1,800 brown trout stocked in the tailwater. These fish were all 6 to 8 inches long. By 1959, when Arkansas began keeping statistics on trout catches, the state record for rainbows fell four times in a single year, increasing from 11 pounds, 3 ounces to 15 pounds, 3 ounces. All of these trout were taken from the Bull Shoals section of the White. By the turn of the century, trout stockings on the White River below Bull Shoals Dam had grown to 1,300,000 rainbows of 9 to 12 inches, plus 100,000 browns, 175,000 cutthroats, and 2,000 brookies.

From the very beginning, the White River's potential for producing lunker-sized fish was apparent. In the early years of the fishery, it was the rainbow trout population that produced the impressive catches. The combination of the 48- to 54-degree water released through the dam, the forage base of sculpins in the river and stunned shad coming through the turbines from Bull Shoals Lake, and a year-round growing season was ideal for trout growth.

In the mid-1950s, the release of browns into the White was discontinued. It was feared that the difficult-to-catch browns would feed too heavily on the freshly stocked rainbows, diminishing the quality of the fishery. Thus, for 25 years the rainbows did not face competition and thrived. Unfortunately, the rapidly shifting water levels in the tailwater are not conducive to rainbow spawning, so almost no reproduction takes place. With estimated yearly carryovers of 10 to 15 percent of the fish, however, rainbows of 2 to 6 pounds became quite common, with some trout of more than 10 pounds showing up as well.

Eventually a total of six Arkansas state-record rainbow trout were taken from the Bull Shoals tailwaters; the final one remains the standard bearer. On March 4, 1981, Jim Miller of Memphis, Tennessee, was fishing a Rooster Tail spinner tipped with a worm near Sylamore when he boated a 19-pound, 1-ounce rainbow.

In the ensuing years, the fishing pressure on the White has grown so heavy that the chances of catching such a monster rainbow have diminished greatly. The estimates of AGFC biologists suggest that up to 97 percent of stocked rainbows are harvested within a year of release in the best trout water from Bull Shoals down to Cotter. Such figures greatly reduce the possibility of anyone tangling with a trophy-sized rainbow. Still, since White River trout grow from $\frac{1}{3}$ to $\frac{7}{8}$ inch monthly, and since harvest rates for rainbows drop to 72 to 82 percent on the portion of the flow below Norfork, some good fish are still possible.

Much the same story can be told of the cutthroat trout that were introduced into the Bull Shoals tailwater in 1982. By 1985, a steady stream of new state records for the species had pushed the mark to 9 pounds, 9.76 ounces. That fish was caught on a combination bait of worm and crawfish by Scott Rudolph of Ozark, Arkansas, on October 6. Since then, overfishing has been a problem for cutthroats as well, and the state eventually mandated a 2-fish creel limit and a 16-inch minimum size limit on the species.

In recent years brook trout have also been added to the list of trout present in the Bull Shoals tailwaters. Stocking numbers for these fish have been small, running from 2,000 to 12,000 per year, and their growth rates have not been as impressive as in the Little Red or Norfork tailwaters. The best place to target the brookies is in the first mile of water below the dam at Bull Shoals.

Despite the good fishing for the staple rainbows and the exotic brookies and cutthroats, the true calling card drawing fishers to the White River is the presence of wild, naturally reproducing, and often huge brown trout. As mentioned earlier, after the initial stockings in the 1950s, the practice was discontinued for more than two decades out of concern for the rainbow fishery. Plantings of browns were not resumed until the 1980s, long after the rainbow trout population had stabilized and then started to decline due to heavy fishing pressure. At about this time it also was discovered that browns were spawning in the river. Eventually, the first mile downstream of Bull Shoals Dam was identified as the major spawning ground, but spawning was also seen below Wildcat Shoals, 12 miles downriver, as well as at Rim Shoals, some 25 miles below the dam.

Although the Norfork and the Little Red Rivers have claimed much of the attention in recent years, due to each having produced world-record brown trout, the river that has most consistently yielded monster fish has been the Bull Shoals tailwater. From the beginning of record keeping in 1959, seven different Bull Shoals browns kept the Arkansas state record on the White River until 1988. The size of the top fish increased from the 10-pound, 13-ounce specimen taken by Frank Tilley of Norfork on a crawfish tail on June 27, 1959, up to the 33-pound, 8-ounce brute hooked on a worm-and-crawfish-tail combination bait on March 17, 1977, by Leon Waggoner of Flippin. This latter fish, which was taken from the White Hole about 4 miles below the dam, held the state record for more than 11 years.

To put the White River brown trout production in perspective, also consider that the stream has produced an average of more than one fish a year of better than 30 pounds since the early 1970s. Additionally, a brown brought to the surface and later released during an electroshock survey in 1990 measured slightly longer than the 39 inches of Huey Manley's 38-pound, 9-ounce former-world-record fish from the Norfork River. One of the more amazing feats of angling on the White River occurred on September 19, 1987, when fishing guide Carl Jones of Flippin boated a 20-pound, 12-ounce brown trout on 2-pound-test line. The fish was subsequently recognized as a line-class world record by the International Game Fish Association.

While the truly huge trout in the Bull Shoals tailwater are the attention grabbers, the sheer numbers of fish that most folks would think of as trophies are even more astounding. A 1986 survey found an average of 266 browns of more than 20 inches for each river mile. Nine of these fish per mile were in excess of 30 inches.

Unfortunately, fishing pressure on these trout was on the increase in the late 1980s as well. When the fish congregated in shoal areas, particularly during spawning season, they became susceptible to legal angling methods—but also to unscrupulous snaggers. A technique was even developed for low-water periods that used several boats to "herd" the browns into schools that produced the same fishing conditions as spawning runs. This herding technique has now been made illegal on Arkansas trout waters. Before it was, however, a 1988 survey showed that the number of trout of more than 20 inches had fallen to 192 per river mile.

At that point the AGFC stepped in to implement the present statewide regulations mandating a 16-inch minimum size and 2-fish creel limit for brown trout. These rules took effect on January 1, 1990. Eventually, even more stringent catch-and-release rules were put into effect on certain portions of the river.

A survey in August 1991 revealed an astounding 700 browns of 20 or better inches per river mile. Such a rebound was logical, however, after the trout were offered some added protection. To begin with, each spawning female lays 10,000 to 12,000 eggs. Given some time to grow and experience fishing pressure, it is easy for mature browns to avoid a hook. The White River is so large that there are plenty of places to hide from the heavy fishing pressure exerted on the waterway. As the fish mature they become more nocturnal, feeding mostly at night when the fewest anglers are fishing. Finally, the shrimp, scuds, sow bugs, sculpins, and shad in the river provide plenty of forage to fatten the browns. The bottom line is that the White River is the best place in the world to seek a brown trout of trophy proportions. A 1994 survey revealed an average of 188 browns of 5 pounds or larger per mile on this river.

Such a reputation does not go unnoticed. From spring through fall, angling pressure on the Bull Shoals tailwater is heavy. There are places and seasons, however, that allow the enterprising angler to beat the crowds. Though the fish continue to bite during the winter months, the number of anglers falls dramatically. The same can be said for after-dark angling. Due to the habits of browns, either of these periods is an excellent time to challenge the fish.

Where you fish on the White River also comes into play in avoiding the crowds. The portion of the river from the dam down to Cotter is noted for being the best fishing stretch; therefore, it receives the lion's share of the pressure. The portion of the tailwater from Buffalo City down to Calico Rock, on the other hand, is its least-fished stretch. The pressure then picks up slightly from Calico Rock to the end of trout water on the White.

As with any resource, not all the story has been pleasant. At times, the Bull Shoals tailwater suffered from some water-quality problems as a result of low water and low oxygen levels. One cause of such conditions was too-low minimum water flow coming through Bull Shoals Dam, which resulted in a major fish kill in the fall of 1990. An additional cause of low oxygen levels involved periods of extremely high rainfall. These washed a lot of nutrients into Bull Shoals Lake, promoting bacterial growth that depleted the oxygen. These oxygen-starved waters then were drawn from the depths of the lake and released into the tailwater. In other words, too much or too little water tended to be the problem in the White River.

Starting in 1991, the Corps of Engineers and Southwest Power Administration began venting the turbines to add oxygen to the water during critical periods. Unfortunately, this limited the amount of power generated, thus costing money. More recently, hub deflectors have been added to the turbines, which accomplishes the same end without sacrificing electrical production.

The Bull Shoals tailwater on the White River is where float-fishing was developed and refined. The standard rig for this angling is a 20-foot johnboat with captain's chairs for the anglers, a cooler for drinks in the middle of the boat, and a 10- to 20-horsepower outboard motor at the rear. Nearly every guide on the river has this type of setup, with only slight variations. Needless to say, many of the local anglers copy the setup for their own use. Expect to see plenty of boats on the White during the prime fishing months of spring through fall.

During high water on the Bull Shoals tailwater (when five to eight turbines are running at the dam), float-fishing is virtually the only option. Practically all of the shoals will be far too deep and swift for wading—the river can rise by as much as 12 feet. Also, trying to anchor a boat in this powerful current is foolhardy. Such an effort can lead to the rushing water capsizing the boat, depositing everyone aboard into sub-50-degree water. Poor boat handling and hypothermia have cost the lives of a number of anglers on this river. As a general rule—but not one on which to bet your life—the lowest water levels occur during the morning hours, from dawn to about 11. As with most tailwaters, Bull Shoals Dam has a siren that announces imminent releases, but it is only useful to anglers immediately downstream of the powerhouse.

The proper way to attack the high-water bait-fishing on the White is to drift downstream, employing what the local folks call "drag fishing." Hooks with standard baits are "dragged" along the bottom as they are fished off the upstream side of the boat. In some cases, the guide uses the outboard to slow the boat's descent, or even employs drag chains. As noted earlier, these chains have been outlawed on the North Fork River because they destroy the aquatic vegetation. Due to the power-generation surges in the White, aquatic weeds and mosses are extremely rare, so chains are allowed here.

When the turbines are running full bore at Bull Shoals Dam, the trout are not bunched up in deeper holes but are dispersed throughout the river. This is a good time to concentrate on areas nearer the bank of the stream, especially around logs or rock piles. The best portion is generally the corridor between the low-water mark and the present shoreline.

For the caster using spinning lures, high-water periods can also yield fish. Artificial baits should be cast into the same areas that the bait-fishers concentrate on. It is usually necessary to slow the boat's drift to provide enough time to properly present a lure. The most popular lures are Rooster Tail spinners, Little Cleo spoons, and Countdown Rapalas. Colors that mimic juvenile rainbow or brown trout are usually successful. These lures are used on all water levels on the White.

When only one to four generators are active at the dam, the tactics employed on the White change a bit. While drift-fishing is still the best choice, much of the action will take place in the middle of the river. The currents at these water levels are not great enough to push the trout out of their feeding lanes, so they hang in midstream eddies and current breaks.

When only one turbine is turning at the dam, or none at all, the White is but a shadow of its former self. The raging lion turns into a meandering pussycat that can be waded in many areas. For the float-fisher, this is the time to cast out the anchor and begin tight-lining into the deeper holes where the fish are concentrated. The water is ordinarily so clear that some guides cruise the river sight-fishing to the larger brown trout. Some locals, including guides, claim that the very best fishing on the White occurs when the river has been low for periods of two to three days.

These low-water periods are also the time that fly-fishers own the river. Although in the early years of the tailwater it was commonly thought that White River trout could not be taken on flies, this has since been very emphatically disproved. Some of the shoal areas produce mayfly hatches in May and June that call for size 14 to 16 Sulfur Duns and hatches of Light Cahills come off throughout the summer in sizes 12 to 14. During the late summer through fall months the Bull Shoals tailwater is noted for its hatches of gray or black midges in the size 18 to 24 range; these take place predominantly on the long, slow pools. Finally, size 14 dark olive caddisflies are prevalent in the early fall.

Despite these hatches, most of the fly-casting action on the White is composed of tossing Gold-Ribbed Hare's Ears, Squirrel-Tailed Nymphs, Woolly Buggers, or Woolly Worms. Brown, black, and olive are the most popular colors for these latter two flies. Sow bug and scud imitations are staples of subsurface angling as well. For the fly-caster targeting big brown trout, a sculpin imitation tied with marabou is a good bet, regardless of the water level.

Opinions differ as to the best time of year to fish the Bull Shoals tailwater. As a rule of thumb, however, a lot of anglers mention that the fishing picks up beginning in mid-May and continues on through June, July, and August, especially during low-water periods. If big brown trout are your quarry, the winter months are probably just as good. But remember to dress appropriately in the fall and winter. The water is always bitterly cold, and the air can be as well.

Access is quite good, with more than 30 commercial trout docks and 18 public access points along the 92 miles of trout water. A large number of these points are located in the first 25 miles from the dam down to Rim Shoals. This portion of the river is noted for the best fishing, thus it gets the heaviest angling pressure. In fact, creel surveys have often documented as many as 200 wading fishermen in the first 7 miles downstream of the dam during low-water periods. Still, with the number of boat ramps and low-water wadable shoals along the stream, anglers can find room to practice their craft regardless of their tackle preference.

The first access point below the dam is in 725-acre Bull Shoals State Park. Located on Corps of Engineers land, the park contains bank access, wadable shoals, a boat ramp, a campground, parking areas, and a state-owned trout dock. All of these are arrayed on the eastern side of the river. The shore access to the river is via the park campground and the Big Bluff Hiking Trail. At the lower end of the park is a major shoal known as Dew Eddy Shoals.

The park is also the site of the Ozarks' largest spawning ground for brown trout. Each winter big browns move upriver to this point with procreation on their minds. To protect these fish, the stretch of water from 100 yards below Bull Shoals Dam down to the upstream boundary of the state park is a catch-and-release area.

The part of the river running through the state park is a seasonal catch-and-release area for brown trout from November 1 to January 31 each year. Also, no fishing is allow from 30 minutes after sunset until 30 minutes before sunrise in this three-month period. In both of these catch-and-release areas only lures with a single barbless hook or one barbless treble hook are

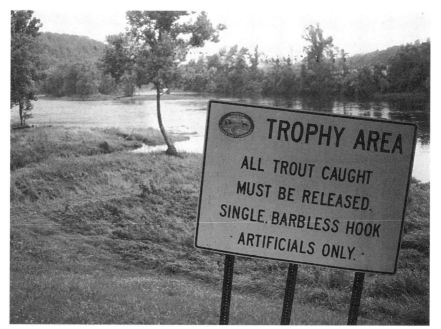

*Public access is now possible from the shore at Rim Shoals on the Bull Shoals tailwater*

allowed. The regulated areas are marked at streamside with signs detailing the regulations.

Access to Bull Shoals State Park is via AR 178, which crosses the dam. The entrance to the park is at the southeastern end of the dam.

The next downstream public access point to the tailwater is at White Hole Access. Located on the western shore of the river, the site contains a boat ramp and parking area. A steep, scenic stone cliff lines the opposite shore at this point, while the near shore features a long gravel bar that is exposed at low water. At medium water levels it provides some wading possibilities around the boat ramp. White Hole is located just downstream of the access point and is noted as a good place to fish for big brown trout in the summer months. A 5-mile paved road runs from the ramp westward to AR 178. A sign at this intersection in the Fairview community indicates the direction to White Hole Access.

Twelve miles downstream of Bull Shoals Dam is Wildcat Shoals Access on the eastern bank of the river. To reach this access point, take Wildcat Shoals Road, which is County Road (CR) 7, west from AR 126 just south of the Whiteville community. When Wildcat Shoals Road dead-ends into

Denton Ferry Road (CR 1), turn right. Follow Denton Ferry Road to its intersection with Waterside Place and turn right. The access point is on Waterside Place.

A paved boat ramp is available at this AGFC site, as are parking spaces. There is a wadable section of water at the ramp, but Wildcat Shoals is actually located around the bend downstream. This is one of the most popular shoals with fly-casters on the White River and another area noted for giving up big summertime brown trout. The shoal can be difficult for boaters to negotiate during low water, but below it Rainbow Hole offers more good fishing prospects for large brown trout in the summer.

The Cotter Access is the next point of public use. It is just off AR 315, south of the town of Cotter. At 18 miles below the dam, this AGFC facility is one of the busiest on the White River. Located just upstream of a railroad bridge and the historic AR 315 bridge, the access's paved boat ramp is next to Cotter Springs, which forms a natural swimming hole before flowing down into the river.

An unnamed island splits the river between the two bridges, and the near-side channel and island are accessible to waders on low water. The fishing is good on the far channel as well, but even slight increases in the water level can leave an unwary angler stranded on the island.

From the US 62 bridge upstream of Cotter down to the railroad bridge below town, a new special regulation area has been established. Beginning in 2003 angling is restricted to artificial lures only, which must have either a single barbless hook or one barbless treble hook. A 12- to 21-inch slot limit applies for rainbow trout, requiring their immediate release. Up to five rainbow trout may be kept, but only one of those may be longer than 21 inches. Finally, a 21-inch minimum size limit and one-fish-per-day creel limit apply to brook, brown, and cutthroat trout taken in this part of the river.

Rim Shoals is another public access site that is worth noting in any description of the White River trout waters. Two small islands, sometimes referred to as Upper Rim and Lower Rim, are found in this shoal. Rim Shoals is one of the areas of the Bull Shoals tailwater most frequented by fly-fishers, and it has also been identified as a brown trout spawning area. Since 1995, the portion of the river from the mouth of Jenkins Creek above Redbud Shoals down to the power line that crosses below Rim Shoals has been designated catch-and-release only, with artificial lures having single barbless hooks mandated.

To reach the Rim Shoals Access, take AR 126 north from the community of Buford, then turn west on Buford Cutoff (CR 3). There is a sign for Rim Shoals at this intersection. Next, turn left onto CR 58 at the sign for Rim Shoals Trout Dock. Follow this gravel road until it crosses the railroad track, continuing through the trout dock property to a gravel parking lot and walk-in access at the head of Rim Shoals.

The AGFC maintains Ranchette Access as the next downriver point of public entry. This site is located 28½ miles below Bull Shoals and provides a jump-off point for Rough Hole, which lies just downstream. There is also some low-water wading available near the paved boat ramp.

The road that approaches the access runs from AR 101, which is 2 miles to the west. At this writing, the approach road does not have a sign identifying it, but the junction with AR 101 has a directional sign for the access point.

Buffalo City Access has dual paved boat ramps at the end of AR 126 on the northeast side of the White River. These are located 4 miles downstream of Ranchette, and just above the junction of the White and Buffalo Rivers. There is some wadable water here, and the far shore of the river is dominated by high, sheer sandstone bluffs.

The boat ramps at Buffalo City are good spots to launch for a short run upriver to Buffalo Shoals. This shoal is considered by many to be the most scenic on the entire tailwater, and it provides a long stretch of wadable water. For the hardy trekker, it is possible to reach the shoals by hiking from Buffalo City up the railroad tracks that parallel the river.

At 36 river miles below Bull Shoals Dam, the AGFC provides the Cartney Access. There is a boat ramp located at the end of a 3-mile drive on CR 72, which is gravel as it approaches the river from AR 341. The ramp is on the southeastern side of the flow.

The next public access to the Bull Shoals tailwater is found at Shipps Ferry Access. On the southeastern side of the river the old ferry-boat landing is still visible, but the access point itself is on the northwestern shore. The approach is via CR 61, but the last ¼ mile of the road is gravel. Besides the ramp and parking area, there is some good fishing around in-stream boulders and ledges on the near side of the river.

The last 6 miles of the White above its junction with the Norfork is the least appealing trout water on the upper river. Through here the stream gets rather warm in the summer months, and trout do not fare well. Fortunately, when the Norfork's cold waters enter the White, the main river is again rejuvenated as a cold-water fishery.

At the town of Norfork, boat ramps are available on either shore in the

Norfork Access. The AGFC ramp on the eastern shore is gravel, while the western ramp is paved. This is a popular site for both bank-fishing and boat launching, so usage is heavy. Both ramps are immediately below the confluence of the two rivers. Access to the western ramp is from AR 341, while the eastern ramp is reached from AR 5.

The next two access points are found at Red's Landing and Chesmond Ferry Accesses. Both of these AGFC facilities have boat ramps. Red's Landing Access is at the end of a 3-mile drive on gravel CR 68 and lies on the northeastern side of the river. You can reach Chesmond Ferry Access via a spur road to the west of the town of Calico Rock. The access is on the northeastern side, and the old ferry landing is visible across the river. Almost the entire western bank from Norfork to Calico Rock lies within the Ozark National Forest.

Midway between these two access points lies another catch-and-release area. This one stretches from Monkey Island downstream to the mouth of Moccasin Creek on the river's east shore. Only single-hooked, artificial lures may be used there and all trout must be released immediately.

At 18 miles downriver from the mouth of the Norfork, the AR 5 bridge spans the White in Calico Rock. The town sits on a high bluff on the northeastern shore of the river and derives its name from the rocky cliff on which it perches. Calico Rock Access is located under the highway bridge at the foot of the cliff below the town. A boat ramp, parking lot, and rest rooms are located here. Wading is impractical through this stretch of water, but bank-fishing is available.

Finding the access at Calico Rock is no easy matter unless you are familiar with the town. Driving south on AR 5 through Calico Rock, you need to turn left on the last street before reaching the river bridge. Next, take the first right turn over the railroad spur track. Once over this spur, the road goes through an underpass beneath the main rail line. From there the road descends steeply to the right approaching the parking area and boat ramp. There are no directional signs at any of these turns.

The next public entry point on the White River tailwater is located near the town of Optimus. Although occasionally referred to as the Optimus Access, the actual name is Boswell Shoals Access. This access is unique in that it is managed by the U.S. Fish and Wildlife Service, due to its location within the Ozark National Forest on the western shore. Also setting it apart from most other accesses is its status as a walk-in area. There is no boat ramp, although it is possible to launch canoes and small boats from the parking area.

The village of Boswell is located directly across the river from this access and lends its name to Boswell Shoals just downstream. These are the last shoals located on the Bull Shoals' trout water. You can reach them by foot from Boswell Shoals Access on the western bank.

To reach this access, travel east on Optimus River Road for 4.1 miles from the village of Optimus (the village is on AR 5) to the parking area. There is a directional sign for the access at the intersection in Optimus. The last 2.3 miles of the approach road are gravel.

The next three access points to White River's trout water are found in the villages of Mount Olive, Sylamore, and Guion (pronounced Guy-on). All of these contain boat ramps for accessing this slower portion of the tailwater, which is characterized by sweeping turns through bottomland.

The final catch-and-release area on the White River tailwater is in the area just upstream of Sylamore. This one mandates single-hooked, artificial lures and the release of all trout caught. It runs from the upstream boundary of the Sylamore National Forest on the west shore in Stone County down to the lower boundary of Jack's Resort, also on the west side of the flow.

At both Sylamore and Guion, access is available on both shores of the river via the old ferry landings. In the case of Guion, the access on the eastern shore is also known as the Wild Haw Landing, taking its name from both an early pioneer family and the 19th-century steamboat landing at the site. All three of these access points are managed by the AGFC.

For up-to-date water-release information for Bull Shoals Dam, the Corps of Engineers maintains a recorded message at the powerhouse. Call 870-431-5311.

# Georgia

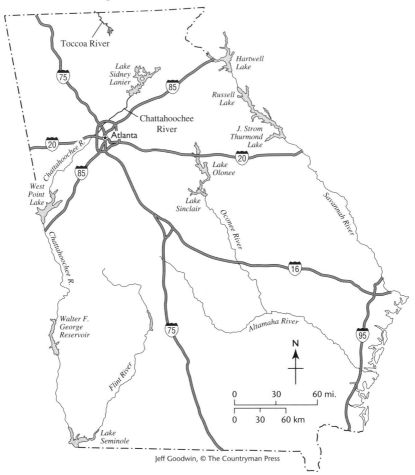

Toccoa River

Lake Sidney Lanier

Hartwell Lake

Russell Lake

Chattahoochee River

J. Strom Thurmond Lake

Atlanta

Lake Olonee

West Point Lake

Chattahoochee R.

Lake Sinclair

Oconee River

Savannah River

Walter F. George Reservoir

Flint River

Altamaha River

N

0    30    60 mi.

0    30    60 km

Lake Seminole

# CHAPTER 5

# Georgia

A mong the states that have traditionally been called the "Deep South," Georgia is unique in that it is the only one containing natural trout habitat. A band of counties stretching from the Blue Ridge Mountains in the northeastern corner of the state to the Cohutta Mountains in the northwest has always been home to native southern Appalachian brook trout. Over the years, through the introduction of brown and rainbow trout, that range has increased to most of the northern third of Georgia. Today, trout are stocked on a seasonal basis well down into the Piedmont region of the state, south of Atlanta.

As a result of these efforts, Georgia vies with North Carolina for the most total trout-stream miles of any southern state, with both claiming around 4,200. Additionally, with 1,500 miles of Class 1 or natural trout waters, the Peach State places third in the region (behind North Carolina and Virginia) in this category. The state's cold-water resources are quite extensive for an area not usually associated with trout angling.

Georgia does not possess a great many tailwater streams, although two of the three located here are of exceptional quality. The Chattahoochee River carries cold water from Lake Sidney Lanier down into the heart of metropolitan Atlanta on the northern rim of the Piedmont, creating an unusual urban fishery. In the northwestern corner of the state, water releases from Blue Ridge Lake add about 16 miles of excellent trout waters to the Toccoa River. Finally, in the northeastern corner of the state, the tailwaters of

Hartwell Lake, on the Savannah River, support a small trout fishery. This last stream is shared with South Carolina—it forms the border between the two states. For this reason, a description of the Savannah River will be found in section 9 of this book, which covers South Carolina.

In recent years an attempt was made to create one more tailwater trout fishery. From 1997 to 1998 Georgia fisheries managers experimentally stocked both rainbow and brown trout below the dam at Strom Thurmond Lake (more commonly known as Clarks Hill Lake in Georgia) on the Savannah River. This area is on the Georgia–South Carolina border, downstream of the fishery at Hartwell Dam and immediately upstream of the city of Augusta.

Beginning in April of 1997, 10,000 rainbow trout and 3,500 browns were released in the rocky shoals that stretch for 15 miles along the waterway. By the summer of 1998, however, the effort had been declared a failure by the Georgia Department of Natural Resources and stocking was discontinued. The area immediately below the dam was found to have water cold enough to support the fish, but the dissolved oxygen level in the water was too low for a healthy fishery. On the other hand, the oxygen levels around the Interstate 20 bridge farther downstream were excellent, but spring and summer water temperatures soared to unacceptable levels.

Although Georgia has a general trout season that lasts from the last Saturday of March through the final day of October, this season does not apply to any of the state's tailwaters. All of these tailwaters are managed as year-round trout fisheries.

A Georgia Trout Stamp is required, along with a regular fishing license, for all resident and nonresident anglers between the ages of 16 and 64. These may be purchased over the phone by calling 1-888-748-6887 or via the Internet at www.ganet.org/dnr. A Visa or MasterCard is required for the transactions.

The creel limit in Georgia is any combination of eight trout per day, regardless of species. There are no minimum or maximum size limits enforced on the tailwaters of the state.

# CHATTAHOOCHEE RIVER

## DeLorme 20, 26

The Chattahoochee River is one of Georgia's best-known waterways. It rises in the Mark Trail Wilderness Area in the north-central portion of the state. From there it courses down to Lake Sidney Lanier, which is the most heavily

Chattahoochee River

Cumming

Buford Dam Rd.
Lake Sidney Lanier
Bowman Island Unit
Sugar Hill

Settles Bridge Rd.

Sharon Road

Chattahoochee River

McGinnis Ferry Rd.
McGinnis Ferry Unit

Suwanee Creek Unit

Abbotts Bridge Unit

Abbotts Bridge

Duluth

State Bridge Rd.

Pleasant Hill Rd.

McClure Bridge

Medlock Bridge

Jones Bridge Unit
East Jones Bridge Rd.
Medlock Bridge Unit

Jones Bridge Park

Roswell

Holcomb Bridge Rd.

Holcomb Bridge Unit

Island Ford Unit
Roberts Drive

Morgan Falls Dam
Morgan Falls Rd.

Johnson Ferry Unit

Sope Creek

Johnson Ferry Road

Cochran Shoals Unit
Interstate North Parkway

Powers Ferry Rd.
Palisades Unit

Mt. Paran Rd.

ATLANTA CITY BOUNDARY

Akers Dr.

Harris Trail
Whitewater Creek Rd.

Akers Mill Road

Peachtree Creek

N

| 0 | | 2.5 | | 5 mi. |

| 0 | | 2.5 | 5 km |

Jeff Goodwin, © The Countryman Press

used Corps of Engineers reservoir in the United States, with between 15 and 20 million visitors per year. After exiting the lake, the Chattahoochee runs through metropolitan Atlanta, then goes on to form the boundary between Georgia and Alabama. Eventually, in Lake Seminole at the Florida border, its waters become part of the Apalachicola River.

The Hooch, as it is referred to by many local anglers, begins its journey to the Gulf of Mexico as a natural trout stream in the mountains above Lake Lanier. By the time it reaches that 38,000-acre impoundment, it is already becoming a warm-water stream. The water drawn through Buford Dam from the 200-foot depths of Lake Lanier revitalize the river as trout habitat. In fact, the Chattahoochee tailwater becomes the Peach State's premier trout water for the next 47 miles.

The story behind the conversion of the Chattahoochee tailwater to a trout fishery is a bit unusual in that the state fisheries managers played no role in the original endeavor. When Buford Dam was closed in 1957, there were no plans to introduce trout into the river. At the time, a program of stocking and stream renovations was in progress in the mountainous northern portion of the state, and the old Georgia Game and Fish Commission was trying to draw anglers to those northern counties. At that time, it had no interest in creating a competing trout fishery closer to the center of population in metro Atlanta.

In 1959 the local chapter of the Izaak Walton League obtained about 5,000 rainbow trout fingerlings and surreptitiously released them into the tailwater below the dam. Once the fish had grown to catchable size, club members invited the state biologists to join them for a day of fishing on the new trout water. Needless to say, such actions today with regard to amateur stocking projects would be illegal, but the state fisheries managers quickly climbed aboard this bandwagon when the river's trout potential was demonstrated.

From this unique beginning, the stocking program expanded. It now releases about 250,000 catchable-sized 9- to 12-inch rainbow and brown trout per year into the Chattahoochee. These fish are stocked in the portion of the river upstream of Morgan Falls Dam, with most released in the spring through fall months.

The lower portions of this tailwater receive an additional 100,000 fingerling browns and rainbows annual. Finally, the delayed-harvest portion of the lower tailwater gets 50,000 adult trout per year, of which several thousand are 14 to 20 inches long when released. These plantings occur from fall through the early spring months.

The Chattahoochee is one of Georgia's most heavily fished trout streams; fortunately, with 47 miles of big water, it is also by far the state's largest. The river is about 200 feet wide at Buford Dam and stretches to twice that width by the time it reaches Atlanta. Also, as mentioned earlier, the entire tailwater is open to year-round fishing, providing more opportunities for anglers. On the downside, the Chattahoochee is strictly a low-water fishery. When generation is taking place at Buford Dam, the river runs very high and muddy, making angling impractical.

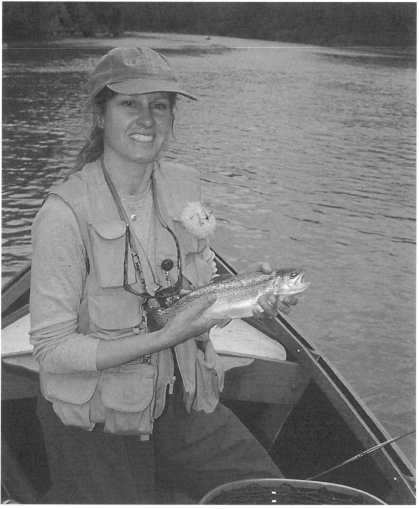

*The delayed-harvest section of the "Hooch" gives up some nice rainbows in the fall and winter.*

Access to the entire Hooch tailwater is very good due to the location of the Chattahoochee River National Recreation Area (CRNRA) along its shores. This "string of pearls" consists of a number of tracts of public land on the river from Buford Dam down to Atlanta. In all, park land totals roughly 4,000 acres.

There are actually four distinct sections of the Chattahoochee between Buford Dam and the end of trout habitat at the mouth of Peachtree Creek in Atlanta. Such variety is a result of the very long tailwater on the Hooch. This distance serves to moderate the surges of water released downriver, allowing for a more diverse habitat in the lower portions of the run.

The first of these sections extends from Buford Dam down to the GA 20 bridge between the towns of Cumming on the west and Sugar Hill to the east. This bridge is roughly 2½ miles downstream of the dam.

Through here the riverbed is subject to the harshest scouring by the rushing waters released during power generation. It is composed of rock, gravel, and sand that is quite barren of aquatic insect life. While the extremely cold water from the lake provides good year-round temperatures for trout, the forage base for the fish is small. This section of the stream is strictly a put-and-take fishery, with only a few carryover trout turning up. Of course, with plenty of fish stocked, the competition for meals is fierce, so the fish are usually hungry and bite readily.

This portion of the Hooch receives regular stockings of brown and rainbow. These fish are supplied by the Chattahoochee State Fish Hatchery located just upstream of the GA 20 bridge. The staple of the fishery is the recent stocker, but occasional browns of 20 inches or better will turn up. The area closer to the GA 20 bridge is best for larger fish.

Much of the fishing pressure in this section is from bait-anglers (the only restriction is that no minnows may be used for bait upstream of Morgan Falls Dam); spin-fishers tossing in-line spinners or Little Cleo spoons place second. This is not the best fly-fishing water on the river, but Woolly Buggers, adult caddis imitations, and attractor dry-fly patterns will take some fish.

There is one easily waded shoal on this part of the river, at Bowmans Island, within sight of the dam. Shore access to the water is good along the west side of the river in the North Bowman Island Unit of the CRNRA, down to the mouth of Haw Creek. At the mouth of this feeder stream is a deep hole that gives up plenty of trout.

This part of the Chattahoochee, however, is a location that calls for extreme caution. Released water can turn it into a raging torrent in a hurry.

Anyone boating, in a float tube, or even wading in the river between the dam and GA 20 must wear a Coast Guard–approved Personal Flotation Device (life jacket) at all times. This dangerous water has claimed the lives of several anglers over the years.

The next section of the tailwater runs from GA 20 downstream to GA 141 at Medlock Bridge and is primarily a float-fishing section of water. This 14½-mile segment of the river is managed under "artificial-lure-only" fishing regulations and is the most heavily fished section of the river. Interestingly, due to metro Atlanta's growing Hispanic population, the signs explaining the regulations are posted along the shore in both English and Spanish.

Fish Weir Shoals, just downstream of GA 20 is the only shoal area on this run, but farther downstream midriver sandbars offer some wading opportunities. Many anglers combine floating with wading by anchoring their boats on the bars, then wading in and casting back toward shore.

Most of the trout through here—both stocked browns and rainbows— are found around the brush piles and blown-down trees along the shoreline.

Although water-release scouring is less intense here, the forage base is still small. More fish hold over here than upstream, with some bruisers in the 5- to 8-pound range taken each year. Brown trout make up the bulk of these larger fish.

The possibility of catching a large brown trout on this part of the river was emphatically reinforced in November of 2001. Charlie Ford of Rome, Georgia, was casting a Yo-Zuri Pin's Minnow lure while drift-fishing when he boated a new state-record brown that weighed 18 pounds, 6.72 ounces. The fish was 32 inches long and sported a girth of 22 inches. It bested the previous state record for the species by almost 5 ounces.

The most popular fishing tactic on this section is casting top-water minnow-imitating jerkbaits or in-line spinners, but you will also encounter anglers like Charlie Ford tossing or trolling sinking versions of the jerkbaits in the deeper portions of the flow. Some anglers use imitation salmon eggs as well, but be aware that the ones permeated with organic oils are not legal on this part of the river. Nymphs, streamers, and attractor dry flies are used by fly-casters. In years when Japanese beetles are present, their imitations can be deadly; grasshopper patterns will also work during the summer and fall months. From late April through June each year the entire tailwater from this section downstream produces heavy hatches of caddisflies. Most anglers resort to casting Elk Hair Caddis patterns in sizes 12 to 18 to take advantage of this surface-feeding action.

Access to this part of the tailwater is available at the McGinnis Ferry,

Suwanee Creek, Abbotts Bridge, and Medlock Bridge Units of the CRNRA. Improved boat ramps are located at Abbotts and Medlock Bridges, providing good put-in and take-out points for a 4½-mile float. Other limited access through here is found at Settles Bridge and at McClure Bridge.

The third section of the Chattahoochee tailwater runs from GA 141 down to the GA 9 bridge at the town of Roswell. The river here is again open to angling by any method and gives up some truly big trout. Browns of 14 to 16 pounds have been taken, while rainbows of up to 14 pounds have also been reported. The extreme water surges abate on this 12-mile stretch of water, and the first aquatic weeds begin to appear.

There are two wadable sections on this run: Jones Bridge Shoals and Island Ford Shoals. Jones Bridge is just over a mile downriver from Medlock Bridge and boasts some hatches of caddisflies during spring and summer. Be aware also that this is the single most heavily fished location on the river, and most of its anglers are bait-casters. With the exception of caddis imitations and natural baits, the fishing tactics used on section two of the tailwater apply through here as well.

Access points for this run are at Medlock Bridge, Jones Bridge, Holcomb Bridge, and Island Ford Units of the CRNRA. Although Jones Bridge is no longer serviceable, there are boat ramps on both sides of the river in the park.

The final section of trout water on the Hooch extends 18 miles from GA 9 down to the mouth of Peachtree Creek in northwestern Atlanta. In recent years a new fisheries management scheme has made this end of the tailwater into a very popular trout-fishing destination.

The first 5 miles of water through here are impounded behind Morgan Falls Dam, a small hydroelectric installation operated by the Georgia Power Company. Although the lake contains trout, it is not considered part of the tailwater fishery.

Though the water rises and falls below Morgan Falls, the surges from Buford Dam have been all but eliminated. As a result, weeds and insects are plentiful. Add to this the presence of four distinct wadable shoals, plus 4½ miles of water under delayed-harvest regulations, and you have the best fly-fishing area of the tailwater. This is not to say that spin-fishers, and to a lesser extent bait-anglers, do not also utilize this portion of the stream. In fact, since the introduction of delayed-harvest fishing in 2000, this has become a very heavily fished piece of water, with the bulk of the anglers being fly-casters.

Delayed-harvest rules call for catch-and-release angling with single hook artificial lures or flies from November 1 until the following May 14 each year.

An exception is made for fly-casters using tandem, dropper-rigs utilizing two flies, as long as each fly has only one hook. From May 15 to October 31, regular trout regulations are enforced, allowing any type of angling, plus the harvest of fish. This portion of the river becomes so warm in the summer months that the carryover of trout from year to year is small. With these regulations, anglers are afforded 6½ months of quality fishing in the fall through early spring, then can take the trout out of the river before the water temperatures rise in late spring and summer.

Below Morgan Falls Dam 100,000 brown and rainbow trout fingerlings of 4 to 6 inches are stocked each fall on a put-grow-and-take basis. Additionally, in the delayed-harvest waters from the mouth of Sope Creek downstream to the US 41 (Cobb Parkway) bridge, another 50,000 catchable-sized trout are releases beginning on November 1 each year. These stockings include both brown and rainbow trout, with 10 percent of the fish 12 inches or longer. Some of the fish even top 20 inches.

Wade-fishing is possible in the delayed-harvest area at Cochran Shoals in the Cochran Shoals Unit of the CRNRA; Devils Race Course and Thornton Shoals at Sandy Point in the West Palisades Unit; at Long Island Shoals at Whitewater Creek in the East Palisades Unit; and in the area around the access point at the Paces Mill Unit adjacent to the US 41 bridge. All of these areas have springtime hatches of caddisflies, plus mayflies that can be imitated with Light Cahills or Sulfurs. Woolly Buggers are another good fly pattern for the deeper runs, while nymphs such as the Gold-Ribbed Hare's Ear and Prince also produce fish.

The last couple of miles of river down to the Atlanta City Water Works at the mouth of Peachtree Creek are not generally fished, although they do contain trout. The shore through here is all privately owned, and there are no take-out facilities at Peachtree Creek for float-fishers.

Anglers should be aware that this lower tailwater now has flip-down signs posted along the shore that warn of times of high bacteria content in the water. This is caused mainly by runoff from feeder streams after periods of rain. If you are fishing when the warning signs are present, be sure to rinse yourself and your gear after a day of angling.

The first access point to the tailwater below Morgan Falls is via Morgan Falls Road on the eastern side of the river at the foot of the dam. Be aware that this site is gated and often closed. Other access points are at the Johnson Ferry Unit of the CRNRA on Johnson Ferry Road and the Cochran Shoals Unit off Interstate North Parkway. Both Devils Race Course and Thornton

Shoals can be reached from the parking lot at the CRNRA Sandy Point Unit off Akers Mill Road, although this requires a ½-mile hike down a steep ridge to the river. Long Island Shoals can be reached from Whitewater Creek Road through the East Palisades Unit of the CRNRA, while the final access point is at the Paces Mill Unit at the US 41 bridge.

The national park service distributes a free brochure with an excellent map showing all the access points and public properties along the Chattahoochee's tailwater. Call 770-399-8070 to order a copy.

The Corps of Engineers' tentative water-release schedule for Buford Dam is available by calling 770-945-1466. For the generation schedule for Morgan Falls Dam, call the Georgia Power Company at 404-329-1455.

# TOCCOA RIVER

### DeLorme 14

Georgia's other major tailwater trout fishery is found on the Toccoa River below Blue Ridge Lake in the northwestern corner of the state. Beginning at the Tennessee Valley Authority's (TVA) Blue Ridge Dam just east of the town of Blue Ridge, the Toccoa's tailwater flows northwest for 15 miles to the twin towns of McCaysville, Georgia, and Copperhill, Tennessee, at the state boundary. As the river crosses the state line its name changes to the Ocoee, which is a well known rafting and kayaking destination, especially since hosting the whitewater events for the 1996 Olympic Games. Along its course through Georgia, the Toccoa is located entirely in Fannin County.

The tailwater on the Toccoa River is only about 60 to 80 feet wide along its entire length—not a particularly large river. Although it is possible to catch trout from the Toccoa at all water levels, most of the fishing pressure occurs when the water level is falling after power generation ends. Once the water level has bottomed out, the fish become difficult to find and catch.

Presently, the Toccoa is stocked only with rainbow trout, with more than 20,000 fish released annually. These stockings of 7- to 9-inch fish take place every 2 weeks from April through Labor Day. State biologists describe the Toccoa as a put-and-take fishery with very low holdover potential. It is quite rare to find rainbows of even a foot long in this river.

There are also some browns present. These are wild, naturally reproducing fish that drop down into the river from feeder streams. (Almost no reproduction is thought to take place in the Toccoa tailwater itself.) A few of the

Toccoa River

browns reach weights of 3 to 5 pounds, but even these fish are probably not year-round residents. One oddity concerning big trout in the Toccoa is that a former state-record brook trout of just under 5 pounds was taken here. It was, of course, a hatchery fish, and brookies are no longer stocked in the tailwater.

Through the mid-1990s very good progress was made in solving a couple of the traditional problems facing the Toccoa's tailwater trout fishery. For years low dissolved oxygen levels and high summer water temperatures limited the quality of the trout habitat. However, in 1995 Blue Ridge Dam was fitted with new generators, which included a miniature unit designed to

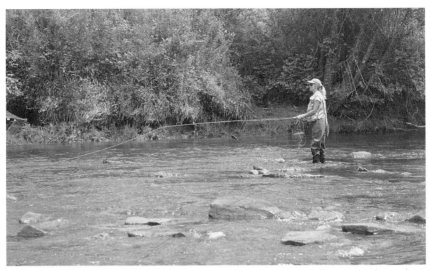

*The shoals in Tammen Park provide easy wading and plenty of room for fly casting.*

maintain minimum water flow. Both dissolved oxygen and water temperature levels have since improved.

The Toccoa's tailwater is made up of long, deep pools broken by occasional shallower runs. It is better suited to float-fishing than to wading, particularly while the water is still falling and fishing is at its best. Since bank access is not abundant on the river, this also adds to the appeal of floating in a float tube, canoe, or johnboat.

Hatches of dark-hued caddisflies in the size 14 to 16 range are seen each spring and summer on the Toccoa, especially in the areas of shallow shoals. These are sporadic and difficult to predict accurately. Another insect to look for is the Japanese beetle. These do not appear every summer in this region, but when they do the trout gorge on those that fall in the water. As on most large streams in the southeastern states, Woolly Buggers in black or olive are good choices for probing the river when no surface activity is visible. With spinning gear, in-line spinners are the most popular offering on this tailwater. Bait-fishers, who are most numerous in the immediate vicinity of the tailrace at Blue Ridge Dam, comprise the largest percentage of anglers. Their favorite baits are corn, worms, crickets, and salmon eggs.

As mentioned, a lack of public access along the Toccoa is the biggest drawback to fishing it. One popular angling location is composed of the two parks near the dam and the water between them. The TVA has a facility immediately at the foot of the dam on the east side of the river. Roughly a half-mile downstream at the GA 515 bridge Fannin County maintains Tammen Park on the western shore of the stream. At lower water levels virtually this entire section of river is wadable. Be sure to listen for the siren announcing water releases, though.

The vicinity of the water outflow from the dam and the area just in front of the parking lot at Tammen Park get very heavy fishing pressure, as they offer easy access to the water. Overall, the rest of the Toccoa tailwater gets light pressure, with more than two-thirds coming from local anglers. Tammen Park is also a popular jump-off point for float trips down the river.

These twin parks near the dam are accessible from GA 515 (also marked as the Appalachian Scenic Highway or Zell Miller Parkway) at its bridge over the river. To reach the foot of the dam, turn south onto the paved road at east end of the bridge. The entrance to Tammen Park is located across the river at the other end of the highway bridge.

The next access points are found off Curtis Switch Road (CR 195) to the north of the town of Mineral Bluff. This paved road runs west off GA 245, but presently has no road markers at the intersection. The intersection is just south of the GA 245 bridge over Hothouse Creek, which does have a sign identifying it. There is limited access to the river where Curtis Switch Road crosses the flow. Additionally, North Toccoa River Road (gravel) runs to the north off Curtis Switch just before the bridge. By traveling $\frac{1}{2}$ mile on this road, you will encounter a small TVA canoe-launch park on the river's eastern bank. The park is marked with a small, inconspicuous sign, and there is no directional sign for it back at the intersection of Curtis Switch and North Toccoa River Roads. This area between Curtis Switch Road and the TVA park offers good wading conditions on low water. The park is also a convenient take-out point for float trips originating upstream at Tammen Park.

Finally, there are two parks in McCaysville proper that offer access to the river and some wadable water. To the southeast of town, 1.3 miles to the southeast of GA 245 on River Road, is Horseshoe Bend Park. This playground and softball complex has over $\frac{1}{4}$ mile of river frontage and easy access to the water. Farther downstream, practically in downtown McCaysville, Toccoa River Park offers easy access to the river and a section of wadable shoals just upstream. There are some old Cherokee fish weirs in the river between these two parks.

To obtain details on the water-release schedule for the Toccoa River tailwater, call the TVA's automated information line at 1-800-238-2254. Press 4 for water releases, then 23 for Blue Ridge Dam. This information is also available online at www.lakeinfo.tva.gov/.

# Kentucky

| | | | |
|---|---|---|---|
| **1** Barren River | | **9** Licking River | |
| **2** Blaine Creek | | **10** Little Sandy River | |
| **3** Carr Creek | | **11** Martins Fork Cumberland River | |
| **4** Cumberland River | | **12** Middle Fork Kentucky River | |
| **5** Dix River | | **13** Nolin River | |
| **6** Johns Creek | | **14** Paint Creek | |
| **7** Laurel River | | **15** Rough River | |
| **8** Licking Creek | | | |

Jeff Goodwin, © The Countryman Press

# CHAPTER 6

# Kentucky

A cursory glance at the atlas would lead one to believe that the Bluegrass State of Kentucky would be a prime location for trout in the South. It shares with Missouri and Virginia the distinction of having the most northerly position among the states of the region. This location, with its resulting colder climate and a mountainous eastern half, would seem to make Kentucky an ideal spot to find cold-water streams.

As is sometimes the case, however, simple geography is not enough to explain the whole story. One must delve into geology to understand Kentucky's cold-water fisheries. While much of the eastern end of the state is composed of highlands, only a very slender rib of truly mountainous land runs down the edge of the state. The Cumberland Plateau and its associated river valleys are to the west of this Appalachian Mountain terrain. Although the land rises to heights of 1,300 to 1,500 feet above sea level, these peaks have little in common with the igneous and metamorphic, hard-rock mountains of the Appalachian chain. The basic building blocks of the Cumberland Plateau are sedimentary rocks formed on the bottom of the ancient inland sea that covered the central United States in prehistoric times.

These sedimentary rocks are much softer than the stone of the true mountain ranges of the South, and less resistant to weathering. As a result, stream water does not tumble over them, but rather cuts through them. Thus, most of the creeks and rivers of the Cumberland Plateau have long since sliced down to form deep valley courses. The result is low-altitude streams that meander sluggishly around the higher ground. Many of the creeks are seasonal, going dry during the summer and fall because they descend into subterranean channels. As for those streams that remain above ground, the only ones that can support trout year-round are fed by cooler waters from the limestone springs and caverns of the region. The number of such streams is small.

In fact, fisheries biologists do not unanimously support the idea that Kentucky ever harbored natural trout populations. (Some creeks along the extreme eastern border are now managed as wild brook trout waters, but the fish had to be introduced into these streams.) Some speculate that trout once inhabited the area but were wiped out by mining and timber cutting; it is equally plausible, however, that they never ranged this far west in the Appalachian foothills.

Due to this topography and geology, the Bluegrass State's modern trout waters are artificial and extensively managed. Most streams support put-and-take, seasonal fisheries. Included among these is the most extensive system of tailwater streams in any state of the Southeast. The Kentucky Department of Fish and Wildlife Resources (KDFWR) manages 15 rivers and creeks as tailwater trout resources. These run the gamut from mighty rivers with scores of miles of water to small streams with only a mile of cold-water habitat. Some are true tailwaters, while others are tailwaters in name only.

There is no closed season for trout in Kentucky. The general regulations mandate a creel limit of eight trout per angler per day, regardless of species. Only three of those may be brown trout, and no more than two brook trout. There is no minimum size limit for rainbows, but all brookies harvested in Kentucky must be 10 inches or longer and brown trout must be 12 inches. There are exceptions to these regulations that apply on some of the tailwaters, but these are discussed in the coverage on specific streams.

Besides a valid Kentucky fishing license, all anglers aged 16 to 64 must possess a Kentucky Trout Stamp to fish for these species. These permits may be purchased by calling 1-877-598-2401, or via the Internet at www.ky-direct.com/kdfwr. A Visa or MasterCard is needed for the purchase.

# BARREN RIVER

## DeLorme 82

The Barren River tailwater is located below Barren Lake in south-central Kentucky, near the Tennessee border. It was created when Barren River Lake was first impounded in 1964. The river below the 10,000-acre lake forms the extreme northern border of Allen County with Barren County at the dam, and then with Warren County farther downstream. The river runs in a northwesterly direction from the dam, eventually flowing through the city of Bowling Green.

The Barren River is only a minor tailwater by southeastern standards. The river is roughly 100 feet wide where it emerges from the dam at Barren Lake, and it broadens to only a couple hundred feet along its course. Barren Lake Dam is just 146 feet high and contains no powerhouse, since this is a Corps of Engineers flood-control project. While the flow of water through the dam varies, its rise and fall is not as drastic as that associated with power surges at hydroelectric facilities. Of course, caution is still necessary when fishing during low water levels. When releases do occur, they raise the river level enough in a short period to merit caution. Even during high water levels, the Barren's flow tends to be sluggish below the tailrace.

In all, the KDFWR presently stocks the Barren tailwaters with 8,500 trout each year. These are all rainbows of standard 9- to 12-inch stocking size, released monthly in varying numbers from April through November. Carryover fish are relatively rare, and no natural reproduction takes place. The Barren's location—close to the major population center of Bowling Green—dictates that it receive moderate to heavy fishing pressure year-round. This pressure is heaviest for the first three days after each month's stocking. Many of the anglers fish from the several gravel bars that jut into the river from the southern shore just below the dam.

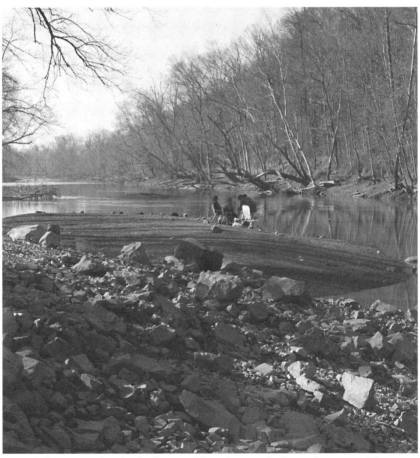

*At low water levels, the Barren River is a gentle flow whose gravel bars are favorites with bait fishers.*

Most of the anglers on the Barren are bait-fishers casting from the bank, with a few tossing spinners from shore as well. Although fly-casting is possible, it is unusual here. The public access portion of the tailwater is not good wading territory. Anglers accustomed to the big waters of hydropower rivers will undoubtedly be disappointed with the Barren. It is, however, representative of the smaller tailwater flows of Kentucky's flood-control reservoirs. While not world-class fisheries, these rivers provide local anglers with trout fishing where it would not otherwise exist.

The prime trout water on the Barren is short, extending only a mile or two downriver. Through this section, public access is limited. The river shore can be reached via the Tailwater Recreation Area from the southern end of Barren Lake Dam on KY 252 (which crosses the dam). A paved drive leads down to a parking area on the river's southern shore. Downstream of the parking area is a Corps of Engineers campground that provides both tent and RV sites, as well as a paved boat ramp. The campground is open from spring through fall. In all, there is ½ mile of riverbank in the corps land. The river then runs through private farmland, crossed only by the KY 101 bridge before it reaches Bowling Green.

# BLAINE CREEK

## *DeLorme 41*

The Blaine Creek tailwater is formed below Yatesville Dam at the reservoir of the same name in northeastern Kentucky, close to the West Virginia border. This creek rises in northern Lawrence County, then flows to the southeast to empty into 2,300-acre Yatesville Lake. Below the impoundment, Blaine Creek runs north and east to empty into the Big Sandy River. Along this entire course, the flow is but a small stream.

Yatesville Dam is a flood-control structure, thus it has no hydroelectric powerhouse. In spite of Blaine Creek's location in the extreme northeast part of the state, the waters coming from the bottom of the reservoir provide only marginal trout habitat. There is very little likelihood of any fish surviving from year to year.

Blaine Creek receives stockings of 3,000 rainbow trout annually, with releases occurring from April into October. All of these are adult, catchable-sized fish.

Public access to the Yatesville tailwater is limited along the roughly one

Blaine Creek

KENTUCKY

WEST VIRGINIA

*Yatesville Lake*

*Big Sandy River*

Louisa

N

0    1.5    3 mi.

0    1.5    3 km

Jeff Goodwin, © The Countryman Press

mile of stream where the trout are most likely to be found. At the foot of the dam there is a park that allows some access to the water and has a paved canoe launch and parking lot. For roughly 200 yards below the dam the creek is wadable at low water levels. Although access is also possible for roughly ⅓ mile downstream on public land, the creek gets too deep and sluggish for wading and the shoreline is heavily wooded. At ¼ mile downstream a gravel parking area is also provided, along with a gated road that allows foot access to the lower portion of public stream bank. This parking lot is reached from the access drive leading to the dam.

To reach the tailwater on Blaine Creek, take KY 32 west from the town of Louisa, which is situated at the Kentucky–West Virginia border, then turn north onto CR 3396. At the intersection of Five Forks, turn west onto CR 3397 and continue until it dead-ends into CR 1185. Turn left; just before CR 1185 crosses the Yatesville Dam, a paved drive on the right leads down to the park at the foot of the dam.

For a recorded message covering water conditions and releases at Yatesville Dam, call the Army Corps of Engineers at 606-686-3161.

# CARR CREEK

## *DeLorme 71, 72*

Carr Creek is located only a mile or so from the coal-mining town of Hazard. Lying in the mountainous southeastern corner of Kentucky, the creek eventually adds its waters to the Kentucky River via that stream's North Fork. The dam on Carr Creek forms a reservoir of the same name that was completed in 1976 mainly to control flooding. It has no hydroelectric powerhouse. Up until 1996, both the stream and the lake were known as Carr Fork, but in that year the U.S. Congress changed the names to Carr Creek.

Carr Creek is only a small stream below the lake. Immediately downstream of the dam is a large pool with riprap walls; this constitutes the major fishing location on the tailwater. Although there is roughly a mile of suitable trout habitat on Carr Creek, only ¼ mile of it has any appreciable public access. This is no handicap to local anglers, however, since almost all of the fishing pressure occurs at the foot of the dam.

Sassafrass Road crosses a bridge over the stream just below the big pool at the dam. According to one local angler I encountered at streamside, the fishing here can be summed up succinctly.

"When they stock them, they just dump the fish off the bridge," he observed. "Everybody crowds around the pool underneath and takes them right back out."

Indeed they do. Biologists for the KDFWR consider Carr Creek one of the most popular trout fisheries in the commonwealth. A total of 12,600 rainbow trout are released into the stream each year, with plantings taking place monthly from April to November. When the stocking truck leaves Carr Creek, expect to find hordes of anglers there for the next couple of days. The shore of the pool just above the Sassafrass Road bridge will be lined with folks, nearly all of them bait-fishers.

After Sassafrass Road crosses the creek, it comes to a parking area with rest rooms and a playground on the stream's northwestern side. From there a set of concrete stairs descends to a paved fishing pier that runs several hundred feet along the shore of the big pool. There is also a walkway and stairs leading over the tailrace gate to a similar, but shorter, pier on the other shore.

Once the stream exits the dam pool, it flows under Sassafrass Road and past the pilings of an old bridge immediately downstream of the present structure. Through the rest of the public access area the creek is only about 30 to 40 feet wide. This downstream access area consists of a Corps of Engineers park containing picnic areas and playgrounds, as well as more rest rooms. It is a seasonal park that closes in the winter months.

Although the stream is shallow enough for wading and has some small shoals and gravel bars through the park area, the crowds from the dam pool spill over into this portion of the creek during stocking periods. These crowds make wading and fly- or spin-casting chancy propositions.

Downstream of the Corps of Engineers land, the creek parallels Sassafrass Road for ¾ mile to where the road intersects with KY 15 (at the crossroads in the town of Sassafrass). Along this stretch of road are a couple of turnouts that offer parking and access to the stream. Below the KY 15 bridge there are no more access points, but the end of trout water is imminent anyway.

# CUMBERLAND RIVER

### DeLorme 82, 83

There can be no doubt that the Cumberland River below Cumberland Lake in south-central Kentucky is the commonwealth's premier trout water. Beginning in Russell County, the river rushes from outlets of Wolf Creek Dam's hydroelectric turbines to create a cold-water fishery that can support trout as far downstream as the Tennessee border, almost 80 river miles away.

Cumberland River

127
boat ramp
Ray Mann Road
Wolf Creek National Fish Hatchery
Helms Landing
379
Creelsboro
Helms Landing Road
Kendall Recreation Area
Cumberland Lake
127
90
127
90

Rockhouse Natural Bridge
RUSSELL CTY.
Winfrey Ferry
379
CUMBERLAND COUNTY
CLINTON COUNTY

912
Crocus Creek
704
Crocus Creek
Cumberland River
Burkesville
61
61
704
90
90
61
485
Ellington

N

0        2        4 km
0        2        4 mi.

Jeff Goodwin, © The Countryman Press

Although trout will show up on the lower end of this tailwater, the best fishing runs only for about 50 miles down into Cumberland County. Still, this makes the river below the 50,250-acre reservoir Kentucky's longest and biggest trout stream.

Unlike many other tailwaters stocked by the KDFWR, the Cumberland is very large, often stretching to widths of several hundred yards. Along its course it can be a raging torrent or a gentle flow, depending upon the amount of water released from the powerhouse at Wolf Creek Dam. When all six turbines are turning, the river rises 6 to 7 feet above minimum flow; it becomes difficult to navigate in a small boat and downright dangerous to unwary waders.

Of particular note is the fact that the releases from Wolf Creek Dam are controlled by computer from the Corps of Engineers' office in Nashville, Tennessee. Although a siren is supposed to warn of impending releases, local anglers have reported that it is undependable, either not sounding or giving false alarms. Obviously, such a record leads to complacency that can end disastrously. If you choose to wade in the ½ mile of park water immediately below the dam, use extreme caution. Pay close attention to water levels and heed the siren every time it sounds. This is a good place to wear one of the newer inflatable fishing vests as an insurance policy.

The turbulence created when the turbines begin turning at Wolf Creek Dam is so great, and the current so strong, that the Corps of Engineers requires all boaters on the tailwater within 0.2 mile to wear a personal flotation device (life jacket) at all times.

The first rainbow trout were stocked in the Cumberland River tailwater in 1952, soon after the dam was completed. These fish thrived over the years, making up most of the cold-water fishing in the river. Presently, the KDFWR stocks 150,000 catchable-sized rainbows in the river annually. The fish are obtained from the Wolf Creek National Fish Hatchery, which is just below the dam. Stocking takes place once a month from April through November. The number of fish involved in these monthly releases varies but is announced in advance. Stockings draw plenty of anglers.

Though the large numbers of fish released is the main attraction of the rainbow trout fishery, bigger specimens do turn up. Rainbows of 3 to 4 pounds are commonly caught, along with the occasional lunker. In fact, the Cumberland has laid claim to the Kentucky state record for rainbow trout since September 10, 1972, when Jim Mattingly of Somerset landed a 14-pound, 6-ounce monster from the tailwater.

In 1982 the KDFWR began releasing sub-adult brown trout into the river as well, adding a new dimension to the fishing. It was this addition to the program, in fact, that turned the Cumberland into a true delight for trophy anglers. Most recently, 60,000 fingerling browns have been added to the flow yearly; stockings take place in the colder months. Since these fish are not of catchable size, the plantings are not announced. They usually occur at up to five locations along the tailwater.

Boasting growth rates of up to 3 pounds per year, the Cumberland fishery produced a state-record brown of more than 11 pounds in 1987. That fish was taken by Randal (Randy) Gibson of Bakerton in the Wetstone Creek area of the tailwater, about 25 miles below Wolf Creek Dam. Apparently not one to rest on his laurels, Gibson later boated browns of 17 pounds, 14 ounces and 18 pounds during 1987 and 1988. Then in June of 1988, Gibson caught a brown trout that raised the Kentucky state-record mark to 18 pounds, 8 ounces. That trout held the number one spot for more than 12 years.

Thomas Malone of Crofton took the present state record for this species while fishing about 3 miles upstream of the boat ramp in Burkeville on April 30, 2000. This monster brown trout tipped the scales at 21 pounds even and measured 33 inches long. Malone hooked the fish while casting a silver and black Rat-L-Trap crankbait on spinning gear.

If you want to tangle with a trophy-sized brown trout, the portion of the Cumberland downstream of the Rockhouse area (roughly 12 miles below the dam) and running as far as 50 miles downriver offers the best fishing. The best bets for a big trout lie downstream of Burkeville, some 30 miles below Wolf Creek Dam. KDFWR electroshock surveys have netted 2.5 browns per hour that were more than 20 inches in length through here. Such big fish are ordinarily difficult to capture with electroshock equipment, so the fact that this many show up hints of a much larger population of magnum-sized browns in the river.

The most effective fishing method for browns is tossing crankbaits in color schemes that mimic either shad or crawfish near shoreline logjams, submerged tree trunks, or root tangles. The browns tend to hold tight to this cover during the day. Rock outcroppings, which are abundant along the tailwater, are secondary locations for casting. When fly-fishing, big, weighted streamer patterns are obvious choices for this water. White, black, or chartreuse colors often attract fish .

The best fishing for the bigger browns occurs when three or fewer turbines are running at the dam, and particularly as the water is first rising when power generation begins. This is probably due to increased food being washed downstream by the rising waters, which provokes feeding binges by the trout. Overcast days are another good time to fish.

The most-targeted times of year on the Cumberland are from late spring (after the runoff from early spring rains has subsided) through mid-November. When the browns get the urge to spawn in October, they are most vulnerable to anglers. This is the time of year when the river is usually at its lowest and even the big fish move into shallow shoal areas.

For those trying to catch rainbows, the first mile of river below Wolf Creek Dam is the prime area, as populations are highest there. Since the rainbow trout are noted for being less inclined to bite during high water, virtually all of the angling from shore occurs when the turbines are still. During these periods the river is reduced to a series of pools with gravel bars jutting out among them, creating excellent access. This ease of access also means the fishing pressure can be very heavy through here. Ordinarily, low-water periods occur from dawn to 9 AM during spring and summer, but there are no set rules on water releases.

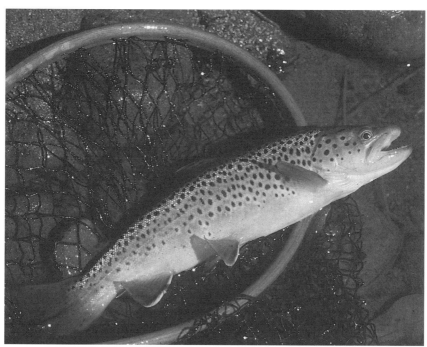

*The Cumberland River is noted for giving up plenty of hefty, colorful brown trout.*

There is one exception to the rule of low water offering the best fishing. In autumn, weakened shad are often sucked through the turbines of the dam during periods of high water, making them easy prey for trout. The presence of stunned baitfish is evident when numbers of gulls are circling and diving in this area.

When this condition occurs, anglers run their boats right up to the tail-race of the dam, fish while floating with the current for several hundred yards downstream, then repeat the sequence. Using lures or flies that imitate struggling minnows can produce plenty of action at these times.

The standard rainbow stocked into the Cumberland tailwater is 8 to 12 inches long. These fish fall for all of the usual baits to which hatchery-reared trout are susceptible. Kernel corn, red worms, salmon eggs, and cheese balls are all popular baits. Spin-fishers cast $\frac{1}{16}$- to $\frac{1}{8}$-ounce Rooster Tail and Mepps spinners, especially in brown colors, or red-and-white Dardevle spoons.

In recent years, more and more fly-casters have begun showing up on the Cumberland River, both wading the shoals of the upper river and tossing their flies from boats farther downstream. For surface-feeding action, the most dependable months are March through October. Throughout this period hatches of tiny black midges in size 20 to 24 are common. From May through August look for Light Cahills in size 12 to 14 to be effective. Sulphur patterns in size 16 to 18 are also good during May and June. Ant and beetle patterns or other terrestrial imitations often work well during August to October, as do olive caddis patterns in the fall months.

When no surface action is evident, switching off to beadhead nymphs, such as a Prince Nymph, can be effective. Woolly Buggers in white, black, or olive usually elicit strikes as well.

Access to the Cumberland River tailwater at the Kendall Recreation Area is at the eastern end of Wolf Creek Dam. An approach road drops down to the river from US 127, which runs across the dam. The Kendall complex contains an RV campground, parking areas, and a boat ramp.

There is a lot of bank-fishing pressure applied to the stream just below the dam, especially during low water. In all, there is $\frac{1}{2}$ mile of shoreline access on the eastern bank, while high stone bluffs overlook the river from the west. Shallow areas are quite limited near the dam, but there is wadable water near the boat ramp. A small creek enters the river just downstream of the campground. During high water it is possible to fish a short way up into it.

Since most land along the Cumberland is privately owned, float-fishing offers the best alternative. A float from the dam through the prime trout water down to the city of Burkesville requires two full days on the water. Fortunately, the Cumberland is such a big river that bass boats and even pontoon boats can navigate it during all but dead-low water levels.

Another access point is via Ray Mann Road, which runs off the approach road to the Kendall Recreation Area. At the end of this $\frac{3}{4}$-mile road, which changes from pavement to gravel, is an unimproved gravel boat ramp. The entire area in front of the ramp offers good wading during low water levels.

Several shoal areas are located along this floating stretch. These offer the drifting angler the opportunity to get out of the boat and do a bit of wading if the water is low enough. At $1\frac{1}{2}$ miles below the dam there is a shoal at the mouth of Little Indian Creek; there is another one at the mouth of Blackfish Creek, at 3 miles downstream.

The first downstream boat ramp is at Helms Landing, off KY 379 in Russell County. This is approximately 10 miles below Wolf Creek Dam. This boat ramp is paved and is managed by the KDFWR. The entire vicinity of the boat ramp is wadable and holds trout during low-water periods.

Helms Landing is located at the end of Helms Landing Road, 1 mile from its intersection with KY 379. That junction is $2\frac{1}{2}$ miles east of Creelsboro, a historic crossroads on KY 379. Today all of the buildings in Creelsboro are boarded up, making it a modern-day ghost town.

Below Helms Landing, you will encounter several shoal areas before reaching the town of Burkeville. The first is 2 miles below the landing, and it is only accessible by boat. Next, in the area of the Rockhouse Natural Bridge, there is a long stretch of wadable water upstream of the site, while Rainbow Run is another wadable shoal located downstream. Rockhouse can be reached by traveling west on KY 379 from Creelsboro. After the road cuts across a cliff overlooking the river, a gravel drive (presently unmarked at the intersection) runs off to the left to a parking area. A trail of only about 50 yards leads to the Rockhouse Natural Bridge and river access.

At roughly 16 miles below Wolf Creek Dam, Winfrey Ferry is located on the south side of the river and is accessible at the end of KY 379. Be aware that KY 379 is on both sides of the river, but there is no bridge connecting the two sections. A gravel boat ramp is provided at this site. Winfreys Rock, a very large boulder sitting in the river near the south shore, is in this area. The riffle downstream of the rock is noted for holding trout.

Farther downstream at the mouth of Crocus Creek is another wadable area that can be reached from shore. Traveling north from Burkesville on KY 61, turn east onto KY 704, then east onto KY 912. This road crosses a bridge over Crocus Creek at its mouth. A gravel parking area is located at the east end of the bridge. You can walk from there back across the bridge and down the trail to a large gravel bar that is accessible during low water. The deep hole at the north end of the bar in the creek mouth is noted for giving up trout as well as striped bass up to 40 pounds.

The Burkesville Boat Ramp is located in the town of the same name and is managed by the KDFWR. It lies on Banks Street between the ends of Lower and Upper River Roads, just upstream of the KY 90 bridge over the river.

Downstream of Burkesville, most of the action is confined to angling from a boat, but there are a couple of places worth mentioning. At the south end of the KY 61 bridge over the river access is available to a riprap channel edge that is wadable on low water. This is directly across the river from the private boat ramp of the Traces On The Cumberland facility. It is possible to wade about 100 yards of this shore.

Five miles below the bridge is an area known as The Islands, which is only accessible by boat. Here, one large and one very small island break the river's flow, offering shoals on the side channel by the larger island. The deep hole near the smaller island usually holds plenty of fish.

Creel limits for rainbow trout on the Cumberland below Wolf Creek Dam down to the Tennessee state border fall under regular Kentucky trout regulations. Each angler may harvest no more than eight trout per day regardless of species. Of that total, no more than one may be a brown trout, and that fish must be 20 inches or longer.

To obtain information on water-release schedules at Wolf Creek Dam, call the TVA toll-free, recorded message at 1-800-238-2264, punch 4 for water releases, then 34 for the Wolf Creek Dam. This information is also available on the Internet at www.lakeinfo.tva.gov/; follow the prompts for Wolf Creek.

# DIX RIVER

## DeLorme 51

The Dix River tailwater forms the boundary between Mercer County on the west and Garrard County to the east. Unlike most of Kentucky's trout waters, the Dix River is located in the Bluegrass Country of the central part of the commonwealth, just south of Lexington. Although the tailwater is just

Jeff Goodwin, © The Countryman Press

over 2 miles long, it is a notable trout fishery before it empties into the Kentucky River near the historic village of High Bridge.

Originating at the foot of Dix Dam, which impounds 1,860-acre Herrington Lake, the Dix River is managed as a trophy brown trout fishery for 2 miles below the dam. Part of the reason for this unusual management scheme is the inaccessibility of the water. Kentucky Utilities, which manages the Dix Dam and the coal-fired electric-generation plant at the location, does not allow any shore access to the tailwater. Farther downstream the shore is lined with massive stone cliffs; this spectacular gorge is on private lands. The

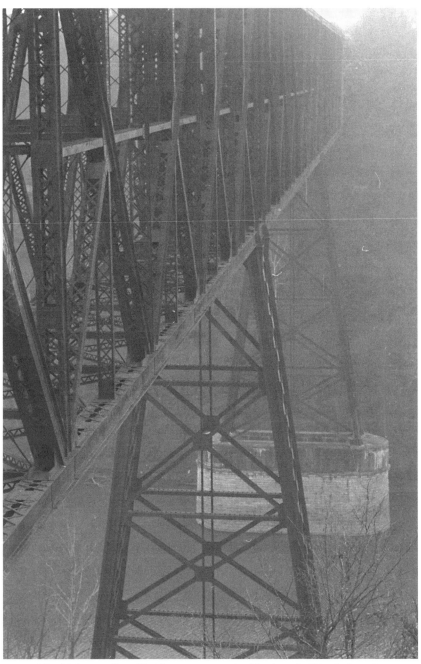

*The highest railroad bridge over a navigable river in North America is just below the mouth of the Dix River. The only access to this tailwater is just downstream of the bridge.*

result is a total lack of bank access to this fishery. Also, the waters run deep in the Dix River, so fishing from a boat is the only option for trout anglers.

The first stockings of trout did not occur on the Dix until 1986, when browns were introduced. These fish—about 3,000 per year—exhibited strong survival and growth rates. At the repeated request of the Bluegrass Chapter of Trout Unlimited in Lexington, the KDFWR established the first 2 miles of water below the dam as trophy brown trout water in 1990. Signs on the river mark the end of this regulated water. Under these regulations, only artificial lures are permitted; the creel limit is 3 brown trout per day, all of which must be at least 15 inches long. This fishery is presently thriving and only an additional 600 browns are added each year.

Overall, this fishery has not attained the level of success for which fisheries managers hoped. The suspected limiting factor is the loss of bigger fish downstream into the Kentucky River during high water levels in the spring. If these fish pass below the Lock No. 7 dam on the Kentucky, they cannot get back upstream into the cold waters of the Dix. One alternative being considered to remedy this problem is stocking trout in the tailwater after May, when spring rains have abated.

Presently, the Dix River below Herrington Lake is stocked with 1,000 brown trout annually, while also receiving 4,000 rainbows. Browns of more than 20 inches have been taken here, as well as rainbows up to 18 inches.

The better fishing in the Dix tailwater is found immediately below the dam. Some anglers cast or troll jigs and heavy spoons on spinning tackle, but this is also a favorite site for fly-casting with large streamers or smaller nymph patterns. Many of the anglers practice catch-and-release here, particularly with the brown trout.

As noted earlier, access is the major problem for fishing the Dix River. The only public access point is located on the Kentucky River at the High Bridge site. This location gets its name from the presence of the highest railroad bridge (308 feet) above a navigable river in the United States. Built in 1876, the span has been updated and is still in use.

Access to the Dix is available by taking KY 29 southwest from the town of Wilmore to the High Bridge community. The road dead-ends at the bridge site. Just before reaching the bridge, Dix Drive descends steeply from the right of the highway down to the riverbank. A park is situated at the site of Lock and Dam No. 7 at this location on the Kentucky River, and a public boat ramp is just above the lock. From this point it is roughly a mile upstream to the mouth of the Dix River.

# JOHNS CREEK

**DeLorme 55**

The Johns Creek tailwater is located in Floyd County in east-central Kentucky, originating at the foot of the dam on Dewey Lake. From there the creek flows to the northwest, then forms an arc as it turns south to empty into the Levisa Fork. The Levisa Fork, in turn, eventually adds its waters to the Ohio River system. Johns Creek is quite small as it exits 1,100-acre Dewey Lake and is a marginal trout fishery.

Dewey Lake is a Corps of Engineers flood-control project and has no hydroelectric facilities. For that reason, there is no true water-release surge in the creek, which flows deep and sluggish when minimum flows are coming through the dam. When more water is being released, it simply rises and runs a bit faster.

Only 5,600 rainbow trout are stocked in Johns Creek each year, with the releases taking place monthly from April to June and September to November. During July and August, Johns Creek is too warm to support the planting of trout. Very little, if any, carryover of fish occurs through the summer. Obviously, this is strictly a put-and-take fishery for catchable-sized stockers of 8 to 12 inches.

Access is available to Johns Creek at the foot of the dam in a Corps of Engineers park that contains playgrounds, a softball field, and rest rooms. In all there is about ¼ mile of shoreline open to the public. All access is on the northern side of the stream. The major features of this tailwater are the huge concrete spillway walls that lie just opposite the park on the southern side of the creek. A large eddy forms where the end of the spillway wall meets the

*The high concrete walls of the spillway beside the tailrace below Dewey Lake give the tailwater of Johns Creek a distinctive look.*

tailrace waters, providing one of the major angling points on this short ½-mile of trout water.

Bait-fishing for rainbow trout is the predominant angling activity here, although some anglers undoubtedly use artificial lures as well. A fly-caster on Johns Creek would be a very unusual sight.

To reach the dam at Dewey Lake, take KY 302 southwest from its junction with KY 3 south of the hamlet of Odds. An access drive to the creekside park is located off the northern side of the highway just before KY 302 crosses the dam.

## LAUREL RIVER

### *DeLorme 69*

The Laurel River originates in eastern Laurel County, where the waters of Callaway and Lick Creeks join. The new river then rushes west through the southeastern corner of the state to empty into 5,600-acre Laurel River Lake, which was impounded in 1974. After passing through the impoundment and

*The flow downstream of Laurel River Lake Dam is one of Kentucky's
newest tailwater trout fisheries.*

the powerhouse at the dam, the river reemerges, carrying cold, clear water
from the depths of the reservoir.

Even by Kentucky standards, the Laurel River tailwater provides little in
the way of a trout fishing resource. The stream is small, spreading to no more
than 50 feet wide. This flow is stocked with only 500 trout per year, with that
number divided equally between rainbows and browns.

The first couple of hundred yards below the dam run very clear and
shallow when the generators are silent. Then the river deepens a bit as it continues its 1.2-mile course down to the high-water mark at Lake Cumberland
on the Cumberland River. Although it is possible to wade farther downstream,
the river runs through a gorgelike area. If you choose to venture into that
stretch, be sure to always have a way out of the water planned as you fish.
When water releases occur the level goes up very fast and the current gets swift.

A park at the foot of the dam provides access to the water, but a walk
down a steep grassy slope is required to get to the river. Large boulders form
riprap along the shore through the park, which has parking areas, rest rooms,
and picnic tables. There are no other access points to the river before it
reaches Cumberland Lake.

To reach the park at Laurel River Dam, take US 25W west from the town of Corbin. Turn north onto CR 1193 and continue along this road until it crosses the Laurel River Dam. At 1.6 miles north of the dam, turn left onto the drive leading to the foot of the dam. It is 1.1 miles along this paved drive to the parking area at the powerhouse.

For information on water releases from Laurel River Dam, visit the U.S. Army Corps of Engineers web site at www.orn.usace.army.mil/pao/lakeinfo. Then follow the prompts for Laurel Lake.

## LICKING CREEK

### DeLorme 56

The tailwater on Licking Creek originates below Fishtrap Lake in Pike County. This impoundment is Kentucky's easternmost major lake, covering 1,130 surface acres. Another of the Army Corps of Engineers' flood-control structures, the dam at Fishtrap does not have hydroelectric facilities. Licking Creek flows for roughly 3 miles below the dam before emptying into the Russell Fork. From there, it flows into the Levisa Fork, then into the Big Sandy River, eventually ending up in the Ohio.

Only rainbow trout are stocked in Licking Creek. The plantings are made monthly from April through November, with 8,500 fish stocked per

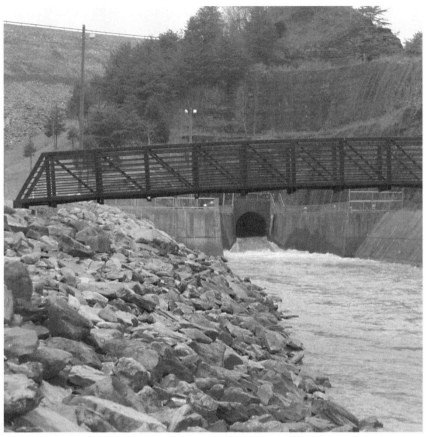

*A footbridge provides access to both shores of Licking Creek at the tailrace below Fishtrap Lake.*

year. Licking Creek is a medium-width stream in this tailwater section and provides only marginal trout habitat. Virtually no carryover of fish occurs from season to season.

The tailrace area of the creek has riprap along both shores as it exits a tunnel beneath the dam. Immediately below the tunnel are concrete fishing piers along both shores. A bit farther downstream, a footbridge crosses the creek. Once the creek exits the roughly 100-yard-long tailrace, it empties into a couple of short, wadable shoals.

There is a parking area at the foot of the dam, along with rest rooms and a Little League baseball field. Parking can be a problem when ball games are being played in the spring and summer.

The Corps of Engineers land runs along both banks just below Fishtrap

Dam and continues downstream for about 1¼ miles on the western shore, providing good access for bank-fishing. Bait-fishing for the fresh stockers makes up almost all of the angling on this stream. Once below the shoals mentioned above, the creek deepens and flows at a sluggish pace.

At ½ mile downstream, there is a picnic area on the western side of the creek. Downstream of this site there is ¾ mile of public access on the corps land, but you can reach the stream only via foot travel. Although the approach road runs along this stretch, there is no place to park. Once below the corps land, Licking Creek flows through private property and is rather trashy. At best, this is a marginal tailwater fishing destination.

To reach Fishtrap Dam and the Licking Creek tailwater, travel 3 miles east from the crossroads of Millard at the junction of the approach road (unmarked) with US 460. The approach road is at the northern end of the US 460 bridge across Licking Creek.

## LICKING RIVER

### DeLorme 40

The tailwater on the Licking River below Cave Run Lake is located in northeastern Kentucky and forms the boundary between Bath County to the west and Rowan County to the east. Positioned just on the northern edge of

Jeff Goodwin, © The Countryman Press

the Daniel Boone National Forest, Cave Run covers 8,300 acres but is not very deep. It is also one of the state's newer reservoirs, completed in 1969. As with most Kentucky lakes that create trout-supporting tailwaters, Cave Run is a Corps of Engineers flood-control impoundment and does not have a powerhouse for energy production.

The Licking River tailwater is fairly large by Kentucky standards, although it does not come close to either the Cumberland or Dix River tailwaters in size. At 75 to 80 yards wide at the end of the dam's tailrace, the stream is large enough to support some float-fishing.

*The point jutting between the Cave Run tailrace and the backwater provides anglers good access just below the dam.*

This tailwater receives a total of 7,500 catchable-sized rainbow trout annually, but due to its low elevation near the edge of the Ohio River valley, conditions become marginal for fish in the summer. No trout are released into this stream from July through September each year.

Bait-fishing is the staple method of anglers targeting trout below Cave Run, but casting or trolling spoons, Rebel Teeny Crawfish, or Rooster Tail spinners (particularly in brown colors) produces fish as well. About the only "hatch" that would interest fly-casters here is the dead and stunned shad that come through the dam when water is released from the lake. These baitfish attract gulls from the lake proper, as well as the attention of the trout. Tossing a minnow-imitating streamer is an option for these occasions. Although the shores are clear enough for casting in the park below the dam, none of the accessible part of the river is wadable.

The Licking tailrace, which is lined on both sides with riprap, is a couple hundred yards long. The flow then spreads into a backwater on the eastern side where a small stream enters the river. The point jutting out between the tailrace and the backwater is a popular spot with local anglers.

Access to the Licking River tailwater is available only in the park at the foot of Cave Run Dam. The park provides ¼ mile of shoreline on both sides of the river. A picnic area, rest rooms, parking lot, and boat ramp are on the park's western shore. A paved walkway leads over the mouth of the tailrace on the dam, providing an easy walk to the abovementioned point between tailrace and backwater.

The boat ramp in the park is an excellent paved one, allowing the launch of anything from a canoe to a bass boat. Due to the river's width, it is possible to float-fish downstream of the park, but the trout-supporting portion of the river is only about a mile long, especially in warmer months.

Access to the park below Cave Run Lake is via a drive originating from KY 801 (this road appears as KY 826 on some maps) at the north end of the dam. This is just to the south of the crossroads of Bluestone on US 60 in Rowan County.

# LITTLE SANDY RIVER

## *DeLorme 41*

The most northerly of Kentucky's tailwater trout fisheries, the Little Sandy River lies below Grayson Lake in Carter County. Nestled in the northeastern

Jeff Goodwin, © The Countryman Press

corner of the state near Ohio and West Virginia, Grayson Lake was completed in 1969 and covers 1,500 acres. This is another of the commonwealth's flood-control reservoirs managed by the Army Corps of Engineers.

Very similar to the tailwater found below Cave Run Lake to the west, the Little Sandy is stocked with 7,500 catchable-sized rainbow trout each year, but none are planted in July, August, or September. The river is actually quite a small stream below Grayson Lake and probably has no carryover of fish from year to year. The suitable trout water extends only about 1 mile downstream to below where a major feeder stream, Big Stinking Creek, enters from the west. All of the angling pressure on this tailwater appears to come from bait-fishers—not surprising in light of its marginal habitat.

Where the stream emerges from the dam, a curved tailrace lined with riprap empties over a shallow shoal to form the main creek channel. A small feeder creek enters from the eastern side at the end of the tailrace, forming a little backwater eddy.

A Corps of Engineers park extends down the western shore, while steep rock walls jut out over the water on the eastern side. These rocky cliffs, which drop right into the creek channel, run for about ½ mile downstream to the junction with Big Stinking Creek. Access to the lower portion of the tailwater is available via the Grayson Lake Nature Trail, which originates in the park on the eastern shore. This trail forms a loop, with one leg running right along the shore of the Little Sandy.

The park below the Grayson Dam contains parking areas, rest rooms, and a playground. It can be reached via an approach drive from KY 7, which crosses the dam. The drive is at the eastern end of the dam. It is located 7 miles south of the town of Grayson, which is situated near I-64 in Carter County.

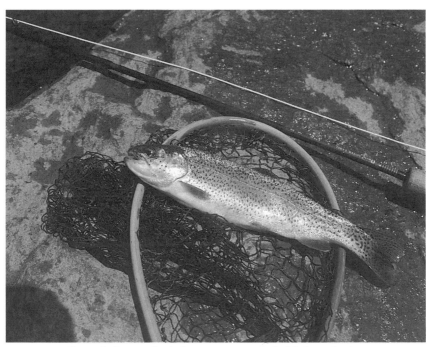

*Several thousand rainbow trout are stocked below the dam*
*at Grayson Lake each year.*

# MARTINS FORK, CUMBERLAND RIVER

## *DeLorme 88*

Among Kentucky's tailwater streams, the Martins Fork of the Cumberland River is unique in that it supports trout both above and below the reservoir through which it flows. Rising in the northeastern corner of Bell County on the edge of the Cumberland Gap National Historical Park, Martins Fork is a major headwater of the Cumberland River. Flowing northeast through

Jeff Goodwin, © The Countryman Press

*High water turns the calm pool at the foot of the dam into
a cauldron of churning water.*

Harlan County, this stream eventually meets the Poor Fork and the Glover
Fork near the town of Harlan to form the Cumberland River. Along this
entire route, however, Martins Fork qualifies as only a small to medium-
sized stream.

Above Martins Fork Lake, the stream is home to the only population of
Coosa red-eye bass in the commonwealth, along with brook and rainbow
trout. In fact, the Kentucky-record brook trout was taken from this creek on

August 21, 1982. R. James Augustus of Louisville caught the 1-pound, 15-ounce brookie. This upper part of the stream is a rough-and-tumble wilderness flow with a 160-foot-per-mile gradient along its course. It is also difficult to reach, requiring a hike in from KY 987, which parallels the stream.

Below the lake, unfortunately, Martins Fork is a less intriguing trout fishing destination. It remains small in size, but its ability to support trout is not much helped by passing through the reservoir (a Corps of Engineers flood-control structure). At best, it is marginal trout water.

Martins Fork receives 5,900 catchable-sized rainbow trout each year, with fish released below the lake every month from April to November, except August and September. When minimum flows of water are coming through the dam, the large pool at the tailrace is quite clear. Trout are visible mixing with bass and bream in the low waters from the dam to the KY 987 bridge just downstream. During higher flows, Martins Fork is turbulent, murky, and churning. Only bank-fishing is practical at those times.

Wading is possible during minimum water levels from the lower half of the tailrace pool down to the highway bridge. Below the bridge, the creek deepens and flows sluggishly toward its junction with the other headwater forks of the Cumberland. Trout undoubtedly move downstream during colder months, but virtually no carryover of fish occurs here. During low water in the summer the stream gets quite warm, even in the mile that holds trout.

Access to Martins Fork tailwater is provided by a gravel parking lot at the foot of the dam on the eastern shore. A steep riprap incline descends to the water on this bank. At the western end of the KY 987 bridge there is a parking area for the Cumberland Shadow Trail. There is about ½ mile of access along the stream below the dam on Corps of Engineers lands. Only foot access is possible below the highway bridge. Downstream of that point, Martins Fork flows on private lands and is not suited to floating.

To reach Martins Fork, travel southeast on US 421 from Harlan to the village of Cawood. Turn right (southeast) onto KY 987 and follow this road until it crosses Martins Fork at the dam.

## MIDDLE FORK KENTUCKY RIVER

### DeLorme 71

The tailwater of the Middle Fork of the Kentucky River lies downstream of 1,230-acre Buckhorn Lake in east-central Kentucky. Buckhorn Dam is 162

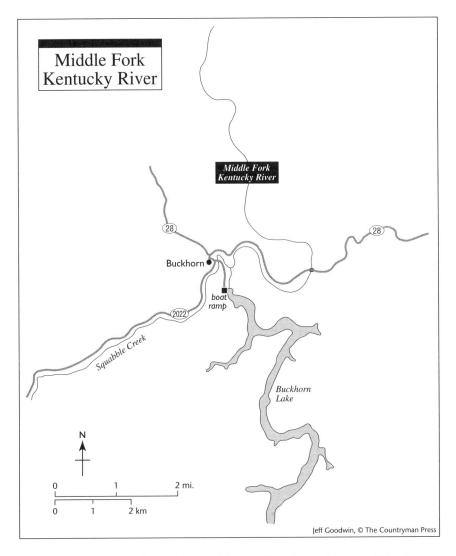

Middle Fork
Kentucky River

Middle Fork
Kentucky River

Buckhorn

boat
ramp

Squabble Creek

Buckhorn
Lake

N

0       1       2 mi.

0    1    2 km

Jeff Goodwin, © The Countryman Press

feet high, was opened in 1961, and is another Army Corps of Engineers flood-control project that supports some trout fishing. As with most of these water-control projects, the Buckhorn Dam's tailwater provides only marginal trout habitat.

Situated in Perry County near the village of Buckhorn, the Middle Fork of the Kentucky is a small stream as it flows to the north below Buckhorn Lake. Eventually it joins the North and South Forks at the town of Beattieville to form the main stem of the Kentucky River.

Mature rainbow trout of 8 to 12 inches are planted in the Middle Fork

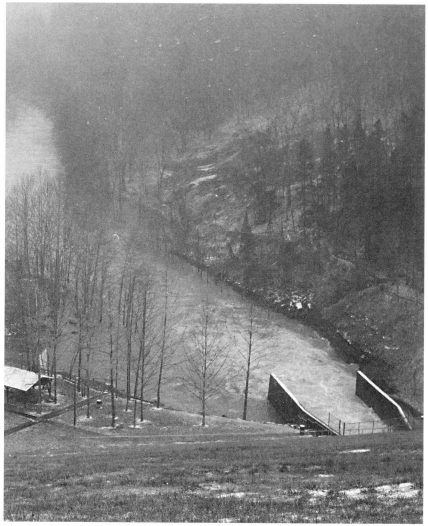

*The tailwater below Buckhorn Lake is a narrow, turbulent flow
when water is being released.*

monthly from April to November. A total of 4,700 fish are released into the
stream annually. It is unlikely that any appreciable carryover of trout occurs
from year to year. As with all of the similar small tailwaters in the Bluegrass
State, bank-fishing with bait is the method of choice for most anglers.
During periods of high water, this tailwater is virtually unfishable. At these
times, however, the mouth of Squabble Creek, which enters the Middle Fork
from the west ¼ mile downstream of the dam, offers a fishing option.

Though the Middle Fork is a murky torrent during high flows, the water backing up into Squabble Creek remains clear. It is accessible from the bank in the Corps of Engineers campground located along its shore.

There is roughly ¼ mile of access to the tailwaters of the Middle Fork on the western shore in the corps park. The park contains a picnic area, a seasonal campground (closed during winter months), and a boat ramp. The campground extends downstream to the mouth of Squabble Creek. Below that point, the Middle Fork flows through private land into the town of Buckhorn.

To reach the park at Buckhorn Dam, travel ¼ mile south of KY 28 in Buckhorn via a paved access road. The road does not have a sign identifying it, but there is a directional sign for Buckhorn Lake at the intersection. The park is directly behind the campus of Buckhorn School, which is visible from KY 28.

For information on water conditions and releases from Buckhorn Dam, call the Corps of Engineers recorded message line at 606-398-7157.

# NOLIN RIVER

### DeLorme 64

The Nolin River below Nolin River Lake is one of the most westerly of Kentucky's tailwater trout fisheries; only the Rough River tailwater lies farther west. It is located in Edmonson County in the west-central portion of the commonwealth. There are 5,975 acres of water in the impoundment behind Nolin River Dam, which opened in 1963. There is no power-generation facility at this Corps of Engineers flood-control project.

Flowing to the southwest, the Nolin skirts the western edge of Mammoth Cave National Park, then empties into the Green River directly north of the village of Brownsville.

The cool waters from the bottom of the fairly shallow reservoir have only a minimal effect on water conditions in the river downstream. As a result, the trout water extends for only about 1½ miles below the lake. The Nolin River is only a medium-sized stream here. Mature rainbow trout are stocked each month from April to November, with an annual total of 16,600. Although most of the angling pressure on the Nolin appears to come from bank-fishing in the immediate area of the tailrace, there is a good boat ramp just below the dam to accommodate float-fishing.

The tailrace at the foot of Nolin River Dam is unique in that there are concrete fishing platforms along both shores for easy access. Then the shoreline changes to riprap that has been poured with concrete to form a solid surface along either bank. At the end of the tailrace the river widens to roughly 100 feet and flows through a shallow riffle area. A small creek feeds into the river at this point as well. Below the riffle, the boat ramp is on the western shore. The eastern bank is dominated by an impressive limestone head that juts a couple hundred feet above the water.

Access to the Nolin River tailwater is afforded by a Corps of Engineers recreation area on the western side of the stream at the foot of the dam. A road from the western end of the dam connects the park to KY 728, which runs across the dam. Parking and picnic areas, a boat ramp, and rest rooms are provided in the recreation area, but no camping is allowed.

Shore access is short on the eastern side of the river, extending only to the end of the tailrace, where the beginning of the stone cliff blocks further movement down this side of the stream. On the western shore, an anglers' footpath leads downstream from the boat ramp area for an additional ¼ mile to the point where a deep ditch and a bluff are located. In all, there is about ½ mile of access on this side of the Nolin River.

Float-fishing is possible on the Nolin farther downstream, for it deepens and slows below the boat ramp. Eventually the river becomes the western boundary of Mammoth Cave National Park. Nolin River Dam is located on KY 728, between the crossroads of Sweeden to the west and Cub Run to the east in north-central Edmonson County.

# PAINT CREEK

### *DeLorme 55*

Paintsville Lake is a Corps of Engineers flood-control facility located in the east-central portion of the state, in Johnson County. Below the reservoir, Paint Creek is managed as a tailwater trout fishery, despite its small size.

*Riffles and pools have been handcrafted in the park on the tailwater
just below Paintsville Lake.*

Created in 1983, it is one of the newest tailwaters in Kentucky. It is also one
of the more interesting and prettiest such fishing sites in the commonwealth.

Presently the number of catchable-sized rainbow trout released in Paint
Creek stands at 18,000 annually, and plantings run from April to November.
Eight hundred brown trout are also released into the flow. These fish are
stocked via a 1-foot-diameter pipe that connects the parking area at the foot

of the dam to the creek, allowing easy access to the hatchery trucks. Thanks to the excellent facilities on this tailwater, fishing pressure is quite heavy immediately following stockings, especially from bank-fishers using bait.

Where the tailrace comes out of the dam, it is surrounded by a concrete walkway that leads into paved fishing platforms along either shore. Below these platforms, steeply inclined riprap lines both banks for several hundred yards down to the end of the Corps of Engineers land. This channel courses through a well-maintained park. Some riprap-sized rocks have also been placed in the water to break the flow into a half-dozen pools. A footbridge crosses here, making for easy access to the entire tailrace area from either bank.

At the downstream limit of the corps land, KY 40 crosses the river on a metal bridge. Just above the bridge, on the western shore, a feeder creek enters the flow. This tributary's flow has pushed a gravel bar out into Paint Creek, creating a natural shoal. Above the shoal a deep, slow pool extends back upstream to the end of the riprap. As in the riprap area, the bank is quite steep on this lower end of the public access.

Below the corps land, Paint Creek flows through private lands as it courses 8 miles down to its junction with the Levisa Fork at the town of Paintsville. It is possible to drift and wade using a float tube through here. There is much less fishing pressure downstream of the public land, and anglers casting small lures or spinners often tangle with smallmouth bass, as well as stocked trout. Also, since Paintsville Lake and the creek have been stocked with river otters, anglers are sometimes entertained by encounters with these frisky critters.

Access to Paint Creek is provided by a Corps of Engineers recreation area at the foot of the dam. There are parking lots, playgrounds, and rest rooms.

To reach Paintsville Dam and Paint Creek, travel 4 miles west from the town of Paintsville via KY 40. The park is located on the north side of this road, 2¼ miles beyond the intersection of KY 40 and US 460.

# ROUGH RIVER

### DeLorme 47

The final trout water covered in Kentucky is the Rough River, the westernmost tailwater trout stream in the state. Rough River Lake is the 4,830-acre Army Corps of Engineers flood-control reservoir from which the trout water flows. There is no hydroelectric generating facility at Rough River Dam. The impoundment and tailwater form the boundary between Breckenridge County to the north and Grayson County to the south. Lying in west-central Kentucky, the tailwater is roughly 70 miles southwest of Louisville.

The KDFWR stocks the Rough River with 8- to 12-inch rainbow trout once per year in June. The total number of trout planted is usually only 3,000. The fishing is mainly bank-angling in the corps park at the foot of Rough River Dam. Fishing pressure is fairly heavy just after the stocking.

During periods of maximum water release, the flow in the tailwater is sluggish, and it becomes murky. A quarter-mile downstream, at the end of the corps property, the river narrows abruptly from about 100 feet to roughly 50 or 60. This causes water to back up, giving this portion of the tailwater a lakelike appearance. Shoreline access is excellent down to the end of the public property on the southern side of the river. It is also possible to walk down the northern side from the dam.

The trout-bearing water on the Rough River is a bit odd in that it stretches for only about ¾ of a mile downstream from Rough River Dam, then, at several miles downstream, trout are once again present around the KY 54 bridge over the river. In the vicinity of the bridge, trout can be found for roughly ¼ mile upstream and downstream just after stocking takes place.

Access to the trout fishing is available in the Tailwater Recreation Area at the foot of Rough River Dam. There is a parking area, plus a seasonal (closed in winter) RV and tent campground. The park is reached via an approach drive off KY 79 at the southern end of Rough River Dam.

Downriver at the KY 54 bridge there is a gravel drive at the southeast end of the span, leading to a small, gravel parking area. Bank access for fishing is very poor, but there is a steep, rough trail leading down to the water. This can be an access point for taking out a canoe after a float trip.

If you decide to try a float trip from the Tailwater Recreation Area to KY 54, be aware that there is a small lowhead dam at Green Mill Historic Site. This grist mill was operated by the Green family continuously from 1823 to 1963. An old metal bridge, no longer used, spans the river here, as well as the lowhead dam that creates a small waterfall. Caution should be exercised in approaching the dam from upriver. The historic site is located at the Falls of the Rough, about ½ mile downstream of the KY 110 bridge.

# Missouri

Jeff Goodwin, © The Countryman Press

# CHAPTER 7

# Missouri

Although Missouri historically had no natural trout populations, the Show Me State nonetheless has a fairly long tradition of trout fishing. The first of these cold-water species introduced to Missouri waters were brook trout transplanted from Wisconsin in 1879. These fish were stocked into several Ozark Mountain streams in the southwestern portion of the state.

As soon as it was realized that the brookies were surviving, rainbow trout from California's McCloud River were planted in Missouri waters; this began in 1880. These West Coast–native fish quickly adapted to the heartland, and by the late 1880s there were reproducing populations in Crane Creek, the Spring River, and Maramec Spring. The stocking of trout, however, was only possible because these rivers are fed by a number of substantial springs that gush forth water at a constant 50 degrees year-round.

In the ensuing years, the Missouri Department of Conservation (MDC) experimented with a number of other exotic species. Eventually, brown trout, steelhead, Pacific salmon, Atlantic salmon, and grayling were introduced. As it turned out, only the brown trout became established and joined the brookies and rainbows in furnishing today's fishery.

Probably the most familiar Missouri trout fishing image for anglers from other areas is opening day in the state parks. Four facilities—Bennett Springs, Montauk, Maramec Spring, and Roaring River—are designated as state trout parks. Here an estimated 400,000 fishing trips per year produce a million trout. The streams in these parks are stocked daily during the spring-through-fall season. Every year, just after Missouri's opening day on March 1, newspapers across America carry photos showing anglers forming large circles of humanity on the streams and fishing inside them. While such angling is productive, its aesthetics are not overly appealing to many trout fishers.

Although memorable, these scenes hardly typify the variety of trout fishing opportunities Missouri provides. During the winter months, the trout parks are open to catch-and-release fishing for a limited number of days each week and offer more solitude. The MDC also provides 12 trout management areas that are stocked periodically with rainbows and browns and open to year-round angling. Finally, there are seven wild trout fishing areas and two catch-and-release trout fishing areas in Missouri. The fishing regulations booklet published yearly by the MDC and available at most sporting-goods outlets identifies these areas and provides complete regulations for each.

Among the MDC's trout management areas is Missouri's only tailwater trout fishery. Located below Table Rock Lake, the White River is the state's premier trout fishing destination. In all, Missouri contains 177 miles of river, creek, and tailwater trout habitat.

All anglers from 16 to 64 years of age are required to have a regular fishing permit, as well as a trout stamp, to catch trout in Missouri. A trout stamp is not required in the trout parks, however; instead, anglers must purchase daily trout tags. On the White River tailwater, neither a trout tag nor a trout stamp is needed. The regular state creel limit is 5 trout per day, regardless of species or size. On the tailwater below Table Rock Lake, only 1 of the 5 may be a brown trout, and it must be at least 20 inches long.

## WHITE RIVER

### DeLorme 62

As mentioned earlier, the White River below Table Rock Lake is the only tailwater trout fishery in Missouri. This is, in fact, the same river that provides tailwater fisheries in the Ozark region of Arkansas just to the south. After passing through Beaver Lake in northwestern Arkansas, the White River enters Missouri and the 43,100-acre Table Rock Lake. Below Table Rock Dam, the river forms an arc that flows into Bull Shoals Lake and, thus, back across the state boundary into north-central Arkansas.

White River

22 River mile markers

Bull Shoals Lake

Railroad

Branson

Fall Creek

Short Cr.

White River

Branson City Campground

Hollister

Shepherd of the Hills Trout Hatchery

Table Rock Lake

boat ramp

Table Rock State Park

Overlook Hole

N

0    0.5    1 mi.

0   0.5   1 km

Jeff Goodwin, © The Countryman Press

The White River's tailwater in Missouri is more commonly known as Lake Taneycomo due to its unusual makeup. The name is derived from the contracted abbreviation of Taney County, Missouri, in which the flow is located. Some 22 miles downstream of Table Rock Dam is Power Site Dam (also known as Ozark Beach Dam), which backs up 2,080 acres of water in Lake Taneycomo. (Power Site Dam is the oldest hydroelectric facility on the White River—constructed back in 1913.) As a result of this configuration, the White's tailwater in Missouri is a hybrid between a lake and a river. Much of the lower end of the tailwater looks and acts like a reservoir, while the several miles just below Table Rock Dam fluctuate between being a river and being a lake. The variation, of course, depends on the discharges of water from Table Rock's four generators. From the practical standpoint of trout fishing, however, this discussion will cover only the 8 miles of river from Table Rock Dam down to the twin towns of Branson and Hollister. Below there, Taneycomo permanently takes on the characteristics of a lake.

Another fact unique to this portion of the White River is that it receives the heaviest stockings of trout per mile of any tailwater in the South. Plantings of rainbow trout began shortly after Table Rock Dam was completed in 1958 and turned Lake Taneycomo into a cold-water resource. The trout come from the Shepherd of the Hills Trout Hatchery. Located in Table Rock State Park at the foot of Table Rock Dam, this is the largest state-owned facility east of the Rocky Mountains. From a high of 1.6 million trout stocked in 1984, the MDC now releases roughly 400,000 pounds of trout into the tailwater annually, or about 760,000 fish.

Beginning in 1980 up to 50,000 brown trout were added to the fishery annually, although that number has since settled to about 15,000 per year. Before 1975, some steelhead trout were also planted here.

With such heavy stocking, up to 90 percent of the trout taken from Taneycomo are rainbows of 8 to 10 inches in length. But that does not mean larger fish are not present. In fact, two of the last three Missouri state-record brown trout have come from this part of the White; it can also lay claim to three previous state records for rainbow trout.

On March 29, 1991, Marty Babusa of Hollister was fishing a Muddler Minnow when he landed a 23-pound, 4-ounce bruiser of a brown trout to claim the record for that species. Babusa's trout was bested on June 27, 1994, by a 24-pound, 15-ounce brown hauled out of the White River by Kevin Elfrink of Jackson. He was fishing a Shad Assassin soft-plastic jerkbait at the time. Finally, on November 10, 1997, Taneycomo lost the state record mark to a 26-pound, 13-ounce brown caught by Rob Caudel of Springfield, who was fishing downstream on the White in Bull Shoals Lake. That fish presently holds the state record for the species.

The first of the Taneycomo record rainbow trout was caught on January 26, 1970, by Charles Gott of Green Forest, Arkansas. He was fishing a Little Cleo spoon near the mouth of Fall Creek when the 13-pound, 14¾-ounce lunker took the lure. The next time the White River produced the Missouri record for rainbows came on July 14, 1976. That 14-pound, 7-ounce fish was hooked by Craig Wolf of Branson, who was fishing a Flatfish lure at the US 65 highway bridge. On December 23, 1984, while fishing the upper part of Lake Taneycomo with a salmon egg, Bill Hecker of Rogersville caught a 16-pound, 12-ounce rainbow. That fish held the record for just under 3 years before being bested by 1 ounce by a Roaring River State Park catch, which continues to set the standard for the species in Missouri.

Despite these impressive fish—all taken from the White River below Table Rock Dam—the rainbow trout fishery has declined noticeably over the years. Many local anglers and fisheries managers point to the 1960s and 1970s, when 5-fish limits of rainbow trout were regularly brought in that weighed a total of more than 35 pounds! Such a catch would raise eyebrows today on Taneycomo. Though occasional 6- to 7-pound rainbows are taken, they are not common.

Part of the decline can be traced to the collapse of the scud population that occurred on this part of the White River in the mid- to late 1980s. Biologists reported that by 1987 the numbers of these small freshwater crustaceans had fallen by 90 percent. Poor water quality resulting from development along the river and a population increase of white suckers—which compete with trout for this food staple—are two possible causes for

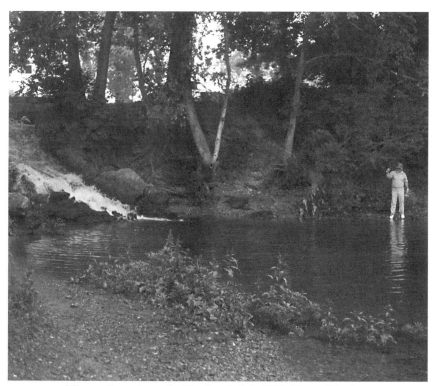

*The outflows from the Shepherd of the Hills Trout Hatchery*
*are hot spots for trout that make spawning runs to the area.*

the scud decline. Another problem may have been that too many trout were being stocked into the river for its forage base. Though a definitive cause for the problem was never found, the number of trout being stocked has declined steadily from the highs of the mid-1980s to present levels.

At the same time that Taneycomo's rainbow fishery has exhibited signs of a decline, its brown trout fishery has been heading in the opposite direction. Besides the two state-record fish of the early 1990s, the same period saw biologists on an electrofishing expedition stun, revive, and release a 36-inch brown. Most anglers and state fisheries managers consider it only a matter of time before the next record-breaking brown trout is brought in from this stretch of the White River.

Supporting that view is the discovery made by Mike Adams, just upstream of Lilley's Landing Resort and Marina on September 10, 1997. Adams found a brown trout floating in the river that had apparently died of old age. The monster fish measured 41.75 inches long, which is $1\frac{1}{2}$ inches longer than the world-record brown from the Little Red River in Arkansas! The carcass also had a girth of 27 inches, and though dead for an estimated 24 hours, still tipped the scales at 37.1 pounds—more than nine pounds more than Missouri's present state record.

In large part, the quality of the brown trout angling here is a result of the regulations covering the species. Since 1982 there has been a creel limit in effect permitting the daily harvest of only 1 brown trout, which must be at least 20 inches in length. This restriction has allowed many of the tailwater browns to grow large.

Since 1997, fishing in the White River from Table Rock Dam downstream to the mouth of Fall Creek has been restricted to the use of artificial lures and flies only. Along this 3.1-mile stretch of water a slot limit for rainbow trout is also enforced on Taneycomo. All rainbows from 12 to 20 inches long must be immediately released. Anglers may still harvest the state creel limit of 5 fish, but the rainbows must be 11 inches or shorter, or longer than 20 inches. The lakewide restriction of only one brown trout of more than 20 inches also applies here.

Most of the trout fishing pressure on Taneycomo occurs from dawn to roughly 11 AM, regardless of the time of year. A lesser period of activity usually follows from 2 to 5 PM. Though the trout are caught at any water level here, local anglers prefer a stable flow. If the river is rising or falling, the fish often seem to be thrown off their feeding routines.

Regarding time of year, trout in Taneycomo are not notoriously picky.

They will take a bait during any month. Still, the period of December through early March is noted for producing the best fishing for trophy-sized brown trout. Another appeal of fishing at this time of year is the chance to avoid crowds on the tailwater. As far back as 1970, the MDC estimated the fishing pressure on Taneycomo to be 5 million angling hours per year. This figure jumped to 15 million by the early 1980s and is undoubtedly much higher today.

By far the most used angling technique on this water is bait-fishing with corn, cheese, marshmallows, or night crawlers. These are employed while drift-fishing on high water or when still-fishing from boats when the generators are silent. Most drift-fishers, however, change over to artificial lures when the turbines quit turning at Table Rock Dam. Little Cleo spoons, Blakemore Road Runners, Mepps spinners, and Rooster Tails are all popular (this latter lure in green is often mentioned as especially productive). Still, the most popular spinning lures for trout on this tailwater are tiny $\frac{1}{80}$-ounce micro jigs. These are often drifted below a strike indicator during low water. The most popular color tends to be brown, but black, olive, gray, pink, and white jigs also take fish. These jigs are also very effective when a shad die-off takes place in Table Rock Lake, loading the tailwater with dead and dying baitfish.

Public access to the shores of Taneycomo is limited. Table Rock State Park, which lies at the foot of the dam, provides the best access to the river. Besides containing the Shepherd of the Hills Hatchery, the park offers gravel and paved parking areas, trail access to the water, and a paved boat ramp. There is just over a mile of streamside access to the fishing on the northern shore of the river in the park.

The three water outlets that empty into the river from the hatchery are a major attraction for anglers in Table Rock State Park. These highly oxygenated and nutrient-loaded flows attract and hold trout. Marty Babusa's 1991 record brown was taken at the mouth of one of these outlets. In fact, many local anglers know this area around the outfalls of the hatchery as the Lunker Hole. Big brown trout are often seen here in the fall and winter, but it is not clear if they are making spawning runs to the outfalls or simply moving to the places where food and oxygen are most abundant. At any rate, these outlets are primary target areas for angling. Be aware, however, that fishing above the high-water mark in these outlets is prohibited.

This is the only area of Taneycomo where fly-casters can be called a common sight. During low water levels some wading is available, and intrepid anglers even wade around the hatchery outfalls during the highest water levels. Minnow-imitating streamer patterns are a good bet at most times, with black Woolly Buggers noted for being particularly good. Fishing scud imitations under a strike indicator should also prove effective. Fish these latter flies 3 to 4 feet below the surface to attract the most attention from the fish.

The next area of note among local anglers is called the Overlook Hole. It is found just below the major island in the river at Mile Marker 21. The markers were placed on Taneycomo by the Empire District Electric Company and are located at 1-mile intervals along the shore. They begin at Power Site Dam and mark the distance from that point upstream to the foot of Table Rock Dam.

The Overlook Hole gets its name from the scenic overlook on MO 165, which is on the southwestern shore above this part of the river. The major fishing feature of the hole is the three large rocks on the southwestern side of the river. These are visible during low water and offer good holding places for trout when the water goes up.

The area with the reputation for the best fishing ends at the mouth of Fall Creek, 3.1 miles below Table Rock Dam. Downstream of this point the river takes on many more of the characteristics of a lake. When using small jigs with spinning gear or scud imitations with a fly-rod through here, fish at depths of at least 7 to 8 feet for best results. There are, however, still some honey holes worth mentioning on this section of river.

Between Mile Markers 18 and 17 is a major submerged gravel bar referred to as Monkey Island. The disruption in the current here generally attracts large numbers of rainbows and is a good area to target year-round. Then, at Mile Marker 17, you will encounter the School of the Ozarks Hole. This spot is noted for having produced some lunker-sized rainbows over the years. It is a deep hole in the riverbed that contains a fair amount of structure and debris, making it best suited for fishing from a stationary boat during low water.

Between Mile Markers 17 and 16 there are no notable structures, nor other distinguished angling hot spots, but this is the area of the tailwater that produced Kevin Elfrink's former state-record rainbow. Obviously, drift-fishing this section can be productive.

The final section upstream of Branson worth special attention is found along the northern shore from the mouth of Short Creek down to the village waterfront. Through here a lot of downed trees are in the water along the bank; either a crankbait or a big minnow-imitating streamer offers a good chance at a lunker brown trout.

Besides the park at Table Rock Dam, the only public shore access on the upper portion of Taneycomo is located in town at the Branson City Campground. In addition to RV and tent-camping areas, the campground offers fishing docks and two public boat ramps. Also, during low water levels, there is the possibility of doing some wading around the US 65 bridge in Branson.

Downstream of town, Taneycomo offers another 14 miles of trout habitat to Power Site Dam, but the water loses all resemblance to a river. This final stretch of tailwater is virtually a reservoir.

While Branson offers various accommodations for visiting anglers, it is far better known for its country music and other theaters. This is a tourist mecca, particularly from spring through fall. The influx of music fans can make for heavy traffic on the roads. Traveling through town can be a nightmare, particularly in the summer.

For information on water releases on the Taneycomo section of the White River, call the Army Corps of Engineers' automated telephone message at Table Rock Dam at 417-336-5083.

North Carolina

ATLANTIC OCEAN

Neuse R.

Raleigh

95

40

85

Cape Fear R.

Wilmington

Haw R.

40 · 85

95

85

Pee Dee R.

Yadkin R.

77

40

Lake Norman

2

26

Asheville

Fontana Lake

4

3

1

Jeff Goodwin, © The Countryman Press

1 Hiwassee River
2 Linville River
3 Nantahala River
4 Tuckasegee River

N

80 mi.

80 km

0   40   80

0   40   80

# CHAPTER 8

# North Carolina

Although the folks in Virginia might argue the point, the Tar Heel State of North Carolina is the epitome of southern trout fishing areas. It has more miles of trout water of every description than any other state in Dixie, ranging from tiny mountain brooklets to large mountain lakes and bold-flowing rivers. The state is probably home to more native brook trout than any other area in the South, as well as thriving populations of brown and rainbow trout.

All of the 4,200 miles of Tar Heel trout streams are located in the 26 westernmost counties of the state. Rainbow trout first came to the Old North State in the 1880s, when the original populations of native brook trout were depleted in many streams. From these original stockings of the West Coast exotics, rainbows eventually became the predominant species in most of the state's trout water.

In 1905 the first recorded introductions of brown trout occurred in North Carolina. Like the rainbows, browns found the new territory to their liking and have expanded their range ever since. It is an expansion likely to continue for some time into the future.

With such an abundance of trout water, the North Carolina Wildlife Resources Commission (NCWRC) has been active in managing the streams, rivers, and lakes of the state. There are more regulations on waters here than in any other state of the Southeast. Regulations run the gamut from fly-fishing-only, catch-and-release waters to hatchery-supported, put-and-take streams. Between these extremes, a number of intermediate management philosophies are applied to some creeks and rivers.

There are also four tailwaters amid this abundance of trout water in North Carolina. The Hiwassee River below Lake Chatuge in Clay County, the Linville River downstream of Lake James in Burke County, the Nantahala River below Nantahala Lake (sometimes identified as Lake Aquone) in Macon and Swain Counties, and the Tuckasegee River below Cedar Cliff Reservoir in Jackson County are all true tailwater trout fisheries.

One other river offers what appears at first glance to be a tailwater, but, due to unique circumstances, it fails to qualify. Technically speaking, the waters downstream of Fontana Lake on the Little Tennessee River, which form the boundary of Graham and Swain Counties, fit the description of a tailwater trout fishery. On closer inspection, however, the Little Tennessee can't actually be called a river through here. Fontana empties its waters directly into Cheoah Reservoir, which in turn flows through its dam into Calderwood Reservoir. Additionally, water from Santeetlah Lake is piped to a powerhouse on Cheoah Reservoir, adding still more cold water to this system of lakes. This results in excellent trout fishing in Cheoah and Calderwood, but entirely in a lake environment.

The Linville, Nantahala and, Tuckasegee tailwaters are managed as hatchery-supported trout waters by the NCWRC and adhere to the statewide regulations for waters carrying that designation, although there is a delayed-harvest section on the Tuckasegee. Surprisingly, the Hiwassee River is not designated as trout water in North Carolina, but it has a naturally developed trout fishery that will be explained in the discussion of that stream. Because of its lack of classification, the NCWRC treats the Hiwassee as a wild trout stream.

The creel limit on hatchery-supported waters in North Carolina is 7 trout per day in any combination of species. The only bait restriction that applies to the tailwaters is in the delayed-harvest portion of the Tuckasegee. Hatchery-supported waters are closed to fishing each year from March 1 until the first Saturday in April.

Stockings of trout in these waters are composed of the Old North State's standard mix of 40 percent rainbow, 40 percent brown, and 20 percent brook trout. These fish are basically 8 to 10 inches in length, but 3 percent of the released fish exceed 10 inches, and 1 percent exceed 12 inches.

To fish for these trout, all persons 16 years of age or older must have a valid comprehensive fishing license. There are some exceptions to this rule for resident anglers, so check the current "North Carolina Inland Fishing, Hunting & Trapping Regulations Digest" for more details. This brochure is available from most outlets that sell hunting and fishing licenses.

Fishing licenses can be purchased in North Carolina over the telephone or by using a computer. You must have a Visa or MasterCard to access the service. Call 1-888-248-6834 or visit www.ncwildlife.org/ on the Internet, then follow the prompts for fishing license purchases.

# HIWASSEE RIVER

### DeLorme 50

As mentioned in the introduction, the Hiwassee River is an oddity among southern tailwaters. The NCWRC has never had a trout-stocking program on the river, it is not natural trout water because of its relatively low elevation, yet it contains a good population of wild rainbow trout, plus some browns.

The Hiwassee rises in the mountains of northeast Georgia, empties into 7,050-acre Lake Chatuge in that state, and emerges from Chatuge Dam in North Carolina. The river then cuts an east-to-west swath across Clay County before being impounded once again at Mission Dam on the Cherokee County border. The reservoir at Mission Dam is a tiny, riverine lake.

Two possible explanations are available for the wild trout fishery now found in the Hiwassee tailwater. One is that private landowners may have placed trout in the river at some point in the past and these fish began to re-produce. The other possibility is that trout stocked in Fires and Tusquitee Creeks moved downstream into the river. While it may have been a combination of the two sources, rainbows have almost certainly entered the Hiwassee from its two feeder streams downstream of Lake Chatuge. Though the Tennessee Valley Authority filled that reservoir in 1942, there is no way of knowing for sure how long the trout fishery has existed there. It is only since the 1990s that it has gained any notoriety.

One factor worth noting that may have been a catalyst for the development of this fishery was the construction of a weir dam less than a mile below Chatuge Dam in 1992. This structure evened out the river's low-water

# Hiwassee River

Tusquitee Road

Tusquitee Creek

Woods Road

Hiwassee River

Fires Creek

Fires Creek Wildlife Road

Lance Cove Rd

Mission Dam Road

Mission Dam

Mission Lake

Sweetwater Road

Hiwassee River

64

Hayesville

69

Chatuge Dam Road

Sanderson Road

Lake Chatuge

64

N

0    1.5    1.5    3 mi.

0    3 km

NORTH CAROLINA

GEORGIA

Jeff Goodwin, © The Countryman Press

flow to 60 cubic feet per second (cfs), while also adding dissolved oxygen to the flow. The dissolved oxygen level has been raised to 6.5 milligrams per liter of water during periods of power generation, just slightly above the level needed by trout to sustain reproduction. Prior to the installation of the weir, the minimum flow of the Hiwassee would sometimes drop to a mere trickle of 10 cfs.

Regardless of the fishery's origins, the Hiwassee River downstream of Lake Chatuge now has more than 15 miles of habitat populated by wild rainbows. Because of the scouring effect of water releases from Chatuge Dam, it is likely that no reproduction of fish takes place until the river passes beneath the Tusquitee Road bridge near Hayesville. On the De-Lorme map this road is shown as Woods Road, but road signs identify it as Tusquitee Road. A survey of the tailwater of the river by NCWRC biologists in 1997 did find young-of-the-year rainbow trout in the Poplar Cove area of the stream, farther downstream. These fish eventually grow to 11 or 12 inches in length, but bigger trout have shown up. In fact, a 7-plus-pound rainbow was taken just downstream of the Tusquitee bridge in 2002. As mentioned earlier, anglers have also reported taking brown trout from the Hiwassee tailwater.

Public access to the shores of the Hiwassee in its trout-bearing areas is the main problem with this fishery. There are only a few points where it is practical to reach the water from shore. The first of these is immediately downstream of Chatuge Dam to the southeast of the town of Hayesville. The weir dam is located just over ½ mile below the dam, off Chatuge Dam Road. There is an improved canoe access immediately below the weir dam. This facility offers the best put-in point for float-fishing the Hiwassee tailwater and there is some limited wade-fishing available at the base of the weir on low water levels. The dam also forms a barrier to keep trout from moving upstream from here.

To reach this site, take US 64 east from Hayesville. At the Hiwassee River bridge, turn southeast onto Sanderson Road. At 0.5 mile, turn southeast onto Chatuge Dam Road. The gated approach drive for the weir dam is at 0.75 mile on the left, but it's presently not marked with a sign. If you reach a bridge crossing the river on this road, you have missed the drive.

The next access spot is at the Tom Day Bridge on Tusquitee Road to the north of Hayesville and just upstream of the mouth of Tusquitee Creek.

Farther downstream and opposite the mouth of Fires Creek, Lance Cove Road provides almost ¾ mile of right-of-way access to the water on the south

*Mission Dam marks the downstream limit of trout habitat
on the Hiwassee tailwater in North Carolina.*

side of the Hiwassee. This entire stretch is composed of shoals and wadable flats
when the river is running at lower levels. To reach Lance Cove Road, travel west
on US 64 from Hayesville for just over 4 miles. Lance Cove Road runs to the
north off the highway. At 1.1 miles it changes from pavement to gravel, then
reaches the river at 1.4 miles, continuing to a dead end along the river.

Less than ¼ mile farther west, Fires Creek Road (the DeLorme map
shows the name as Lower Sweetwater Road) also runs north off US 64,
crossing the Hiwassee River at one mile. At the southeast end of the bridge is
Sweetwater Community Park, a joint venture between Clay County and the
TVA. A parking lot and concrete-step canoe access point are located in this
facility. It also provides access to a ¼-mile wadable shoal just upstream of the
canoe launch.

Downstream of Fires Creek Road, the Hiwassee flows through the small
lake formed by Mission Dam. Some trout show up in the tailrace below this
facility. The tailrace exits the dam on the north side of the river at the foot
of the structure. Trout are encountered in the water immediately below this
point. A small island splits the flow at the foot of the dam, with the water on

the south side of the river coming over the dam via the spillway. Fishing that side of the flow is likely to yield smallmouth bass instead of trout.

To reach Mission Dam, continue north across the bridge on Fires Creek Road. At its intersection with Mission Dam Road, turn west. At 1.6 miles a gravel drive runs left off the road to the foot of the dam.

To obtain information on water-release schedules at Chatuge Dam, call the TVA's toll-free, recorded message at 1-800-238-2264, punch 4 for water releases, then 19 for Lake Chatuge. This information is also available on the Internet at www.lakeinfo.tva.gov; follow the prompts for Chatuge.

# LINVILLE RIVER

### DeLorme 33

The Linville River tailwater fishery is often overlooked in North Carolina. This situation is not hard to understand, since the state is blessed with such wide-ranging, diverse trout water. The stretch of tailwater on the Linville is only about 1 mile long and has rather poor access, making it of only marginal interest to most anglers.

Located entirely in Burke County to the west of Morganton, the Linville tailwater originates at the foot of Linville Dam on 6,500-acre Lake James. While many anglers may be familiar with the Linville's trout fishing, their knowledge is generally limited to the river's upstream portions. North of the Blue Ridge Parkway in southern Avery and northern Burke Counties, the Linville is one of the Tar Heel State's most fertile trout habitats, producing

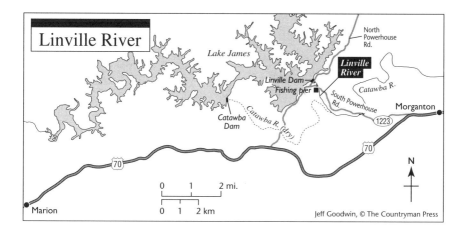

chunky stockers and wild fish. Then the river plunges over Linville Falls and through the wilderness lands of the Linville Gorge for more than a dozen miles. In the gorge's seemingly enchanted landscape of stone chimneys and steep rock cliffs, the Linville is a big, brawling river that supports brutish brown trout. These browns are planted as fingerlings, produced in NCWRC hatcheries from half-wild brood stock. Once out of the gorge, the river empties into Lake James.

Lake James's configuration is a bit unusual in that there are dams on both the Linville (to the east) and Catawba (to the west) Rivers. As the waters of the lake rose, they spilled through a gap in the hills dividing the two river valleys, thus forming a single reservoir. The Linville Dam is the only one with a powerhouse, so all of the water exiting Lake James goes down the Linville. The bed of the Catawba is dry from its dam down to where the Linville empties into it.

The trout water on the Linville tailwater is listed by the NCWRC as running from the Linville powerhouse down to the mouth of Muddy Creek. A look at a map, however, shows that Muddy Creek actually empties into the Catawba upstream of where the Catawba and Linville join. The confusing terminology probably results from the fact that all of the water in the Catawba at the junction came from Muddy Creek, even though it is flowing in the old bed of the Catawba. Anyway, whether you choose to call it Muddy Creek or the Catawba River, the point at which this stream joins the Linville is the downstream limit of trout habitat on the tailwater. Below the junction the stream is known as the Catawba River.

The trout fishery on the Linville below Lake James is a purely put-and-take resource. It is unlikely that any appreciable carryover of trout occurs, let alone any reproduction. This is marginal trout habitat. The NCWRC releases roughly 9,000 trout into the Linville tailwater each year from March through July. The fish are equally divided between catchable-sized brook and rainbow trout. These stockings take place at the State Route (SR) 1223 bridge near the foot of Linville Dam.

Just below this bridge is a large pool that features a public fishing pier. This is the only public access on the Linville tailwater, and it gets heavy usage at all water levels from bait-anglers. It is a placid pool when minimum flows are coming through the powerhouse, but turns rowdy when the water level goes up. There are some shoals just downstream of the pool where wading is practical, especially during low water.

It is also possible to float the tailwater in either a canoe or a float tube.

The take-out point is a second SR 1223 bridge, about 2 miles downstream of the first. Unfortunately, the last mile of the float is through water where trout are scarce.

There is a parking area on the western side of the Linville at the upper SR 1223 bridge. The public fishing pier is also located on that side of the river, beside the parking lot. The Linville tailwater is open to fishing under standard North Carolina regulations for hatchery-supported waters.

To reach the Linville River tailwater, travel east from the town of Marion via US 70. Turn north onto South Powerhouse Road (SR 1223) and stay on this paved road until it crosses the river for the second time, just downstream of Linville Dam.

## NANTAHALA RIVER

### DeLorme 51

The Nantahala River is one of the more celebrated streams of western North Carolina. The renown the river has achieved, unlike that of most tailwater streams, does not rest with the trout fishery created by humanity's tinkering with the environment. The headwaters of the river, far upstream of Nantahala Dam, have enjoyed the reputation of being a fine natural trout stream that even supports native brook trout in its more remote portions. Add to this a legacy of some of the best white-water canoeing, kayaking, and rafting in the eastern United States and the package is so appealing that the tailwater fishery is actually often overlooked.

Another feature setting the Nantahala apart from most of the South's artificially created trout fisheries is that the tailwater does not start at the foot of the dam. Rather, almost all of the water exits Nantahala Lake via a pipeline that bypasses roughly 8 miles of the riverbed. Through this section the Nantahala is dependent upon its feeder streams for all of its water. The upper portion of this bypassed water is very marginal trout habitat, but it is stocked with several thousand trout each year. The lower 4 miles is open under special delayed-harvest fishing rules that have proven so popular since being instituted back in 1993 that this portion of the stream has also drawn attention away from the tailwater farther downriver.

When the pipeline ends at the Nantahala Powerhouse in Macon County, just south of the Swain County border, the water empties out of the turbines to refill the riverbed. For the next 8 miles the river flows through

Swain County and the Nantahala Gorge. In the process it earns its name, which in the Cherokee language means "land of the midday sun." Steep mountainsides drop precipitously to both shores of the river valley, shutting out the sun except in the early afternoon.

Unlike some other southern tailwaters, there are only two water levels on the Nantahala. When the water is "off," the flow is that of a medium-volume creek meandering along the bed of a full-sized river. Wading is possible on virtually the entire stream at this stage; its pools are fairly placid throughout. Such conditions are usually found during the night and early-morning hours, especially during the peak fishing months of spring through fall.

Periods of low water tend to be favored by fly-casters on this tailwater. In fact—and in another departure from other southeastern tailwaters—fly-fishers are usually more common on the Nantahala than are bait- or spin-fishers. This is, in part, due to some large hatches of aquatic insects on the river. Unfortunately, while they can be expansive in size, these hatches are no more predictable than those on other waters of the southern highlands.

Fly-fishers usually employ one of two methods in their fishing. The first is to try to match the insect action taking place with dry flies of the appropriate color, in sizes from 16 to 18. This approach usually produces a lot of smaller fish. On the other hand, some local anglers cast large, bushy attractor patterns, like the Royal Wulff, in sizes up to 8. These folks get fewer strikes, but the fish they raise are often the larger rainbows and browns of 16 to 20 inches.

Bait- and spin-anglers on the Nantahala tailwater use all of the usual trout baits and lures. In the case of spin-fishing, in-line spinners or small Rapala minnow patterns are most common.

Another oddity about the Nantahala is its status as the only trout stream in North Carolina open to night-fishing. The use of large streamers or attractor dries after dark offers the fly-fisher the opportunity to tangle with one of the big nocturnal brown trout that inhabit the stream. It is wise, however, to be thoroughly familiar with the portion of river to be fished before attempting to tackle it in the dark.

When fishing the Nantahala, be aware that the water will rise without

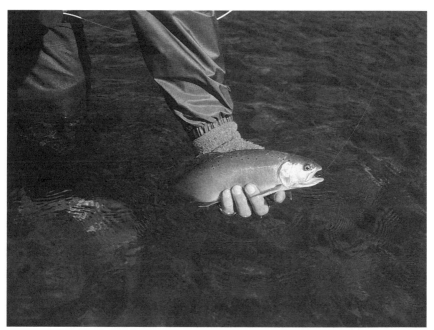

*The stretch of water running through the Nantahala Gorge yields some hefty rainbows; they may be holdover or wild fish.*

warning. Wading anglers should keep a close eye on the water for any hint that it is rising. Keep an ear alert as well. A noticeable rushing noise will become audible from upstream when the river begins to rise. When its volume begins to increase, it is wise to head for shore.

The other fishing condition encountered on the Nantahala occurs when the turbines at the powerhouse are on. During these periods, the river is a boisterous, rowdy, powerful flow that careens down the gorge. It is this water that attracts crowds of boaters to the river; hundreds of them descend the chutes and shoals in kayaks, rafts, and canoes. Such crowds discourage most anglers from approaching the water. Those who do, however, will find that the high water and numbers of watercraft do not seem to affect the fish. The trout have apparently become used to the mass of humanity floating over them and continue to feed just feet from passing rafts.

The rafters and kayakers descending the river head for the rougher current, while the trout look for big eddies or obstructions breaking the current. This puts the fish in a different part of the river from most of the raft traffic. During high water, other good places to look for the trout are in the side channels behind islands or around logs and boulders in the river.

Regardless of the water level or the fishing method employed, the trout on the Nantahala can be impressive. Although both browns and rainbows reproduce naturally here, these populations are annually supplemented with about 5,000 catchable-sized fish. The plantings of brook, brown, and rainbow trout take place from March through July, and due to their presence, the Nantahala is managed under regular North Carolina hatchery-supported regulations. The nutrient-rich waters released from Nantahala Lake support a forage base that turns both stocked and wild fish into plump, energetic battlers. Most of the fish will be under 12 inches, but trout of up to 20 inches are fairly common.

As with any brown trout water, there is the chance of hanging a fish measured in pounds rather than inches as well. This point was punctuated on April 17, 1998 when Robert Lee Dyer caught the present North Carolina state-record brown trout from the river. The fish measured 36 inches long, had a girth of 24 inches, and tipped the scales at 24 pounds, 10 ounces.

When the angler hooked the fish, he was casting a Rapala top-water lure in the channel that runs from the Nantahala powerhouse down to the main course of the river. Although there is no barrier to keep fish from moving from the river into and out of this channel, the channel itself is not open to the general angling public. Fortunately for Dyer, he was an employee of Nantahala Power and Light Company, so he had fishing privileges on this water.

Access to the Nantahala tailwater is excellent through nearly the entire gorge. US 19 parallels the river from just below the powerhouse down to Nantahala Falls (previously known as Little Wesser Falls) at the foot of the gorge. At that point, the river leaves the highway to plunge over Big Wesser Falls and empty into Fontana Lake. There are a number of parking areas along the highway in the gorge. During rafting season, the highway and parking areas can be very crowded around midday.

To reach the Nantahala tailwater, follow US 19/129 north from the town of Andrews. Stay on US 19 when the two routes separate at the crossroads of Topton (US 129 heads northwest). US 19 strikes the Nantahala near the village of Beechertown, just downstream of the powerhouse.

To hear a recorded message giving water-release schedules for the Nantahala River tailwater, call the Nantahala Power and Light Company at 828-369-4556.

# TUCKASEGEE RIVER

### DeLorme 29, 51, 52

The Tuckasegee River rises in southern Jackson County, then flows northwest to eventually empty into Fontana Lake at the southern rim of the Great Smoky Mountains National Park. The headwaters contain a stretch of river that supports wild, native brook trout, while lower down reproducing populations of rainbows and brown trout are present. Finally, in its larger, lower section hatchery-raised fish of all three species are stocked.

The tailwater portion of the Tuckasegee is the most complicated to describe of any in the Southeast. Four small dams on its feeder streams or on the river itself control the flow of water in the main river. These begin with the Tanasee Creek Reservoir, which receives the flow of Tanasee Creek and the headwaters of the Tuckasegee River. Immediately to the north of this impoundment lies Wolf Creek Reservoir, on the creek of the same name. Pipelines exit both of these dams to join and run to the west to a powerhouse, where the water empties into 475-acre Bear Creek Reservoir.

Bear Creek is the only one of the four small impoundments along the upper Tuckasegee that receives regular stocking of trout. From March until June a total of 5,000 fish are planted in the lake. These releases consist of 2,000 rainbows, 2,000 browns, and 1,000 brook trout. Bear Creek, however, offers only a lake fishing environment.

Tuckasegee
River

Jeff Goodwin, © The Countryman Press

From Bear Creek Reservoir the Tuckasegee dumps directly into the upper end of Cedar Cliff Reservoir. When the river reemerges from Cedar Cliff, the tailwater section of the Tuckasegee begins, but no trout are stocked for roughly the first mile down to the junction with the West Fork of the Tuckasegee.

Adding to the complexity of this watershed is the presence of two more impoundments upstream on the West Fork, which also affects the water flow in the main river. Thorpe Reservoir, built in 1941, is the first and larger of these two. It spreads over 1,470 acres, with its waters directed into a pipeline that bypasses roughly 5 miles of the West Fork, down to the powerhouse at the head of Little Glennville Lake. There is a 3-mile portion of the bypassed part of the Tuckasegee that is stocked with trout and open to fishing under hatchery-supported regulations. From the mouth of Shoal Creek down to Little Glennville Lake, the West Fork provides a put-and-take fishery, but the first 2.25 miles are down in a gorge beside NC 107. There is very limited roadside parking through here, making the fishing very difficult to access.

Although Little Glennville Lake does not receive regular stockings of trout, it is worth noting that it did produce the North Carolina state-record rainbow trout. Terry L. Gregory caught that 16-pound, 5-ounce fish in 1989. Below Little Glennville Lake the West Fork of the Tuckasegee flows for about another mile to its mouth on the Tuckasegee. No stocking, however, takes place on the West Fork upstream of that junction.

It is below the junction of the two branches of the Tuckasegee that the tailwater trout fishery begins on the river, with the rise and fall of water mainly dictated by the operations of the Thorpe and Cedar Cliff dams. For the next 20 miles, the Tuckasegee offers several levels of trout fishing.

From the junction of the West Fork, the main body of the Tuckasegee is a large flow, offering plenty of room for fishing, including adequate space for fly-casting. Open under hatchery-supported rules, until recently the Tuckasegee's main claim to fame was that it produced a North Carolina state-record brown trout. That 15-pound monster stood atop the state list for a number of years before being bested. The hatchery-supported section of the river receives 11,000 fish annually in March through August, with stockings composed of the usual mix of rainbows, browns, and brookies.

Within this section lies a 5.5-mile stretch from the NC 107 bridge at Love Field down to the low-head dam at Dillsboro that is open as a delayed-harvest stream. This part of the river gets an additional 42,000 stocked trout. About 10,000 are browns, with the rest divided equally between brook and rainbow trout. Plantings of fish take place monthly from March through May, with additional releases in October and November. In fact, this is one of the most heavily stocked portions of trout water in the state.

Much of the Tuckasegee is wadable when no water is being released from the dams on either of its upstream forks. If only one of the dams is releasing water it is also low enough to wade. On the other hand, when both the Cedar Cliff and Thorpe dams are generating power, floating in a canoe or small boat is more practical. Although there are no boat ramps, a site for entering the water for such a float is located at the East LaPorte Access Area. This

TVA/Jackson County park is located off NC 107 at the mouth of Caney Fork Creek. It offers a picnic area, canoe launch access, and some wadable water. The park is on the west side of Caney Fork Creek and open from 8 AM to dusk each day. Other possible points of access are at the NC 281 bridge at the junction with the West Fork and at a number of spots along Wayehutta Road down to its junction with Old NC 107. Wayehutta Road runs along the northeast shore of the river and even offers access to several wadable shoal areas.

Near the point at which Wayehutta Road bears off to follow the creek of the same name away form the Tuckasegee, a small dam blocks the waters of the river, but there is a portage path for detouring around it. Downstream, Old NC 107 runs at streamside but offers very minimal public access to the water.

Another portion of the river with some shoal access is located in the delayed-harvest area directly south of the town of Sylva on North River Road. To reach this road, take NC 116 to the west off NC 107 north of the village of Cullowhee. At about 1 mile, North River Road runs to the north to parallel the river for a couple of miles to Dillsboro.

Be aware that another small dam is located on the Tuckasegee at Dillsboro. This one lies near the junction of North River Road and US 441/23. It is a more difficult portage, demanding extra caution during the approach. The roughly ¾ mile of river upstream of the dam and at the end of the delayed-harvest area forms a small lake.

Below the dam, down to Wilmont, public access to the Tuckasegee is virtually nonexistent. There is, however, access from a park on the north side of the river at the foot of the dam, just east of US 441/23. The entrance to the park is off North River Road. From the dam downstream to the Valley Road (SR 1392) bridge at the village of Wilmont, the Tuckasegee is once again open under hatchery-supported trout fishing regulations.

To listen to recorded water-release messages from the Nantahala Power and Light Company for both Thorpe and Cedar Cliff Reservoirs, call 828-369-4559.

# South Carolina

1 Saluda River
2 Savannah River

ATLANTIC OCEAN

Pee Dee River

Little Pee Dee R.

Black River

Santee River

Lake Moultrie

Lake Marion

Wateree Lake

Catawba R.

Lake Wylie

Columbia

Lake Murray

South Fork Edisto River

Savannah River

Lake Keowee

Harwell Lake

Russell Lake

J. Strom Thurmond Lake

N

0    30    60 km
0    30    60 mi.

Jeff Goodwin, © The Countryman Press

# CHAPTER 9

# South Carolina

It comes as a surprise to many anglers to learn that South Carolina has always had a population of trout within its borders. Their range has traditionally been quite small, however. In fact, the natural trout waters of the Palmetto State are confined to the three counties comprising its westernmost corner. Oconee, Pickens, and Greenville Counties today contain about 200 miles of streams and rivers that support some type of trout fishing for at least part of the year.

As with the other natural trout waters of Dixie, South Carolina's native fish was the southern Appalachian strain of brook trout. Unfortunately, these holdovers from the last Ice Age were virtually eradicated from the state's waters during the last half of the 19th century by logging and farming in South Carolina's small portion of the southeastern highlands. Today, relics of the original brook trout population maintain a tenuous hold in a few remote headwater creeks and brooks.

Introductions of rainbow and brown trout soon followed the decline in native brookie numbers and, as elsewhere, accelerated that downward trend. Since the early 1950s, the South Carolina Wildlife and Marine Resources Department (SCWMRD) has been actively managing and stocking most of the state's suitable trout waters. Presently, 250,000 catchable-sized trout are released into state waters annually, along with another 150,000 sub-adult fish. Almost all of these are rainbows and browns. These go into more than 30 creeks and rivers, as well as 7,500-acre Lake Jocassee. This reservoir on the Greenville and Pickens County boundary is the state's bona fide trophy trout fishery, regularly producing browns and rainbows in the 2- to 6-pound range. The impoundment is managed by the Duke Power Company.

When a pair of tailwaters were stocked by the SCWMRD, the range of trout in the state was increased to include two more counties. The Saluda River below Lake Murray and the Savannah River below Hartwell Lake constitute the man-made trout resources of this state.

To fish for trout in South Carolina, anglers 15 to 64 must possess a valid state fishing license; nonresident anglers under 64 must also have a license. These licenses can be purchased over the telephone by calling 1-888-434-7472 or by using the Internet. The web site to visit is www.dnr.state.sc.us; follow the prompts for license purchases.

The creel limit on trout is 10 per day, regardless of species. There are exceptions to these rules on some state waters (especially the Savannah River), so check the SCWMRD brochure, "Hunting and Fishing Rules and Regulations." This annual publication is available from many bait and tackle shops, by mail from the SCWMRD offices, or on the Internet at the site mentioned above. There is no closed trout season in South Carolina.

# SALUDA RIVER

## DeLorme 35, 36

The tailwater of the Saluda River is located deep in the Piedmont region of central South Carolina in Lexington County. This area, west of the state capital of Columbia, is far removed from the portion of the state ordinarily thought of for trout fishing.

The tailwater originates from the 90-foot depths of Lake Murray, an almost 50,000-acre reservoir built in 1930. The Saluda flows to the southeast from the dam, joining the Broad River to form the Congaree River at Columbia's western edge. Along the Saluda's roughly 10-mile course from Lake Murray to the river junction, the entire flow is capable of supporting trout. In fact, during cooler months it is not unusual for trout to turn up for a mile or more down the Congaree below the mouth of the Saluda.

In general, the Saluda tailwater is a large river with limited public access. Also, very little wadable water exists along the flow. The few wading areas it has are most accessible when the five generators at the dam at Lake Murray are not in use.

Jeff Goodwin, © The Countryman Press

The Saluda trout fishery has had a spotty history, with a number of peaks and valleys. Until recently, the South Carolina Electric and Gas Company managed the Saluda Hydroelectric Plant for the generation of electricity alone, with little regard for the fishery downstream. As a result, water containing almost no oxygen would be released into the river in late summer and early fall, leading to fish kills. The local chapter of Trout Unlimited in Columbia has since brought pressure on the company to be more cognizant of how its management practices affect the fishery. In response, the energy company has now instituted a program of venting the turbines in the powerhouse at critical times to maintain the oxygen levels.

The SCWMRD stocks the Saluda monthly with trout from November through May. The annual stockings total 60,000 fish, composed of catchable-sized 9- to 10-inch rainbows and sub-adult brown trout in the 6-inch range. Because of the lack of easy access points along the Saluda, trout are now stocked using helicopters in order to disperse them throughout the entire tailwater.

Although water temperatures are low enough to support trout even in the summer, no fish are released from mid-June through October. Striped bass from the Santee-Cooper Lakes downstream migrate into the Saluda tailwater in search of refuge from the warming lake waters. Trout stocked during the summer would be little more than forage for these stripers, but rainbows and browns released earlier are streamwise enough to avoid the large predators.

Due to the airborne stockings dispersing the trout along the Saluda, and the fact that fishing pressure on the river is ordinarily only moderate, some of the browns and rainbows stay in the river long enough to grow in size. In these fertile waters trout can grow as much as one inch per month, and fish of 16- to 17-inches are taken routinely from the tailwater. A few 20-inchers have even shown up in the area several miles downstream of the dam.

While most tailwater fishing tactics prove successful here, the bulk of the pressure comes from bank-anglers using natural baits. There are, however, some notable hatches of caddisflies on the river during spring and summer evenings. These tend to occur farther downstream toward Columbia, attracting local fly-casting enthusiasts.

The major drawback to fishing the Saluda is its lack of public access. There is an access road at the northern end of Lake Murray Dam, but it is only open at the discretion of the South Carolina Electric and Gas Company and is not a dependable route to the river.

On the southern shore of the stream, the only public access is found at Hope Ferry Landing. This park is open from sunrise to sunset daily and provides a paved boat ramp and limited parking. The accessible portion of the river is minor here, since the park is surrounded by private farmland.

To reach Hope Ferry Landing, travel south on SC 6 from the point at which the highway crosses Lake Murray Dam. Turn east onto Corley Mill Road and drive 1¾ miles to its junction with Hope Ferry Road, which enters from the left. Follow this paved road until it changes to gravel and reaches the parking area and boat ramp at ½ mile.

*Saluda Shoals Park provides access to some wadable areas of the river's tailwater near Columbia.*

The northern bank of the Saluda is bit more accommodating to anglers. Directly across the river from Hope Ferry Landing is the Saluda Shoals Park, operated by the South Carolina Electric and Gas Company. The park is roughly 1½ miles downstream of the Lake Murray Dam and is open daily from sunrise to sunset. Parking, picnic areas, and fishing docks are provided, along with paved boat and canoe launch facilities. A fee is charged for entry to the park.

To reach Saluda Shoals Park, travel northward from the dam on SC 6 to the intersection with SC 60 and Bush River Road (SC 107). Turn southeast onto Bush River Road and drive 2.1 miles to the park entrance on the west side of the highway.

Although there is no shore access upstream from the park, there is a shoal ¼ mile upstream of the facility. A small island and shoal offer some opportunities for wading at all water levels, but they are ideal for such activity on low water. At higher levels it is possible to run small boats with outboard motors upstream through this shoal.

Saluda Shoals Park offers ¼ mile of river access downstream of the boat ramp via the paved Greenway Trail. Through here there are two bands of rocks crossing the river that are shallow enough for wade-fishing during non-generation periods. Access using the trail presently ends at the mouth of Rawls Creek. Phase two of the park, which is in the planning stage, will eventually offer another ½ mile of shore access and another canoe landing downstream.

One other area worth mentioning with regard to wading is found directly behind the Riverbanks Zoological Gardens, which sit on the river's northeastern shore. This site is just upstream of the Saluda's junction with the Broad River in Columbia. The zoo lies along a rocky section of the flow that is shallow enough to wade during low water.

The South Carolina Electric and Gas Company maintains a toll-free number that provides information on water conditions on Lake Murray and release schedules for the Saluda tailwater. Call 1-800-830-5253.

# SAVANNAH RIVER

### DeLorme 23

The final tailwater in South Carolina is located on the Savannah River. Due to its location on the border between Anderson County, South Carolina, and Hart County, Georgia, the Savannah River trout fishery is claimed and managed by both states. Unfortunately, the resource that they have to manage has been greatly reduced over the last decade and a half.

When trout were first introduced into the Savannah River tailwater, their range stretched for 14 miles downstream of the dam and power plant at Hartwell Lake. Then in 1982 the gates were closed on Russell Lake just downstream, creating a new reservoir that backs up almost to the foot of Hartwell Dam. In the process, the demand for electric power destroyed nearly all of the trout fishing area. Today the Savannah River trout fishery is but a ghost of its original self. At virtually any level, the river resembles a lake more than flowing water.

Presently, South Carolina and Georgia each stock 12,000 catchable-sized rainbow trout in the Savannah River annually. The efforts of the two states are coordinated so that they do not release fish at the same time. Stocking is generally done twice a week from February through June. Additionally, Georgia has from time to time planted some brown trout in the Savannah.

Any trout that hold over in the tailwater below Hartwell Dam have the potential to put on some size. A former South Carolina state-record rainbow

Savannah River

Hartwell Lake

SOUTH CAROLINA

GEORGIA

Savannah River

Russell Lake

Jeff Goodwin, © The Countryman Press

of 5 pounds, 8 ounces was taken from the river in April 1971. More recently, 10-pound rainbow and brown trout have been caught by anglers fishing from the Georgia shore.

As a result of its position on the border of two states, the Savannah's fishing regulations represent a compromise between the South Carolina WMRD and the Georgia Wildlife Resource Division. Fishing is allowed with all types of flies, lures, and natural baits. The creel limit adheres to Georgia's standard of 8 trout per day regardless of species. Consistent with South Carolina's streams, there is no season closed to fishing on this tail-water. Also, anglers may fish the main branch of the Savannah River from

*Below Hartwell Dam, the Savannah River tailwater is more like a lake than a stream—at all water levels.*

either bank as long as they possess either a Georgia or a South Carolina fishing license.

Almost all of the fishing that takes place on the tailwater of the Savannah is in the form of bait-fishing from shore. Although some rocky portions of the river just below the dam are visible and shallow enough for wading, signs are posted along this section warning that no one is allowed on the rocks even during low water. Even boats coming upstream from Russell Lake are denied access to several hundred yards of the tailwater by a cable and buoys strung across the river below the dam. Anglers occasionally try casting in-line spinners or crankbaits from the bank, but a fly-caster is a rare sight on the Savannah.

The U.S. Army Corps of Engineers maintains parks on both shores of the Savannah River below Hartwell Dam. On the South Carolina side, three concrete fishing piers are provided. The Georgia shore has a walkway for fishing near the dam and one pier farther downstream. Access to the Georgia park is via an approach drive off US 29 at the western end of the

186

highway bridge, immediately below Hartwell Dam. To reach the South Carolina bank access, go 0.5 mile east of the bridge on US 29, then turn south onto Utz Lane. This dirt road dead-ends in the river park at 0.75 mile. Boats can be launched at ramps on the upstream end of Lake Russell near the SC 181 bridge.

To hear a recording of the water-release schedule at Hartwell Dam, call the Corps of Engineers at 706-376-3500, then follow the prompts for generation schedules.

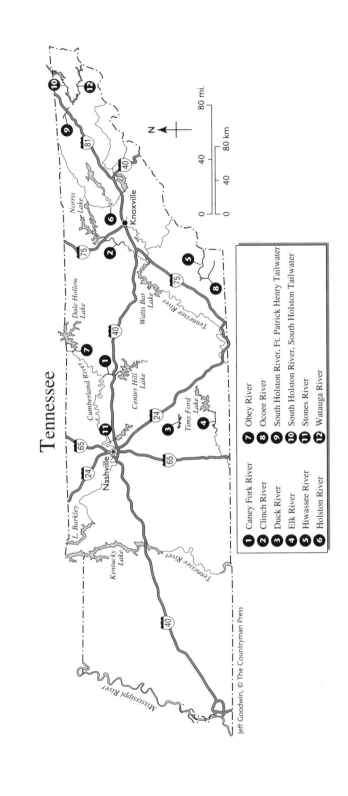

Tennessee

| | |
|---|---|
| 1 Caney Fork River | 7 Obey River |
| 2 Clinch River | 8 Ocoee River |
| 3 Duck River | 9 South Holston River, Ft. Patrick Henry Tailwater |
| 4 Elk River | 10 South Holston River, South Holston Tailwater |
| 5 Hiwassee River | 11 Stones River |
| 6 Holston River | 12 Watauga River |

Jeff Goodwin, © The Countryman Press

# CHAPTER 10

# Tennessee

When trout fishing in the Volunteer State is mentioned, the inclination is to think of the Great Smoky Mountains National Park or the Cherokee National Forest of extreme eastern Tennessee. The 10-county strip of mountainous land along the North Carolina border where the national park and forest are found does contain some of the wildest and most beautiful trout streams in eastern North America. The presence of these gems among Tennessee's 1,900 miles of trout water, however, means that many of the state's other trout fishing resources are overlooked. This is especially true of the man-made resources.

Tennessee's "artificial" trout waters fall into two categories—stocked streams and tailwaters, both of which are managed by the Tennessee Wildlife Resources Agency (TWRA). In the case of stocked streams, the planting of fish has extended the range of trout in free-flowing water westward all the way to the lower Tennessee River valley, some 50 miles west of Nashville, the state capital. Here some spring-fed tributary streams in the ridge country along the Tennessee and Cumberland Rivers now provide habitat for hatchery-raised brown and rainbow trout.

In the other form of man-made trout habitat—tailwaters—the Volunteer State is blessed. Although its tailwaters are less numerous than Kentucky's and may not be quite as awesome as those in Arkansas, Tennessee still lays claim to some of the top blue-ribbon fishing destinations in the eastern portion of the nation. There are 12 tailwater trout fisheries, totaling roughly 135 miles of rivers.

Three of the tailwaters—the Clinch, Hiwassee, and South Holston—deserve mention in any listing of the top trout rivers in America. The other nine—Caney Fork, Duck, Elk, Holston, Obey, Ocoee, Stones, South Holston–Fort Patrick Henry, and Watauga—rate from good to very good as fishing destinations.

The statewide creel limit in Tennessee is seven trout, regardless of species. There is no minimum size limit for brown or rainbow trout, but all brook trout must be at least 6 inches long. There is no closed season for trout on Tennessee's tailwater rivers. There are exceptions to these regulations on some tailwaters, which will be discussed with each specific river.

To fish for trout in the Volunteer State, a resident angler over 13 years of age and born after March 1, 1926, must possess a regular fishing license and an annual trout permit. For nonresidents over 13, an All Fish License is required. These licenses and permits may be ordered over the telephone by calling 1-888-814-8972, or via the Internet at www.wildlifelicense.com/twra/index.html.

## CANEY FORK RIVER

### *DeLorme 55*

The Caney Fork River is noted as the best trout water in Middle Tennessee. Since this region did not originally support trout, one might assume that the competition for this title is not very tough. There are, however, 39 streams in this part of the state that now hold rainbow and brown trout. Most of these are spring-fed tributaries of the Cumberland or Tennessee Rivers. These feeder streams drop down from the highlands of the Cumberland Plateau and flow into the rivers from the south or east. Although some are good trout fisheries, the Caney Fork tailwater stands head and shoulders above the rest.

From Center Hill Dam near the community of Laurel Hill, the Caney Fork flows for 28 miles to the northwest, eventually emptying into the Cumberland River at the town of Carthage. Located about an hour's drive due east from Nashville, the Caney Fork is the midstate area's most popular trout fishing destination. Particularly in spring and summer, this tailwater attracts a lot of canoeists, bank-fishers, and wade-anglers. Due to its limited shoreline access, float-fishing in a canoe is the best option for covering the water

Caney Fork
River

Caney Fork River

Carthage

Cumberland R.

0    1.5    3 mi.
0    1.5    3 km

N

264

Club Springs Road

St. Marys Road

St. Marys Road

40
53
Gordonsville

264

Kirby Lane

Bettys Island
Access

SMITH CTY.

96

40

Bettys Bend
Road

141

Happy Hollow
Access

96

PUTNAM COUNTY
DE KALB COUNTY

141

SMITH COUNTY

DE KALB COUNTY

141

Laurel Hill

Long Branch
Campground

96

Center Hill Lake

Jeff Goodwin, © The Countryman Press

during its low periods. There are so many shallow riffle areas that venturing out in a float tube requires plenty of downstream walking along the way.

It is, of course, the trout fishing that attracts most of the visitors to the Caney Fork below 18,220-acre Center Hill Lake. Each year from March through September, the TWRA releases up to 125,000 brown and rainbow trout into the flow (usually 80 percent are rainbows). The TWRA uses boats to stock the Caney Fork along its entire length, unlike the procedure on most tailwaters, in which fish are simply dumped from bridges or other access points. For this reason, the entire 28 miles of water provide fairly dependable fishing.

The Caney Fork is noted for producing quality trout as well as quantity. Rainbows of 2 to 3 pounds are common, while fish in the 6- to 10-pound range also occasionally turn up. As with any water in which brown trout are found, catching a large fish is a consistent possibility. These battlers regularly turn up in the 5- to 10-pound range, and 15-pound behemoths have been reported.

Two distinct patterns are used by anglers on the Caney Fork, depending on whether they are after a limit of fish or a lunker. To produce numbers of trout, corn, worms, or other natural baits are hard to beat. Tossing Rooster Tail, Panther Martin, or Beetle Spin spinners will take the stockers as well, along with Little Cleo spoons or small jigs. Fly-casters have particularly good results using Woolly Buggers in dark hues or Tellico Nymphs. Despite the presence of rising trout in downstream areas, aquatic insects are scarce on the Caney Fork's rocky bottom.

For larger trout, fish during low water and look for deeper runs, rocky banks, and downed trees in the water. Especially where the trees and rocks are found together, expect to encounter some bigger brown trout. Most such areas are located 4 to 5 miles below Center Hill Dam. During hot summer months, browns will be in this type of cover almost exclusively during daylight hours.

Spin-casters often resort to crawfish-pattern crankbaits for the big browns and rainbows and will even tie on large top-water jerkbaits like the Red Fin, Thunderstick, or Rapala. Fly patterns to use for the lunker trout are leech, crawfish, or minnow imitations.

Although the most often cited problem with fishing the tailwaters of the Caney Fork is lack of shoreline access, there are several places open to the public. The most popular is at the foot of Center Hill Dam. This part of the river comprises the tailrace from the dam, plus a backwater eddy. An underground creek empties into the eddy via a waterfall after popping out of

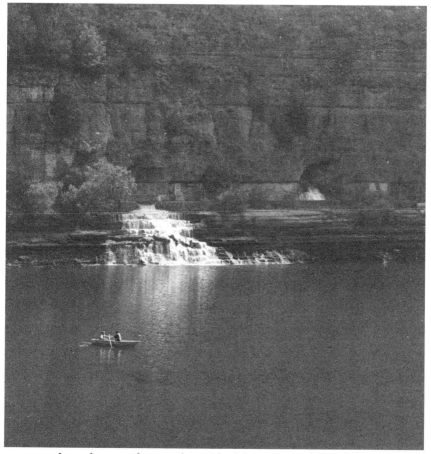

*An underground stream bursts forth into a waterfall and drops into the pool at the foot of Center Hill Dam.*

the rocky cliffs on the northeastern shore. Some of this flow is also seepage from the lake above. In all, there are several acres of water backed up here in an area sometimes referred to as the Pond. The flow exits the Pond to the northwest through a shallower riffle area.

When the flow from the dam is low, the best area to fish for browns is around the waterfall. For rainbows, the vicinity of the boat ramp on the eastern shore is good. The water between these two points is deep, but at the foot of the falls it becomes quite shallow. It is not unusual to see anglers wading around the east-side boat launch during low water. However, when wading this pool, be aware that the water can rise up to 8 feet when all three of the dam's generators are operating.

Also visible in low water are carp, gar, bass, bream, and other warm-water fish. Some of the anglers you encounter here will be using heavy gear to target the striped bass that inhabit the pool.

When the water begins to rise, angling interest is redirected to the western shore along the riprap below the tailrace. Through here, stunned minnows will surface after coming through the turbines. Fishing this area with minnow-imitating lures may yield some of the biggest trout in the river.

Below the pool, foot access is possible for roughly a mile down the eastern shore, along the part of the tailwater that is more riverine. Access to the western side is via the Long Branch Campground and the paved boat ramp beside it. The campground and parks on both shores are managed by the Corps of Engineers. There are drives off TN 141 (which crosses the dam) at either end of the dam that lead to both parks. The east-side access is through the Center Hill Lake Resource Manager's office parking lot.

On the western shore, some access is available off TN 141 along the first 2 miles of river below the dam. At 1½ miles downriver there are parking spaces for three to four cars, with trails leading down to an outside bend with deep water. Just ¼ mile farther down, at the point the road leaves the river at the Smith County border, a long gravel bar gives ½ mile of water access. Parking is in short supply at this point as well, consisting of a few roadside turnouts. Both of these areas appear to get heavy fishing pressure on weekends.

The first "official" downstream access to the river is found at the TWRA's Happy Hollow Access. A parking area is provided at the Putnam-DeKalb county line on the southeastern side of the river, along with a paved boat ramp. The river skirts a long gravel bar at this point, and the river bottom is made up of marble- to baseball-sized rocks. This provides excellent footing for wading. Walking the bar or wading provides about a mile of access along the river from this entry point. When water is released at the dam, it takes about an hour for the surge to reach Happy Hollow Access.

One unique aspect of the Caney Fork's gravel bars is that when the water falls rapidly in nongeneration periods, isolated pools of it are left on the bars. These often contain trout and provide beaver-pond-type fishing. The trout cruise these pools, continuing to feed as they await rising water and an opportunity to escape back to the main flow. Since the water in the pools is very clear, use extreme caution when stalking these fish.

Expect fishing pressure and competition for parking spaces to be heavy on weekends at all of the access points along the river. Also expect to see a lot of cars in the Happy Hollow parking area bearing license plates from Nashville's Davidson County.

To reach Happy Hollow Access, take TN 96 north for 2.5 miles from its intersection with TN 141 just east of Center Hill Dam. The parking area is on the western side of the highway.

The next downstream access point is Bettys Island Access, which is managed by the TWRA. This spot is just upstream of Laycock's Bridge. Though the high iron-and-wood bridge is still in use on Bettys Bend Road, it can be unnerving to cross. Positioned on the northeastern shore, a gravel bar, from which small boats or canoes can be launched, runs for about ½ mile along the river. All of this area is wadable during low water.

Through here, there are more of the "beaver ponds" described at Happy Hollow. Be aware that you do not want to leave a vehicle on the gravel bar even though it is possible to drive onto it. When the river rises during power generation, the bar is inundated. It takes the rising water roughly 2½ hours to reach this point from the dam. The gravel bar also provides a take-out point for a good 6-mile day of float-fishing beginning at Happy Hollow.

To reach Bettys Island Access, take St. Marys Road west from TN 96. This intersection is 5.5 miles north of the junction of TN 96 and TN 141 near the dam. Follow St. Marys Road until it changes to Club Springs Road (the transition point is not clearly marked, but proceeding straight at each intersection will keep you on the proper road). Also, most maps show the road as Stonewall Club Springs Road, though the street signs on the road show the shorter version of its name. At 4.1 miles a gravel spur marked with the access sign is on the left. It runs down to the gravel bar on the river.

Another point of access is located just downstream of Bettys Bend, where Kirby Lane skirts the shoreline of the Caney Fork. At the point where Kirby Lane first strikes the river, there is a gravel bar and a mild shoal that is reached by wading. Then, for a little over ¼ mile, the river runs deep and slow along the roadside. Where the river and Kirby Lane run under I-40, there is more wadable water.

Kirby Lane runs south off Club Springs Road and it is 0.8 mile from that intersection to the river. Kirby Lane then follows the river for 0.3 mile, passes under the I-40 bridge and comes to an end. The property downstream of I-40 is posted. The intersection where Kirby Lane leaves the Club Springs Road is located 1.8 miles west of Bettys Island Access.

To obtain the Caney Fork water-release schedule, call the Tennessee River Authority's recorded message at 615-548-8581. This information is also available at 1-800-238-2264. Punch 4 for water-release schedules, then 37 for Center Hill Dam. The information is also available on the Internet at www.lakeinfo.tva.gov/.

# CLINCH RIVER

### *DeLorme 59*

The Clinch River is located in northeastern Tennessee's Anderson County, just over 20 miles to the northwest of Knoxville. This tailwater has some distinctive history and geographic features that set it apart from similar waters in the Volunteer State. The Norris Dam, from which the tailwater originates, was the first building project begun by the Tennessee Valley Authority (TVA); it came on-line in 1933. The Clinch was also the first tailwater in the South to be stocked with trout, receiving its first fish in 1936. The success of those plantings provided the impetus to introduce trout below other TVA and Corps of Engineers projects where the habitat looked promising.

The Clinch is a big river. For the entire 14 miles of its trout-bearing tailwater, from 24,000-acre Norris Lake down to the town of Clinton, the river is up to 100 yards wide. It is pretty easy to find supporters for the position that it is also the best big-trout destination in Tennessee. Backing up this view is the feat accomplished by Greg Ensor on August 30, 1988. While fishing about 2 miles below Norris Dam, the angler from the nearby hamlet of Powell hooked and landed a 28-pound, 12-ounce brown trout, which remains the Tennessee record for the species. Many anglers believe that the river holds browns of over 30 pounds as well. In the spring of 1993, TWRA biologists performing an electroshock survey raised a brown that was longer than the record fish and pulled their 25-pound scale all the way to its limit. Browns of 8 to 15 pounds turn up in the Clinch every year, and rainbows in excess of 10 pounds have been caught as well.

Despite these glowing tales of big fish, however, up until the last decade or so the Clinch was not highly thought of as a trout destination. A quick look at its history reveals why and also explains why the stream's reputation has improved markedly.

During the early years the brown and rainbow trout stocked by the TWRA and federal agencies did fairly well in the river, but a triumvirate of problems dogged the tailwater. Wildly fluctuating water levels scoured the

Jeff Goodwin, © The Countryman Press

river bottom at all times of the year, while in summer water coming through the powerhouse turbines contained low levels of dissolved oxygen. Finally, minimum releases in June and July raised water temperatures in the tailwater to marginal or lethal levels for trout. Until the Little Tennessee River tailwater was inundated by Tellico Lake in the late 1970s, the Clinch languished in the shadow of that famed fishery as well.

The Clinch's turnaround began in 1984, when a weir dam was built some 2 miles downstream of the reservoir to even out the flow of water during power-generation releases. Another benefit of the weir is the waterfall effect created when water plunges over it during low levels. This helps add oxygen to the tailwater downstream.

More recently, hub baffles have been added to the turbines in the dam's powerhouse. These are designed to suck air into the flow when electricity is being generated. Along with this innovation, release schedules have been altered to ensure that a minimum flow is maintained downstream.

While these physical and management changes were taking place, some biological tinkering was also being effected on the Clinch. The flow's sand-and-gravel bottom is among the richest in nutrients of any trout water in Tennessee, but was made barren by scouring. To address the absence of insect life in the river, some insects common to the highland streams of southern Appalachia were transplanted to the tailwater. As conditions improved in the Clinch, the TWRA and the U.S. Fish and Wildlife Service increased the stocking of rainbow and brown trout by 40 percent in the mid-1980s. Now the Clinch is stocked annually from March through September with roughly 70,000 adult rainbows and 40,000 brown trout. Up to 150,000 fingerling rainbows are also released in most years.

It would appear that all of these efforts have borne fruit. Recent tagging studies revealed that the Clinch's rainbows grow at a rate of 1 inch per month. There are also indications that brown and rainbow trout may spawn in the river, but some of these wild fish could be coming from Clear Creek, a feeder stream that enters the eastern side of the river just upstream of the weir dam. Because of the big trout running up into this stream to spawn, it is closed to fishing from December 1 until March 31 each year. It would be hard to imagine a trout fishery in America that improved any more in a single decade than did this river below Norris Dam.

Another effort to improve the fishing on the Clinch did not fare quite as well. Back in 1993, a Quality Trout Fishing Area was established for the 4.1 miles from the mouth of Cane Creek to the downstream end of Llewellyn Island. On this portion of the flow, the original regulations called for artificial lures only and a daily creel limit of 2 trout over 14 inches long. In 1994 the rules were changed to allow any type of bait and liberalize the creel limit to 3 fish per day, only 1 of which could be 14 inches or longer. Finally, in 1995, the Quality Trout Fishing Area rules were rescinded. The entire tailwater below Norris Dam now is open under general Tennessee trout regulations and creel limits.

Despite all of this activity to improve the fishing, most of the trout taken from the Clinch tailwater are still rainbows of 10 to 12 inches. These stockers are vulnerable to anglers at all water levels and during all seasons. The same, however, cannot be said of the larger trout.

During periods of low water the lunker-sized browns and rainbows will hug the bottom in deeper water, usually around any structure available. Much of the Clinch runs shallow and calm on minimum flows, and all of the trout become quite spooky. This is particularly true of the bigger fish.

It is during medium to maximum water releases that the angling for large trout picks up. Although virtually the whole river becomes unwadable at these times, it is possible to float the stream in a float tube, canoe, or john-boat. This allows anglers to get to the big trout that feed more recklessly in the stronger currents. High water levels are most prevalent on the Clinch from July through September when energy demands are at their peak.

For bait- and spin-fishers, the lures and the natural baits that work on other tailwaters will score here as well. For fly-casters who challenge the heavy currents, weighted streamers and sinking lines are needed. Black Woolly Buggers are a favorite with local anglers.

When the river is running at minimum water levels it becomes a fly-fisher's dream. Although both caddis and mayfly hatches occur on the Clinch, one bug of particular interest is the Light Hendrickson. Due to the constant temperature in the tailwater, these mayflies, in sizes 14 to 16, are likely to appear at any time of the year. Midge hatches are fairly common during the summer months as well. A Griffith's Gnat in sizes 20 to 22, fished on a 7X tippet, is often needed to fool the fish during this action.

If no surface feeding is evident, attractor flies such as the Royal Wulff and the Adams are good options. Elk Hair Caddis will also work, along with Tellico, Hare's Ear, and George's Nymphs. By far the most popular fly for fishing wet, however, is a scud imitation suspended beneath a strike indicator. This should be in the size 18 to 20 range; black, brown, gold, and green are dependable colors.

Although access points are not abundant on the Clinch tailwater, the TWRA has improved the situation in recent years by adding several public areas. The first access points below Norris Dam, however, are provided by the TVA. On the western side of the river the TVA Historical Area provides a paved drive down to a picnic area at the foot of the dam. This shore is fairly steep, but the River Bluff Trail runs down the river and is a better way to approach the water at about a mile from the trailhead. The drive to the picnic area and trailhead is off the Norris Freeway (US 441, which crosses the dam) at the western end of Norris Dam.

*During low water, much of the Miller Island Access is wadable.*
*It is also a good spot from which to begin a float trip.*

On the eastern side of the river, the Songbird Canoe Access and Song-bird Trail provide almost a mile of shoreline access. Through here the river is like a very shallow lake when no turbines are in operation at the power-house. Although there is no boat ramp here, it is possible to launch canoes and johnboats. This access point along with the next two—one downstream at the weir dam, the other at Miller Island—are all reached by following the Norris Freeway south along the Clinch.

At the weir dam, which is roughly 2 miles downstream from Norris Dam, the river is split by an island. There are weir dams on both channels of the river, along with a canoe portage to make it easy for floaters to get around these drops. On low water, the area just below the dams breaks into multiple small channels coursing through the rocky riverbed. Just below the island are State Record Shoals, where Greg Ensor took his mammoth brown trout.

One mile below the weir dam is the Miller Island Access, also on the river's eastern shore. Access here is excellent and includes a paved boat ramp. During low water, a long stretch of the river in front of the ramp and down both sides of Miller Island downstream is easily waded. In fact, around the island the river is almost too shallow for fishing in many spots.

From this point down to Massengill Bridge, the eastern shore is paralleled by River Road. There are several spots with turnouts and trails to the water along the 1¼-mile stretch, but there is also much private land. A lot of bait-anglers fish from Massengill Bridge during higher water levels.

The next access point encountered heading downriver is the most recent one established by the TWRA. The Peach Orchard Access provides only limited shore or wading access. When traveling north from Knoxville, you can reach it by turning southwest off I-75 onto TN 61. Go to the intersection of TN 61 and Peach Orchard Road, then turn northwest to drive 3 miles to the access point.

Access to the section of river around Llewellyn Island is possible just upstream of the town of Clinton. Park at the county jail on the southwestern side of the river at the TN 61 bridge. There is a park with soccer fields adjacent to the jail at this point as well. A streamside trail leads from the jail parking lot up to the island. This area of the river is noted as a good place for fly-fishers to try scud imitations.

On the northeastern side of the river and at the other end of the TN 61 bridge is the 61 Bridge Access. This TWRA access provides a boat ramp, but the river is too deep to wade here. The same conditions exist about a mile downstream at the last public access point at Eagle Bend Access, off Dismal Road.

To obtain information on water releases at Norris Dam, call the TVA's recorded message at 1-800-238-2264. Next punch 4 for water releases, then 17 for Norris Dam. The same information can be retrieved via the Internet at www.lakeinfo.tva.gov/.

# DUCK RIVER

*DeLorme 22*

The Duck River tailwater is located in south-central Tennessee, almost directly north of Tims Ford Lake and the Elk River tailwater (see page 205). The river emerges from the foot of Normandy Dam at the Bedford-Coffee county line, then flows westward through Bedford County. This close proximity to the Elk, along with some problems with water quality, have combined to make the Duck an often overlooked trout fishing destination. Still, the river does have some following as a trout fishery, because it and the Elk are the most westerly tailwaters in the Volunteer State. Virtually all of the anglers encountered on the Duck River will be local residents.

Normandy Lake

Frank Rd.

Normandy
Fish Hatchery

TVA Park

269

Normandy

Cortner Road
Bridge

269

Normandy Road

41A

16

Three Forks Road

Three Forks
Road Bridge

U.S. 41A
Access

Duck River

41A 16

Shelbyville

Duck River

N

0        1        2 mi.

0    1    2 km

Jeff Goodwin, © The Countryman Press

At only 3,230 acres, Normandy Lake is a small reservoir, and it has had recurrent problems with releases of poorly oxygenated water over the years. There is no powerhouse at this dam, because it is strictly a flood-control structure. Even at its best, this river offers only a 10-mile stretch of marginal trout habitat. To combat this, a multilayered piping system draws water from varying levels of the lake, and the TVA, which manages the dam and lake, has installed ½ mile of "soaker hoses" on the lake floor to release air bubbles into the water. This oxygenates the water before it is released into the river.

As late as 1994 the Duck's flow failed state criteria for water contact. In other words, swimming and wading wet are not advised in this river. The major problems noted by the TVA are excess nutrients, resulting from the high phosphorus content of surrounding soils, plus runoff silt and bacteria from dairy farming and other agricultural activity in the region. Anglers have complained that the Duck sometimes looks cloudy and even gives off a faint sulfurous odor.

Despite these dreary water conditions, the TWRA has continued to stock rainbow trout in the river. Between 5,000 and 7,000 rainbow trout are stocked in the Duck River annually from March through December. In the late 1990s, some brown trout were also released into the river. On the brighter side, TVA sampling has shown a slight improvement in the condition of the tailwater's fish community in recent years. Still, the likelihood of any carryover fish in the Duck is small. Although there are wadable stretches at a few access points, the best way to fish the Duck is floating in a canoe or johnboat.

Be aware that the river is narrow and its banks are fairly steep. For those reasons, the stream can only be safely waded when releases from Normandy Dam are less than 140 cubic feet of water per second.

Access is provided to the Duck River tailwater between the foot of Normandy Dam and the upper bridge on Frank Road by a TVA park on the western side of the stream. Below the park, the Normandy Fish Hatchery property borders this shore between the two bridges on Frank Road, all the way downstream to the town of Normandy. Much of the river between the two bridges is wadable, but access is only possible from the bridges at each end. Most of the hatchery land is used for wastewater filtration spraying and is closed to public access.

The water in the park is usually wadable during low water, and the eastern shore just below the dam is lined by a steep wall of layered sedimentary rock. The park provides a boat ramp and a stairway to the canoe access,

*Normandy Dam on the Duck River does not have a powerhouse,
but still supports a downstream trout fishery.*

but no camping facilities. The park is 1 mile northeast of the village of Normandy via Frank Road.

Downstream of the town, the TWRA has constructed three other public access points along the river. At the Cortner Road Bridge (TN 269) there is a parking area and a stairway down to the water. There is also an old, abandoned highway bridge standing to the west of the one now in use. Just downstream of the two bridges is a short stretch of shallow water that is wadable at low levels.

The next access point is located where Three Forks Road bridge crosses the stream, about 6 miles below Normandy Dam. A stairway to the canoe launch and a parking area are provided. There is a gravel bar and wadable riffle downstream of the access point.

The final point of access is upstream of the US 41A/TN 16 bridge just east of Shelbyville. A gravel drive intersects the highway from the west on the northern side of the river, then loops back under the bridge and follows the flow upstream for $\frac{1}{4}$ mile to the parking area. A gravel bar along the northern shore provides wading and boat-launch possibilities. This site is the end of practical trout water. It also receives heavy use and is rather trashy.

To hear a message detailing the current water-release schedule for Normandy Dam, call the TVA's automated phone line at 1-800-238-2264. Punch 4 for water releases, then 56 for Normandy Dam. Similar information can be accessed via the Internet at www.lakeinfo.tva.gov/.

## ELK RIVER

*DeLorme 22*

As noted in the previous chapter, the Elk River is located south of the Duck River tailwater. The reservoir spawning the Elk's tailwater is 10,700-acre Tims Ford Lake. Tims Ford Dam is located in western Franklin County, but the river soon becomes the north-south dividing line between Franklin and Moore Counties. It then turns west to form the border between Moore and Lincoln Counties. Eventually, the Elk River flows into Lincoln County, with its trout-holding water ending near the town of Fayetteville, roughly 28 miles below Tims Ford. The best trout water is found in the first 12 miles of river below the dam.

This river, which was known to the Native Americans of the area as the Chuwalee, is for the most part a small flow, alternating between shallow riffles running over a gravel bottom and pools that drop to depths of 10 feet. In most places the stream is no more than 50 to 80 feet wide.

The Elk is stocked with catchable-sized brown and rainbow trout by the TWRA annually from April to November. Some of these fish obviously carry over from year to year, since trout of both species show up in the 4- to 7-pound range. The gravel bottom and clear waters of this river are ideal for trout. Surveys done by the TVA, however, have shown that the stream has only a fair population of aquatic insects and crustaceans. Probably the most important of these organisms to trout is the sow bug.

The lack of insect life is probably tied to the same type of problems mentioned earlier for the Duck River. Nutrient loading is a concern on the Elk due to the phosphorus-based soil it flows through, as well as agricultural runoff. Low oxygen levels in the water released from Tims Ford also plagued the Elk in the past. Fortunately, a pilot program to increase oxygen levels was begun by the TVA at Tims Ford Dam back in 1981, running through the summer of 1991. This resulted in a small, constantly running turbine being placed in the powerhouse; later, an aeration and an oxygen-injection system were added. Oxygen levels in the Elk are no longer a problem, due to the equipment installed during the pilot program.

Elk River

Tims Ford Lake

50

121

TN 50 Access

Garner Ford Road

Garner Ford Access

Farris Creek Bridge Access

Lexie Crossroads

Farris Creek Bridge Rd.

LINCOLN COUNTY
FRANKLIN COUNTY

Lois Ridge Road

Eddie Bend Road

MOORE COUNTY

Elk River

Old Dam Ford Access

121

MOORE COUNTY
LINCOLN COUNTY

Shiloh Bridge Access

Fish Hatchery Road

Flintville Fish Hatchery

Smithland Road

Champ Road

Dickey Bridge Access

64  15

Kelso

Fayetteville

N

0    1.5    3 mi.

0    1.5    3 km

15

64

121

Jeff Goodwin, © The Countryman Press

On the other hand, the lack of aquatic life has not been adequately addressed. TVA surveys in recent years have shown a decline in variety and mass of insect and fish life in the river. Additionally, at five of the six TWRA access points on the trout-bearing part of the tailwater, the TVA monitoring has shown the river's water quality to be too low to allow swimming.

Having noted all this bad news, the Elk River remains a popular fishing and canoeing destination in Middle Tennessee. Angling pressure just below the dam is usually fairly heavy on weekends, and all of the canoe access points get at least medium usage.

The bulk of the fishing pressure on the Elk is from bait-casters using corn, worms, and the other usual trout offerings. Casting small in-line spinners or floater-diver minnows such as the Rapala is also popular. Growing numbers of fly-fishers are showing up on this river as well. The area just downstream of the dam and the gravel bars found at several of the access points are popular with these long-rod enthusiasts. Some sporadic hatches of caddisflies or, in the summer, midges take place on the Elk.

Access to the Elk River tailwater is possible off TN 50, only a couple hundred yards below Tims Ford Dam. A large pool forms just below the tailrace, then the river narrows as it flows under the highway bridge. A long gravel bar composed of fossil-bearing sandstone and limestone runs several hundred yards down the southeastern side of the river. This part of the stream is composed of slick pools and mild riffles, almost all of which are wadable during low water. The parking area is located on the southeastern side of the river just above the highway bridge. There is no boat ramp, but canoes and johnboats can be launched here.

The next point of entry to the Elk is at Garner Ford Access. This site is managed jointly by the TWRA and the Tennessee Elk River Development Agency, as are the rest of the downstream access points. It consists of a parking area at the end of Garner Ford Road. Again, a gravel bar on the northern side of the river provides a place to launch small boats. There is also room at the end of the road for some primitive camping.

For a couple hundred yards upstream of the access it is possible to wade the river along the gravel bar. This is an area where late-evening hatches of caddis and midges often occur. This part of the river also demonstrates why a float tube would be a poor choice for the Elk. The water is so shallow that for long stretches, more walking than floating would be required. A canoe is a much more practical choice.

To reach this access point, take TN 50 northwest from Tims Ford Dam

*The long gravel bar downstream of the TN 50 bridge below*
*Tims Ford Dam is a good place for wadefishing.*

to the intersection with Garner Ford Road. Turn south and travel ½ mile to the river.

The next downstream public access point is at the Farris Creek Bridge Access. There is a parking area at the end of a dirt spur running off the road at the bridge on the eastern side of the river. Both up and downstream of the bridge there are a couple hundred yards of water that are shallow enough to wade.

Take Farris Creek Bridge Road northwest from the community of Lexie Crossroads on TN 121 to reach the access point.

The Old Dam Ford Access is the next public site. At this location the river widens to a couple hundred feet, and most of the water is quite shallow. Needless to say, this makes for excellent wading. Several small islands and exposed gravel bars also break the river up into small channels.

Old Dam Ford is located at the end of a ½-mile gravel road running off Edde Bend Road. To reach this intersection, take Lois Ridge Road (the same road as Farris Creek Bridge Road—the name changes once it crosses to the northwest of the Elk) 1.3 miles northwest of Farris Creek Bridge Access. Turn left onto Edde Bend Road. It is 4 miles along this road to the gravel spur entering from the right, but presently there is no sign at the intersection indicating the presence of the access point.

The next public access is the Shiloh Bridge Access. This part of the river offers no practical wading water, but has parking and a launch site for canoes. To reach Shiloh Bridge, take Fish Hatchery Road north from US 64 in Lincoln County. After passing the Flintville Fish Hatchery, you will encounter a three-way junction. Smithland Road (gravel) forks to your left. Take the right fork, Champ Road, and follow it to the bridge. It is 4.6 miles from US 64 to the bridge.

The final access point on the Elk before its waters become too warm to support trout is the Dickey Bridge Access. Through here the river runs deep and slow, offering no wading, though there is a canoe landing. The portion of the Elk from Shiloh Bridge to Dickey Bridge is very marginal trout water. To reach Dickey Bridge, take Champ Road to the northeast from the village of Kelso on US 64.

To obtain up-to-date water-release information on the Elk River tailwater, call the TVA automated message line. The number is 1-800-238-2264. Punch 4 for water releases and 50 for Tims Ford Dam. You may also get this information via the Internet at www.lakeinfo.tva.gov/.

# HIWASSEE RIVER

*DeLorme 26*

Located in southeastern Tennessee, approximately 50 miles to the northeast of Chattanooga, the Hiwassee River below Apalachia Lake rates as one of the premier trout fisheries in the Southeast. It also has the distinction of being one of the few tailwaters to run through a good deal of public land. In fact, most of the tailwater is located in the Cherokee National Forest. For its first 10 miles below the dam, however, it is not much of a stream. The water is diverted through a pipeline along this part of its course, reappearing at the Apalachia Powerhouse. It is at this point that the Hiwassee tailwater begins.

As with all tailwaters, the Hiwassee's flow fluctuates according to the need for electricity. Fortunately, this is a broad, shallow river for several miles below the powerhouse, so wading is possible in some areas even on high water. Of course, caution is necessary at those times, since the current can be quite strong.

During low water most of the riverbed is exposed, appearing as small

Hiwassee River

Apalachia Lake

pipeline

Apalachia Powerhouse

FR 108

Big Bend Recreation Area

(315)

John Muir National Recreation Trail

Reliance

(30)

*Hiwassee River*

FR 108

(30)

Gee Creek Campground

Quinn Springs Campground

(33)

(411)

Clemmer Ferry Road

Patty

boat ramp

Benton

*Ocoee R.*

N

0        1.5        3 km

0                1.5        3 mi.

Jeff Goodwin, © The Countryman Press

channels running through a rocky maze. This situation is particularly prevalent during the month of April when water releases are rare. Although this low water offers the best wade-fishing conditions, many anglers continue to take fish even at the highest water levels, especially when fishing from rafts, canoes, or float tubes.

The fish in the Hiwassee tailwater consist of stocked rainbow and brown trout, but holdover fish are common. More than 100,000 rainbows of 9 inches in length are released into the flow year-round. As a result, the average rainbow caught is 10 to 14 inches long and shaped somewhat like a football. This is a fertile river, providing plenty of insect life for the fish, which explains their oval shape. In past years, brook trout were also routinely stocked in the tailwater, accounting for the Hiwassee yielding the Tennessee record for that species. Back in 1973, Jerry Wills hauled a 3-pound, 14-ounce brookie from the river to establish the mark.

From the powerhouse to the U.S. Forest Service's Big Bend Recreation Area, the river is open to fishing under Tennessee's general trout regulations and creel limits. The next 3 miles—down to the Louisville & Nashville railroad bridge just above the town of Reliance—are managed under trophy trout regulations. Artificial lures are mandated along this stretch, with a creel limit of 2 trout per day, each of which must be at least 14 inches long. These waters have been managed for trophy fishing since 1986 and the plan has worked admirably. Trout of 16 to 20 inches are regularly hooked on this part of the Hiwassee. Browns of 15 pounds and rainbows to 9 pounds have also been reported.

These larger trout, whether in the trophy or open sections of the river, fall victim to anglers more often during periods of high water. This is pretty typical of southern tailwaters, where larger fish do most of their feeding when they feel safe in the stronger currents.

From Reliance to the end of trout water on the Hiwassee, the river is again open under general regulations. On the portion of the flow down to the US 411 crossing, the angling is similar to that found above the trophy section, with plenty of 10- to 12-inch stockers present. There are some privately held lands along the river in the vicinity of Reliance, and just above US 411 the river flows out of the Cherokee National Forest.

Below US 411 the Hiwassee is usually cold enough to support trout down to its junction with the Ocoee River, but access is a problem. Almost all of the land is private on both shores, and there is little road access. The tailwater here is more suited for float-fishing. One unimproved boat ramp is located near the junction of the Hiwassee and Ocoee Rivers to the north of the town of

Benton and downstream of the village of Patty. This portion of the river is not very accommodating to fly-casters and gets little attention from them.

Needless to say, the upper reaches of the tailwater get plenty of attention from bait-fishers and anglers using in-line spinners or small minnow lures. This part of the river also is noted as a fly-fishing destination. It is one of the rare streams of the southern highlands on which insects hatch with some measure of predictability. Beginning in April, Blue-Winged Olives and caddis are the mainstay of the daily activity, followed in May by Sulfurs and Light Cahills. When no surface action is visible, many anglers turn to floating Royal Wulffs in sizes 12 to 14 through the riffles.

Despite all of this glowing information on the Hiwassee's trout fishing, there is a downside. The portion of the tailwater immediately below the powerhouse has for some reason never supported the numbers of trout it seems capable of sustaining. Recently the TVA and local Trout Unlimited chapters have been looking into possibilities for improving this situation.

Also, the TVA has begun "pulsing" the generators at the powerhouse to maintain a minimum flow in the Hiwassee. Instead of running the generators for eight hours, then shutting them off for eight hours, for instance, this method runs the generators for two hours, turns them off for two hours, and so on. Thus, just as much electricity is produced, but the river level is not allowed to bottom out. Without pulsing, the extremely low water levels experienced when no water was being released were particularly detrimental to the insect life in the river. Aquatic insects unfortunate enough to be in shallow water when the river began to fall found themselves high and dry, wiping out much potential trout food. Keeping a minimum level of water in the river should largely alleviate this problem.

Along the 8 miles of river from the powerhouse down to US 411, access to the Hiwassee is excellent. Forest Service Road FR 108 runs along the northern side of the river from the powerhouse to Reliance. The only point at which it leaves the flow is the Big Bend section. There is a foot trail along the 3 miles of water that are not at roadside. The John Muir National Recreation Trail follows the northern side of the river here and takes in most of the trophy trout water. Parking areas are provided at Big Bend, Towee, and the Hiwassee River Recreation Areas. This is by far the most popular portion of the tailwater, and anglers flock to it on weekends.

Below the bridge at Reliance, TN 30 parallels the southern side of the Hiwassee tailwater. Due to the presence of some private land, not all of the water along this stretch is readily accessible. The water can be reached with

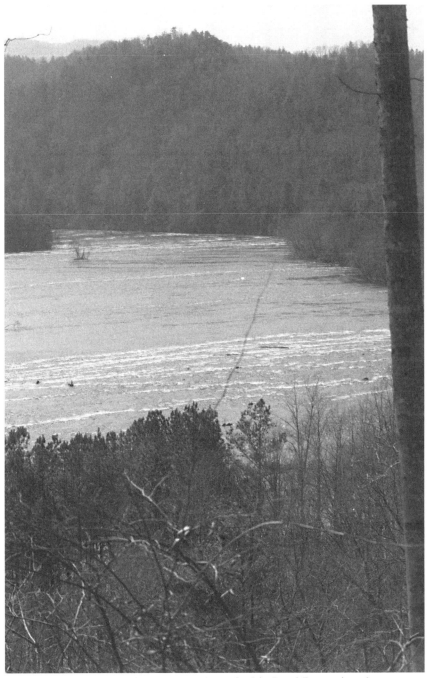

*The Hiwassee tailwater just above the Big Bend Recreation Area
is a wide river with many shoal areas.*

ease in Reliance, or at Cherokee, Taylor Island, and Quinns Springs Recreation Sites, by driving west along TN 30 from the town. All of the recreation areas on the Hiwassee are managed by the U.S. Forest Service as part of the Cherokee National Forest. A state-run campground is located on FR 108 at Gee Creek on the northern side of the river, while the forest service maintains one at Quinn Springs.

The lower portion of the river below US 411 can only be fished by floating, since there is practically no shore access. A boat ramp at Boyd Bottoms can be reached by taking Clemmer Ferry Road west from the Benton town square. The road makes several sharp turns along the route. At 1.7 miles, turn left onto the road (it presently has no sign) marked ROAD CLOSED. At 0.75 mile, the boat ramp is down the steep gravel spur on the right.

Water-release updates for the Hiwassee tailwater can be obtained by calling the TVA at 1-800-238-2264. Press 4 for water releases, then 22 for Apalachia Powerhouse. This information is also available on the Internet at www.lakeinfo.tva.gov/.

# HOLSTON RIVER

### DeLorme 60

The Holston River is formed in northeast Tennessee by its Middle, North, and South Forks. These tributary rivers flow down from the highlands of southwest Virginia before joining just east of Kingsport, Tennessee, to create the main stem of the Holston. In turn, the main river joins the French Broad River at Knoxville to form the Tennessee River.

Within this system there are three tailwaters in Tennessee that offer some level of trout fishing. Two of these are found on the South Fork at Fort Patrick Henry Lake and South Holston Lake and are discussed in later sections. The other is found below Cherokee Lake on the main branch of the Holston.

The Native Americans who lived along the shores of the Holston River called it Hogoheegee. Today, the impounded waters of the river are named in honor of those people as Cherokee Lake. Located on the river roughly 20 miles to the northwest of Knoxville, the waters coming from Cherokee Dam make up one of Tennessee's newest tailwater fisheries.

Although 30,300-acre Cherokee Lake was first impounded on December 5, 1941, its tailwaters did not become trout water until the last year of the 20th

Holston River

92

Holston River

Cherokee
Lake

TVA Park

34
11E

N

0     1     2 mi.

0   1   2 km

Jefferson City

11E 34

92

Jeff Goodwin, © The Countryman Press

century. In February of 1999 the TWRA stocked 20,000 rainbow trout from the dam downstream for 12 miles to the Indian Cave area.

Rainbows are now stocked in the Cherokee tailwater in March and again in October each year. Although this is a put-and-take operation, some trout may hold over in deeper pools of the river. Overall, however, the stream gets too warm for the fish in the summer months.

The Holston is big water where it emerges at the foot of Cherokee Dam to form the boundary between Jefferson County on the south and Grainger County to the north. In the area immediately below the dam the river flows too deep for wading at all water levels. There is a public area on the southwest side of the river at the dam, providing a parking lot and paved boat ramp. Anglers can access the riprap shore both up and downstream of the launch site. Pilings of an old bridge also break the current in the river just above the boat ramp.

Farther downriver the Holston contains few shallow shoals, and these cannot be reached from shore because of private, posted land. The only practical way to fish this tailwater is from a boat. That boat needs to have a motor,

*The only shoreline access to the Holston River tailwater
is immediately below Cherokee Dam.*

because the ramp at the dam is the only one on the river. If you float down-river, you will have to run back upstream to get out at the end of the day.

To reach Cherokee Dam, take TN 92 north from Jefferson City. An access drive runs off the highway to the west at the southern end of the dam.

To hear a recorded message detailing the power generation schedule for the Cherokee tailwater, call the TVA's automated telephone line at 1-800-238-2264. Press 4 for water releases, then 5 for Cherokee Dam.

# OBEY RIVER

### DeLorme 66

The Obey River tailwater lies below Dale Hollow Lake in north-central Tennessee, tight against the Kentucky border. In all, the trout habitat stretches downstream for about 8 miles, to the town of Celina at the junction of the Obey and Cumberland Rivers. Prior to the completion of the Cordell Hull Dam on the Cumberland, trout showed up for more than a half-dozen miles down that flow as well. The new lake, however, now backs up into the mouth of the Obey at higher water levels.

Despite the loss of the free-flowing portion of the lower Obey, the river still offers some quality trout fishing. From its emergence from the Corps of

Engineers' 27,700-acre Dale Hollow Lake (4,300 of those acres lie across the state line in Kentucky), the river travels a contorted course to the west, through Clay County to Celina. Along that route it is only a medium-width stream, but much of it is deep and carries a large volume of water. As a result, it is capable of floating even bass boats during periods of water release. On low water, a canoe or a johnboat is a better choice for float-fishing.

At all but the lowest water levels, the Obey is a float- or bank-fishing destination. Bank-fishers are most common and much more prevalent during low water. There are a couple of shoals that offer wading access at low levels of water release.

One problem with fishing the Obey is the relative scarcity of shoreline access for the public. Basically, there are three parks along the river from the dam to Celina, with the rest of the Obey flowing through private property.

The Obey is a fertile river that supports a healthy insect population. In fact, back in its glory days—before the construction of the Cordell Hull complex—this tailwater at one time or another laid claim to the Tennessee records for both brown and rainbow trout. In 1955, a 26-pound, 12-ounce brown was wrestled from the Obey's water. That fish stood for a number of years not only as the Volunteer State standard, but also as the largest brown trout taken in North America. In 1971 the Obey yielded a rainbow that tipped the scales at 14 pounds, 5 ounces. That trout held the top spot in the state record book for more than a decade.

During those early years, cutthroat trout were also stocked in the Obey on an experimental basis. Today, however, the fishery is composed of freshly stocked rainbow and brown trout. A fair amount of carryover must take place in the river, since trout of both species in the 12- to 15-inch range are not uncommon. And of course, that rare fish measured in pounds rather than inches does still show up on the Obey. The dominance of stockers is ensured by the presence of the Dale Hollow National Fish Hatchery on the banks of the river. Needless to say, a large number of trout reared here find their way into the tailwater.

Fishing tactics on the Obey are similar to those on other southern tailwater rivers. Bait-anglers lean toward corn, salmon eggs, and worms. These anglers tend to dunk their baits in the deeper pools, especially during low water. In the case of spin-anglers, spoons and small minnow-type lures are popular. Nymphs and streamers tend to be the favored offerings of the rare fly-casters who tackle the Obey.

The Dale Hollow Recreation Area is a Corps of Engineers park located at the foot of the dam and stretching downstream for ½ mile. The entrance to the recreation site is on the western side of Dale Hollow Road, ½ mile north of the dam (Dale Hollow Road crosses the dam). Picnic and camping areas are in the recreation area, along with a paved boat ramp.

The campground stretches downriver from the boat ramp and separates the stream from the hatchery grounds. There are a couple of wooden fishing piers at the boat ramp, along with a sign warning of rising water. Believe the sign. At full generation the piers will be underwater. The pier just above the boat ramp will be completely submerged when the river is at high levels, with only a small ripple in the stream to mark it.

Downstream of the boat ramp, a trail runs along the river above the high-water mark. This path leads past the camping area, ending at the creek carrying the hatchery's outflow into the river. This creek is a good place to fish when the river is running at full bore. Trout will be backed into it all the way up to the miniwaterfall at the outflow pipe. Unfortunately, most of the really big fish spotted in the creek at these times turn out to be carp. There is a paved walking trail that follows most of the creek bank.

Another tip for high-water angling is to walk the path along the river watching the area around the bases of the trees standing in the edge of the flow. Trout usually are visible holding on the upstream side of some of the tree trunks. A fly or bait dropped in front of these fish will often tempt them.

When no generation is taking place at Dale Hollow Dam, a large gravel bar appears in the river at the mouth of the hatchery outlet. This provides a good wading site, offering casting possibilities upstream into the deep run in front of one of the fishing piers. The river channel runs against the south shore beside the bar and can be easily covered with all types of angling gear. Below the bar another deeper run can be fished as well.

The next downstream public access on the Obey is at the Corps of Engineers' Moody Boat Ramp. This site is located on TN 53, 2.5 miles east of this road's junction with TN 52 in Celina. There is an improved boat ramp and several wooden fishing piers along the river, as well as a paved parking lot and rest rooms. In all, about ¼ mile of shoreline is available to the angling public here. When the river is high, up to a foot of water will be running over the fishing piers.

About 100 yards downstream of the parking area at Moody Boat Ramp, a gravel bar juts out from the north shore at minimum water-release levels. This can be accessed via an anglers' trail along the shore, and it offers one of the river's rare wading locations.

The final point of access to the Obey tailwater is in the town of Celina. Donaldson Park is a Corps of Engineers day-use facility containing about a mile of shoreline and a boat ramp. There are also playgrounds, rest rooms, and parking and picnic sites in the park.

Through the park, which is on the southern side of the river, the water is too deep to wade, but it does offer some bank-fishing possibilities. To reach Donaldson Park, turn north off TN 53 onto East Lake Street, just ¼ mile east of the courthouse square in Celina. The park is at the end of the street.

To obtain information on water releases for the Obey tailwater, call the TVA recorded message center at 1-800-238-2264. Punch 4 for water releases, then 35 for Dale Hollow Dam. This information is also available via the Internet at www.lakeinfo.tva.gov/.

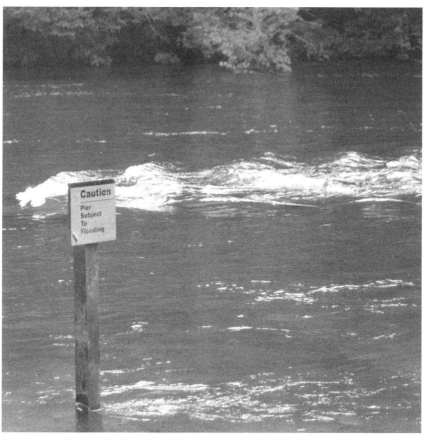

*At high water levels, the fishing pier near the foot of Dale Hollow Dam is nothing but a ripple!*

# OCOEE RIVER

### *DeLorme 26*

For a stream that is millions of years old, the Ocoee River had to wait until very recently to be recognized for its recreational values. Although it is one of the premier destinations in the eastern U.S. for white-water rafting and kayaking enthusiasts, those sports did not come to the flow until 1976. In the case of the tailwater trout fishery, it was the turn of the 21st century before it was developed.

The course of the Ocoee River through southeast Tennessee, from the point it enters the state at the town of Copperhill until it empties into the Hiwassee River, is entirely contained within Polk County. As noted in the earlier discussion of the Toccoa River in Georgia, this is one of the few streams in the nation that changes names when it crosses a state border. In Georgia it is the Toccoa River, becoming the Ocoee at the Tennessee state line.

Once in the Volunteer State, the Ocoee passes through three hydroelectric operations in the Ocoee Gorge, each creating different conditions on the river. The first of these to be built were Ocoee No. 1 at the Parkville community. Constructed in 1910 by the Eastern Tennessee Power Company, it was soon joined in 1913 by the Ocoee No. 3 Dam. The Tennessee Valley Authority (TVA) acquired both of these in 1939. During World War II that agency added the Ocoee No. 2 Dam between the two earlier structures on the stream.

At the Ocoee No. 3 Dam, water is diverted through a tunnel for $2\frac{1}{2}$ miles downstream to a powerhouse, leaving the streambed virtually dry. A similar situation occurs at the Ocoee No. 2 Dam, which is a low diversion structure. This dam is only 30 feet high, but water flows into a wooden flume positioned high on the mountainside above the streambed. By the time the flume reaches the powerhouse 5 miles downriver, the water plunges 250 feet straight down through pipes to turn the generating turbines. As with the upper portion of the Ocoee, the riverbed is virtually dry when power is being produced.

It was during reconstruction of the wooden flume in 1976 that white-water paddlers discovered the Ocoee River. For a year the river flowed unfettered through the gorge and paddlers flocked to it. Today the TVA provides a limited number of days with water flowing over the top of Ocoee No. 2 Dam each year to accommodate the boaters. During the 1996 Atlanta Olympic Games, a white-water paddling venue was constructed in the river below Ocoee No. 3 Dam. Water releases now take place for special events in that portion of the stream as well.

Trout fishing came to the Ocoee River when the TWRA began releasing fish into the flow below Ocoee No. 1 Dam. This dam holds back 1,890-acre Lake Ocoee (also known as Parkville Lake), which is the largest of the three impoundments on the river.

Though it is improbable that there is any reproduction of trout in the river, the TWRA now stocks the stream each year in March and April, then again in September and October. These stockings of 500 fish each are composed of 9- to 10-inch rainbows, with all of the fish concentrated in the area immediately downstream of the dam. Because the water warms quickly in the river, the trout rarely venture far downriver.

The only access point to the trout water on the Ocoee is at the foot of the Parkville Dam. Located on the south side of US 64 and on the north side of the river at the foot of the dam, there is a park with rest rooms, picnic area,

*A miniature replica of the 1996 Olympic white-water paddling venue is located at the foot of the Parkville Dam beside the Ocoee tailwater.*

and paved parking. A unique feature of the park is a miniature reproduction of the Olympic white-water course that was built at streamside. This model was used for hydrologic testing prior to the construction of the actual course farther upstream. There is also a concrete-step canoe launch site in the park.

The Ocoee No. 1 park is open until sunset, but it is closed on Mondays and Tuesdays.

For anglers, the Ocoee No. 1 site provides bank access to roughly ¼ mile of the stream. Although the river runs fairly deep through much of this length, some wading is possible. Just below the dam some anglers wade across the river to fish the deep hole along the sheer cliff on the south side of the river. Also, beneath the abandoned bridge in the park there is a rocky area jutting out from the north shore that affords some wading possibilities. Be aware that signs in the park mandate the wearing of a PFD (life jacket) by anyone who is in the riverbed.

To check water-release schedules for Ocoee No. 1 Dam at Parkville, call the TVA's automated telephone line at 1-800-238-2264. Punch 4 for water releases, then 26 for the Parkville Dam.

# SOUTH HOLSTON RIVER–
# FORT PATRICK HENRY TAILWATER

## *DeLorme 63, 71*

The tailwater of the South Holston River below Fort Patrick Henry Lake is located in Sullivan County in extreme northeastern Tennessee, very close to the Virginia border. This site is just upstream of where the North and South Forks of the river join to form the main branch of the Holston River. Fort Patrick Henry Lake is a relatively small Tennessee Valley Authority impoundment, with a dam that is not particularly high. The result is a tailwater that supports trout for only about 2½ miles—from the dam down to the city of Kingsport.

The fishery consists of stocked adult brown and rainbow trout of 10 to 12 inches. These fish are released into the flow from February through May each year. There are reports of trout of 2 to 3 pounds being caught occasionally, so

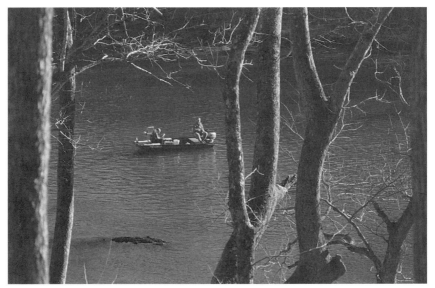

*Virtually all of the fishing access to the South Holston tailwater below Fort Patrick Henry Lake can only be gained by boat.*

there apparently is some carryover. Anglers on the river generally are bait-fishermen, while some cast spinning lures or use fly-rods to fish nymph patterns. Dry-fly fishing prospects are noted for being rather poor here.

For such a short tailwater, access to the river is quite good, particularly in the first mile below Fort Patrick Henry Dam. There is a 100-yard trail from a parking area at the southeastern end of the J. Mack Ray Bridge on TN 36 (Fort Henry Road). The bridge is to the southeast of Kingsport and within sight of the dam. Rock Springs Branch empties into the tailrace pool beside this trail. This location offers only bank-fishing access to a hundred or so yards of water.

The next access point is at the opposite end of the J. Mack Ray Bridge. Immediately west of the bridge, Wesley Road runs south off Fort Henry Road. From Wesley Road a loop drive descends beneath the highway bridge, offers a small parking lot under the structure, then goes on to connect to the powerhouse drive on the west side of the highway. Along this bank, beneath the highway bridge, the shore is cleared of most vegetation, allowing open enough access to the water to permit even fly-casting. The stream, however, is too deep for wading along here.

The best access point to the South Holston in this area can be reached by continuing south on Wesley Road to its end in a parking area on TVA property. This is ½ mile south of TN 36. From this point a trail runs along an old dirt road for another ½ mile downriver. Fifty yards along this path from the parking area is the only shoal area that offers wade-fishing. It requires climbing down a steep bank to reach the water.

Along the rest of the trail, rocky outcroppings and shallow shelves along the shore offer fishing areas. All the water downstream of the single shoal tends to run deep and slow. At about 150 yards below the parking area an old metal barrier blocks the road. At ½ mile the trail ends at a private camping area.

The final access point is at the TN 93 bridge at the edge of Kingsport. There is a parking area at the northeastern end of the bridge and an unimproved boat-launch site under it. Anglers often launch boats here to run upstream to the better trout fishing areas. This site also marks the practical end of trout water on the Fort Patrick Henry tailwater. Though trout may venture farther down the stream in cooler months, that area is not very pleasing aesthetically. The shores through here are lined by the Eastman Chemical Company complex, the U.S. Army Holston Ammunition Plant, and other industrial sites. Unfortunately, these industrial activities sometimes leave a chemical odor hanging over the South Holston in this region.

To obtain the most recent water-release information for the Fort Patrick Henry tailwater, call the TVA's automated telephone service at 1-800-238-2264. Press 4 for water releases, then 4 for Fort Patrick Henry Dam. This information is also available online at www.lakeinfo.tva.gov/.

# SOUTH HOLSTON RIVER– SOUTH HOLSTON TAILWATER

### DeLorme 63, 70, 71

A good way to start a debate in East Tennessee is to begin comparing the trout fishing in the Clinch, Hiwassee, and South Holston tailwaters. The argument may swirl on endlessly, with proponents of all three rivers claiming that their choice represents the blue-ribbon trout destination in the eastern United States. And none of them will be far from wrong.

In truth, all three tailwaters offer excellent fishing, but the natural ebbs and flows of nature will make one a little "hotter" for a season or two, only to be overtaken by one of the others later on. Over the last couple of years, a very good case could be made for the South Holston being the best of the best in southern trout fishing. In this period the Clinch has suffered through some summers when the fish have been hard to catch, and on the Hiwassee the larger fish have played hide-and-seek as well. But on the South Holston the rainbows have been plentiful, with their average size pushing 12 to 13 inches and lunker rainbows and browns of over 20 inches turning up regularly.

Much of the credit for the South Holston's outstanding fishing can be laid at the door of the TVA for improvements they have undertaken on the tailwater. Chiefly, they installed a labyrinthine aeration weir about a mile below South Holston Dam. By creating a long, crested waterfall across the river, the dam adds a great deal of oxygen to the downstream water. The weir, which was the first of its kind anywhere in the world, also aids the fish population by evening out water surges. This lessens the scouring effect on the bottom, allowing for more in-stream insects and plants. The decreased surge also makes the South Holston a bit safer for anglers when the turbines start to turn. The moderating effect of the weir allows them more time to react when the water begins to rise.

The South Holston tailwater originates at the foot of the 285-foot-high, earthen South Holston Dam, which was constructed by the TVA in 1947. Above the dam South Holston Lake backs across the state boundary into Virginia. Below the dam the river's trout-bearing water, which was first stocked in 1952, stretches for 14 miles through Sullivan County to the south of Bristol in extreme northeastern Tennessee. Eventually, the tailwater dumps into Boone Lake just north of Johnson City.

Along its course the South Holston is one of the more conveniently located tailwaters in Tennessee. It is almost constantly in sight of paved roads as it flows through a semiurban area mixed with some farmland. This ease of approach, coupled with the river's position among the Tri-Cities of Bristol, Johnson City, and Kingsport, makes it a popular destination. Adding to the pressure is its proximity to both Virginia and North Carolina. Many anglers in search of big trout find their way across those borders to sample the South Holston fishery.

Regardless of where they come from, the visiting anglers find a medium-width stream composed of slick, glassy pools broken by gentle shoals. These pools and shoals are home to hordes of stocked rainbow and brown trout, which are planted annually from March to September. Up to 150,000 fish are released, with about two-thirds of the number composed of fingerlings. Natural reproduction has also been documented in the river, especially for brown trout. Added to this mix is a healthy sprinkling of trophy-sized rainbows and browns in the 7- to 10-pound range.

Virtually all of the South Holston is wadable when the water is running

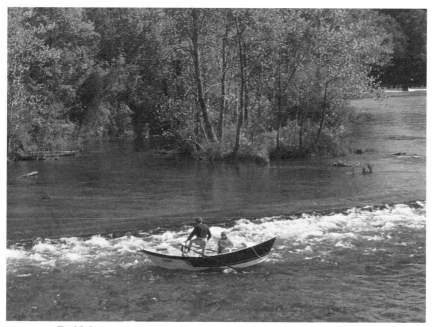

*Drift boats are commonly used on the South Holston tailwater for fishing during periods of high water.*

low, while high water levels make the stream ideal for floating in a johnboat, canoe, or float tube. There are only a very limited number of points where anglers can get to the river. Besides the public land sites, there are usually a number of enterprising land owners along the South Holston who rent parking spaces and access across their property to anglers. This is a constantly changing circumstance, but worth investigating while driving along the flow.

Due to its shallow and clear waters, the South Holston is one river where even many bait-anglers forsake the shore to wade. This allows them to get into position to float their baits under and around logs, rocks, undercut banks, and other structure. Wading is easy on the South Holston, since it flows at a much slower rate during low water than do many other tailwaters. Whether the bait-anglers take to the water or stick to the shore, they are armed with all the usual tried-and-true trout baits. Night crawlers, corn, and crickets predominate.

The easily waded and gentle flow of the South Holston makes it perfect for fly-casting. Indeed, a large percentage of anglers here carry a long rod. The insect populations in the tailwater are strong and active. In March through June good hatches of caddisflies come off regularly. The Elk Hair

Caddis pattern in sizes 16 to 20 is a local favorite for this fishing. Hatches of sulfurs, which often take place in late afternoon on most southern streams, are common in May to June and are likely to occur anytime during the day on the South Holston. This is particularly true when the day is overcast. Another insect hatch important on this flow is the blue-winged olive. These bugs appear in February through May and require imitations on hook sizes 18 to 20.

Most of the fly-fishing here involves casting to rising fish. When no such action is visible, using any of a number of regionally popular nymph patterns should turn up some fish. A Tellico Nymph or Gold-Ribbed Hare's Ear is a good option.

Finally, if the fish you are targeting are the big rainbows and browns, your best bet is to float the stream during high water. Casting minnow or crawfish imitations on spinning gear will bring the best results. The fly-fisher should try a big, weighted streamer. These are often dressed with a gold spinner blade.

In order to protect and enhance the natural reproduction of trout in the South Holston, special quality trout regulations were introduced on the tailwater in 1999. A slot-limit is now in effect that mandates the immediate release of all brown and rainbow trout from 16 to 22 inches in length. Additionally, although the total creel limit is still the same as the normal statewide 7 trout, only one of these may be larger than 22 inches.

Two sections of the river are closed to all fishing from November 1 through January 31 each year to protect the mature trout during their spawn. One of these runs is from the mouth of Bottom Creek downstream to the Hickory Tree Bridge. The other spans the water from the upper end of the first island upstream of the Webb Road Bridge, down to the lower end of Boys Island, which is the first island below Weaver Pike Bridge.

The best public access to the South Holston River is located at the Osceola Island Recreation Area at the weir dam. This TVA park is 1 mile below South Holston Dam. Above the weir the river is almost like a lake as it flows sluggishly along. Below the weir it offers plenty of wadable water. The weir dam is located on both channels of the river on either side of the island.

The parking area for Osceola Island is on the southern shore of the river off Holston View Dam Road. There are walking trails on the island that are accessible via a footbridge below the weir dam. It is also worth noting that even on high water levels there are limited wading possibilities around Osceola Island. These are found on the southern side of the island between the weir dam and the footbridge, but especially on the downstream tip of the northern side. There is limited room for casting on the island just below the weir dam on the northern channel of the river. Though not wadable, this site can be fished from shore on higher water levels.

A hiking trail runs ½ mile down the southern shore from the Osceola Island parking lot to the Holston View Dam Road bridge over the river. Another section of trail continues under the bridge, running for another mile along the river and offering several access points to the water. All of this stretch is open to public fishing.

Below the bridge there are several turnout parking spots offering access to the flow along TN 44 (Rockhold Road) and off Big Springs Road. Both of these roads border the river at several points on its southern side. Riverside Road also offers some access to the river's northern shore, upstream of the Weavers Pike Bridge. The final access consists of boat landings at the head of Boone Lake in the town of Bluff City.

For information on water releases from South Holston Dam, call the TVA's automated phone system at 1-800-238-2264. The code for water releases is 4, then press 1 for South Holston Dam. This information can also be accessed via the Internet at www.lakeinfo.tva.gov/.

# STONES RIVER

### DeLorme 53

There are several unique aspects regarding the tailwater trout fishery on the Stones River below 14,200-acre J. Percy Priest Lake. To begin with it is located farther west in the Volunteer State than any other trout-supporting tailwater. While it is only 15 minutes from downtown Nashville and is acknowledged by all to be a warm-water stream, it does provide a wintertime trout fishery.

Since 1999 the TWRA has stocked 3,500 catchable-sized rainbow trout at the base of 130-foot Priest Dam each month from December through March on a strict catch-and-keep program. There is no possibility of any of these fish lasting through the heat of summer in this part of Tennessee, so the idea is to provide area anglers with some fishing fun and fish dinners in the winter months.

Although a few of these fish may drift downstream after stocking, surveys of the early experimental phase of this fishery found most stayed within ¼ mile of the dam. From a fisherman's standpoint that is just as well. There is

Stones River

Cumberland River

Cumberland River

Stones River

Dodson Chapel Road

Nashville

Stewarts Ferry

Bell Road

Road

N

J. Percy Priest Lake

0    1    2 mi.

0    1    2 km

Jeff Goodwin, © The Countryman Press

no public access to the river except in the parks at the dam. Both sides of the river have parking areas, with concrete fishing platforms and riprap banks. These are found between the dam and the Interstate 40 bridge. Virtually all angling is from the bank, especially during periods of water release.

Obviously, the tailwater trout fishery on the Stones River is not of the quality to entice anglers to drive any distance to visit it. But for local anglers it is a benefit, plus anyone visiting Music City USA in the winter months might want to take a day off from touring Opryland and wet a hook here. If so, expect to share the water with a number of anglers using bait, lures, or flies. Spin-fishermen cast in-line spinners, gold or silver spoons, and shad-imitating crankbaits for best results. Fly-casters usually turn to nymphs and other sinking patterns to fool the fish. Flies that sink slowly through the water column are noted for provoking plenty of action.

To reach the southwest shore of the river at the dam take the Stewarts Ferry Road exit off I-40. Go south to the intersection with Bell Road and turn left. This road runs across the J. Percy Priest Dam. Just prior to reaching the dam, a drive runs off the north side of the road and leads to the parking area.

To reach the northeast side of the river, continue across the dam on Bell Road, then turn left (north) onto Dodson Chapel Road. The entrance to the drive leading to the parking lot appears immediately on the left side of the road.

For water release updates on Priest Dam, call the Corps of Engineers recorded message line at 615-883-2351. This information is also available via the Internet at www.orn.usace.army.mil/pao/lakeinfo. Follow the prompts to J. Percy Priest Lake.

# WATAUGA RIVER

## DeLorme 63

The Watauga River below Wilbur Dam is a large stream characterized by long, deep pools. In all there are just over 16 miles of trout water down to the point at which the tailwater empties into Boone Lake. The Watauga traverses Carter County in northeastern Tennessee, finally reaching the lake in Washington County.

The Watauga's tailwater gets a rather unusual start on its course. It flows out of Watauga Lake, which was built in 1948 by the TVA, through a rock tunnel under the Iron Mountains, and into Wilbur Lake. Wilbur Lake was formed in 1912 and purchased by the TVA in 1945. The water is then released from this small impoundment into the Watauga tailwater. Pulsing generators have been installed in the powerhouse to help maintain water and oxygen levels downstream, but due to the influx of water from the Doe River several miles below, neither of these has been a problem on the Watauga.

The Doe River, however, creates a problem of its own. It muddies up quickly, especially during rainy weather, and will stain the Watauga as well. While bad for the fishing, this is also harmful to the habitat due to the amount of silt it brings into the tailwater.

Along its course, the Watauga passes through an area known as Siam, then runs through the towns of Hunter and Elizabethton. Just downstream of Elizabethton the river passes the historic site at Sycamore Shoals where frontier settlers gathered before crossing the Appalachian Mountains to defeat the British at the Battle of Kings Mountain during the Revolutionary War.

Much of the country traversed by the Watauga is flat, providing gentle shoals that are easily wadable during low water. Like the South Holston, the Watauga is basically a float-fishing river at high levels, but a wader's paradise when the turbines are silent.

Watauga River

Jeff Goodwin, © The Countryman Press

The fishery has seen some ups and downs in past decades. To begin with, up through the early 1980s, surveys found that the portion of the river from Elizabethton down to Boone Lake was heavily degraded. Only the most pollution-tolerant insect life and fish species were found there. Reductions of effluents into the stream were implemented and by the end of that decade, the river had recovered to the point that the TWRA began stocking that stretch with trout. Eventually, even a Quality Trout Fishing Area with special regulations was added.

Unfortunately, in February of 2000 a fire struck the North American Rayon textile mill in Elizabethton, resulting in a major spill of chemicals in the Watauga. An estimated 24,000 trout were killed and the fishery destroyed for 10 miles downstream to Boone Lake. At the time predictions were made that the river would need a decade to recover from the disaster. Thankfully, those prognostications proved overly pessimistic. By the fall of 2001, after restocking, trout were again thriving in the lower Watauga tailwater, with no apparent after effects from the spill.

The Watauga tailwater is stocked with brown and rainbow trout annually from February through June. Fish are released as adults for put-and-take fishing, but fingerlings are also planted in the river for put-grow-and-take fishing. The TWRA has noted that there is some natural reproduction of

*The Revolutionary War mustering ground at Sycamore Shoals lies right on the bank of the Watauga tailwater.*

brown trout. Some of these browns end up being taken when they have reached weights of 3 to 9 pounds.

In the summer of 2001 brook trout also were released in the lower Watauga, downstream of Elizabethton, on an experimental basis. It is hoped that these fish will provide a put-grow-and-take fishery on this stretch of water. Any of these brookies caught outside of the Quality Trout Fishing Area must be at least 6 inches long to be harvested.

Fly-fishers will find the same insect hatches on the Watauga as are found on the nearby South Holston tailwater. The Elk Hair Caddis is popular for imitating the abundant caddis hatching during falling water levels. Sulphurs in size 16 are also present, as are midges in the summer months. When the fish start attacking the midges, flies in sizes 20 to 22 are needed.

The most popular areas for fishing on the Watauga are along the first 6 or 7 miles below Wilbur Dam down to Elizabethton. Through here Tennessee's general trout regulations apply, but there is a Quality Trout Fishing Area located farther downstream. From the Smalling Bridge down to the bridge in the village of Watauga, only artificial lures are legal, and the creel limit is 2 trout per day, which must be at least 14 inches long. From Watauga down to Boone Lake, the river continues to support trout and is again open to fishing under general regulations, but access is extremely limited and the river is not heavily fished. It is possible to float-fish through this stretch. The TVA ordinarily maintains a water-release schedule to accommodate afternoon and evening high water levels for recreational floating.

Access to the river at Wilbur Dam is available via Wilbur Dam Road to the southeast of the town of Hunter. From the point where the road crosses the river on the old metal, one-lane bridge at Siam, it follows the river upstream to the dam. There is a parking area on the southwest side of the dam, with foot trails down to the stream. On low water there is good access to the main stream and a large backwater pool here. Both offer conditions open enough for some fly-casting and limited wading access.

Back downstream at the Siam Bridge access is also good, though there is very limited parking available along the roadside. The water under the bridge is quite deep, but a shelf protrudes from the northwest shore offering some wading access. At the first bend below the bridge the water shallows up for better wading. Overall, this upper portion of the river is better for float-fishing, even on low water levels. To reach Wilbur Dam and the Siam Bridge, travel south from TN 91 in Hunter via Siam Road. At the northwest end of the Siam Bridge turn left onto Wilbur Dam Road.

The next downstream public access is found in the village of Hunter. Where Old TN 91 crosses the river there is a TWRA parking area under the southern end of the span. Besides parking spaces it offers a canoe launch. On low water levels it is possible to wade this entire area, both upstream and downstream of the bridge.

Probably the most convenient area for wade-fishing on low water levels is found in the city park along West Riverside Drive in Elizabethton. There is easy access, plenty of parking, and good wading shoals along about a mile of the facility's paved bike/walking trail on the south side of the stream. This trail continues downstream of the open parkland as well. The river features mild ripples interspersed with deeper runs through here. This park is located just west of the TN 400 bridge over the Watauga in downtown Elizabethton.

The next access point is at Sycamore Shoals State Park on US 321, at the western edge of Elizabethton. A long, broad, and shallow stretch of water upstream of the actual shoals can be waded on low water, plus there is shore and wading access to Sycamore Shoals itself.

Access to the river at Sycamore Shoals can be a bit tricky, however. The state park is open only from 8 AM until 4:30 PM daily, which can be a problem for anglers, especially in the summer months. Fortunately, Joe LaPorte Jr. City Recreation Area lies adjacent to the eastern side of the state park. It is possible to park in the lot for the swimming pool and tennis courts there, which is open from dawn to sundown. From there, get on the state park hiking trail that runs 200 yards to the river. Turn downstream and it is ½ mile to the shoals from the parking area.

Two final possible access points are located farther downriver. The Smalling Road and Watauga Road bridges lie at either end of the Quality Trout Fishing Area to the northwest of Elizabethton.

For details on water releases from Watauga and Wilbur Dams, call the TVA message center at 1-800-238-2264. Press 4 for water releases. The code for Watauga Dam is 2, and the code for Wilbur Dam is 42. This information is also available online at www.lakeinfo.tva.gov/.

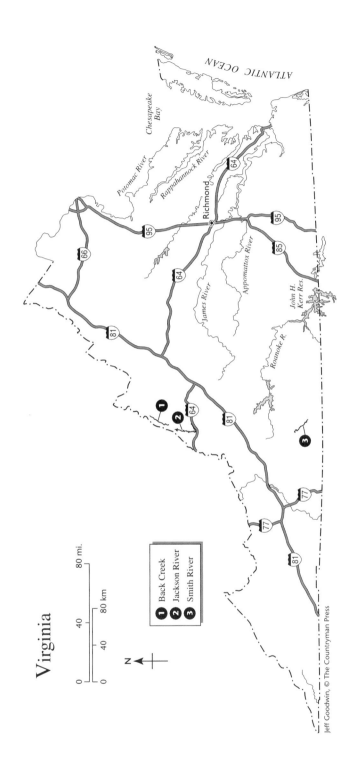

Virginia

ATLANTIC OCEAN

Chesapeake
Bay

Potomac River

Rappahannock River

Richmond

95

64

95

85

66

64

Appomattox River

James River

John H.
Kerr Res.

81

Roanoke R.

64

81

77

77

81

① Back Creek
② Jackson River
③ Smith River

N

0    40    80 mi.

0    40    80 km

# CHAPTER 11

# Virginia

Virginia is the northernmost of the states covered in this book and, due to the position of the Allegheny and Blue Ridge Mountains within its boundaries, has some of the most beautiful natural trout waters of the region. In all, the Old Dominion contains 2,800 miles of trout streams, of which only 600 miles require stocking to supplement natural reproduction. These include both high-elevation freestone streams and spring creeks flowing through lower valleys. The higher-elevation streams are noted for having the best native brook trout fishing south of New England.

With such outstanding natural trout water, it is hardly surprising that Virginia's tailwater fisheries have not received as much publicity or cornered as large a share of fishing interest as have the man-made trout streams of other southern states. Contributing to this situation as well is the relative scarcity of tailwater fisheries in Virginia. The state contains only three such flows: Back Creek, the Jackson River, and the Smith River.

Another stream that is sometimes lumped with the tailwaters is the North River below Elkhorn Lake in Augusta County. Although it bears some similarity to a true tailwater, it is not generally considered one by state fisheries managers. A 1½-mile stretch of this river in the George Washington National Forest between Elkhorn Lake and the Staunton City Reservoir is managed as a delayed-harvest stream. However, the North River is a trout stream upriver of Elkhorn Lake as well as below the dam. The 54-acre lake is not particularly deep, and it exerts very little influence on the river downstream of the dam. For these reasons, the North does not actually qualify as a true tailwater fishery.

Year-round trout fishing is legal in all of Virginia's waters, including the tailwater flows. The standard Virginia creel limit for trout is 6 fish per day with a minimum size limit of 7 inches. All three of the state's tailwaters, however, are managed under special regulations, which are covered in the appropriate sections.

To fish for trout in Virginia, a regular fishing license is required. If you are fishing in any of the state's designated stocked trout waters, an additional permit is needed. However, fishing is allowed in these waters from June 15 each year to September 30 without the special trout license. Finally, when fishing on national forest lands, a special national forest fishing permit is necessary. An exception is the Jackson River. Although a portion of it crosses the George Washington National Forest, no permit is required.

Virginia fishing licenses may be purchased by calling 1-800-986-2628. A major credit card is needed for this service.

With such a maze of permits and the possibility of changes in the regulations, it is wise to check the latest edition of "Virginia Freshwater & Saltwater Fishing Regulations" before venturing onto the tailwaters of the Old Dominion. The booklet is available at many retail sporting-goods outlets or by contacting the Virginia Department of Game and Inland Fisheries (VDGIF). Their phone number in Richmond is 804-367-1000. The fishing regulations may also be viewed online by visiting the VDGIF home page at www.dgif.state.va.us/fishing/; follow the prompt for the "Fishing Law Digest."

## BACK CREEK

### DeLorme 65

Undoubtedly the least known of the tailwater trout fisheries is Back Creek in Bath County. Located in the Allegheny highlands in west-central Virginia, Back Creek flows from north to south through a scenic valley less than 10 miles east of the West Virginia border.

The history of the Back Creek tailwater is a short one. The headwaters have always been good trout water, but the lower section did not come into its own until the Virginia Power Company created the Bath County Pump Storage Station reservoir and power station on the creek in the mid-1980s. At that time the company also created a recreation area below the dam, as

## Back Creek

0      1      2 mi.

0     1     2 km

N

Bath County
Pump Storage
Station Reservoir

Beaver Run Bridge

Haul Road Bridge

Virginia Power Company
Recreation Area

600

Back Creek

39

Mountain
Grove

Jackson River

39

220

Blowing Springs
Campground

Back Creek

Jackson River

39

Warm Springs

Jeff Goodwin, © The Countryman Press

well as making extensive modifications to the stream itself. As a result, the creek has more holding water for trout in its tailwater portion than existed before the work began.

For several years after the creek below the reservoir dam was opened to fishing, it was stocked only with fingerling trout. The idea was to create a trophy brown trout fishery, so the regulations mandated single-hooked artificial lures only and a daily creel limit of 2 trout, which had to be at least 16 inches long. Fishing was permitted on the creek year-round. These rules were in effect from the Beaver Run Bridge on County Road (CR) 600 (Big Back Creek Road) just below the dam downstream for 1½ miles to the Haul Road Bridge (the next bridge downstream, also on CR 600).

Unfortunately, the water coming through the 60-foot-high dam was too warm in the summer for the trout to carry over in large numbers. As a result, in the fall of 1992 Back Creek was changed to a delayed-harvest stream. Under this management scheme the portion of the tailwater below the dam is heavily stocked with catchable-sized trout in the fall, winter, and spring. From October 1 until May 31 each year, fishing is permitted under catch-and-release regulations with only single-hooked artificial lures allowed. From June 1 to September 30 the stream reverts to general trout regulations, using the state creel limit and allowing any type of bait or lures. Also, during the period when delayed-harvest rules are in effect, a special trout license is required for fishing the Back Creek tailwater. The resulting fishery has proved to be a popular one that provides quality angling experiences to a large number of fishers each year.

From its beginning at the foot of the dam, Back Creek's tailwater is never more than a medium to large mountain stream. It averages no more than 25 feet wide along all of its trout water. Even during releases from the power-house, it is still possible to wade portions of Back Creek. When the water is low, virtually the entire run provides good wade- and fly-fishing. Most of the trout encountered are freshly stocked rainbows, but some fish do carry over, so it is possible to take a larger brown or rainbow. Also, expect to see some smallmouth and rock bass in all areas of the stream.

Once below the lower CR 600 bridge at the end of the Virginia Power Company's property, Back Creek is open to fishing as "designated trout water." This is the Old Dominion fisheries managers' way of identifying stocked trout water. Back Creek receives plantings of mature rainbow trout through here in the spring and again during the fall. No trout are stocked during the summer, when water temperatures sometimes soar above the tol-

*At any water level, Back Creek is only a medium-to-large-sized stream in its tailwater section.*

erance level of the fish. There are some holdover browns that attain respectable size through here, however.

In spring, Back Creek is noted for its mayfly hatches. Quill Gordons and March browns are reported to be important. More often, fly-casters use attractor patterns in sizes 14 to 16. Royal Wulffs and Adams patterns are good for this fishing. Through the open, meadowlike areas of the Virginia Power Company's land, grasshopper imitations work well in late spring. For fishers wanting to challenge the brown trout in Back Creek, in-line spinners, spinner-fly combinations, or—for the fly-caster—minnow-mimicking streamers are appropriate.

Access to the Back Creek tailwater begins at the Beaver Run Bridge below the dam. No angling is allowed in the tailrace upstream of this bridge. There is no parking allowed at this point either, but just downstream is the entrance to the Virginia Power Company Recreation Area. Besides offering parking (for a small fee), the recreation area has a campground, playgrounds, picnic pavilions, and two warm-water lakes (the smaller of which has a swimming area).

At the second bridge on CR 600, at the lower end of the Virginia Power

Company land, there is a parking area beside the old bridge (which is no longer in use). This is an ideal spot to begin a day of wading upstream.

The next 8 miles down Back Creek along CR 600 and VA 39 are on private property and are not open to public fishing. The creek here is not large enough for float-fishing, so this portion is off-limits. From the VA 39 bridge, located to the southwest of the crossroads of Mountain Grove, the creek flows for 1¼ miles along VA 39 through U.S. Forest Service land. Through here there are a number of roadside turnouts, a water-gauging station, and the forest service's Blowing Springs Campground. Below the campground, a foot trail along the shore leads down into the Back Creek Gorge portion of the tailwater. In the portion of Back Creek on national forest land trout are stocked from November through May 15 each year, with the heaviest releases of fish taking place in the spring months.

To find Back Creek, take VA 39 west from its junction with US 220 near the village of Warm Springs. Continue past the Blowing Springs Campground to the intersection with CR 600, then turn right (north) to reach the delayed-harvest portion of the stream and the Virginia Power Company Recreation Area.

# JACKSON RIVER

## *DeLorme 52*

The Jackson River below Lake Moomaw in Allegheny County is Virginia's newest tailwater trout fishery. It was created when the river was first stocked in 1989. It is also the site of the Old Dominion's oldest ongoing controversy over trout fishing.

The Army Corps of Engineers first received congressional authorization for a dam on the Jackson in 1946. No work was begun, however, and in the 1950s the VDGIF purchased 18,000 acres of land, which included 12 miles of the river, to create the Gathright Wildlife Management Area. When the corps actually received funds for the lake project in the mid-1960s, Virginia's fisheries managers and many sportsmen opposed the construction of the dam. Basically, they did not want to lose the Gathright Wildlife Management Area or the free-flowing river.

In the end, the Gathright Dam was built, impounding 2,530 acres of water in Lake Moomaw. As part of a mitigation agreement, however, the corps invested $10 million in a 260-foot mixing tower that releases water

Jackson River

Gathright Dam

Lake Moomaw

687

605

638

Johnson Spring Access ■ Natural Well

Jackson River

687

220

600

666

640

641

Old Smith Bridge Access ■

Indian Draft Access ■

North Smith Bridge Road

220

600

687

Petticoat Junction Access ■

Clearwater Park ●

N

0        1        2 mi.

0    1    2 km

64
60
Covington ●

64 60 220

Jeff Goodwin, © The Countryman Press

*The Indian Draft Access offers a couple of hundred yards
of wadable water at lower river levels.*

from nine different depths in the reservoir. This creates ideal temperature
and oxygen levels for trout in the Jackson tailwater. Oddly enough, Gathright Dam does not have electric-generation capacity, thus no powerhouse
or turbines.

Even before the dam was closed, however, landowners along the river
downstream began efforts to block the stocking of trout and the use of the
river by the public. In October 1978, the river was declared navigable by the
Corps of Engineers since the stream had been used for commercial hauling
in historical times. This opened the way for the public to float the Jackson.
The landowners appealed the decision and the battle dragged on in court
until 1984, when the corps' decision was upheld. Meanwhile, in 1981, work
on Gathright Dam was completed and the lake filled.

At this point the landowners changed direction and challenged public
use of the river based on crown grants made by George III before the American Revolution. These had given grantees the title to the riverbanks, the bottoms, and the fish in the stream. The present landowners contended that they
still held that right. Under their interpretation, only the water in the river
could be claimed by the state of Virginia.

Finally in 1989, the VDGIF stocked the first trout in the Jackson River.

But the controversy did not end. In 1991 a landowner sued a guide and his clients for floating and fishing through his property. In the end, the landowner lost the case, but the ruling only established that the public could float down the Jackson. Unless you really enjoy court proceedings, you'd still be wise to skip fishing when floating across posted areas of the river (particularly the posted lands just above the public access point at Johnson Spring) until the courts decide the issue once and for all. And, of course, it is certainly illegal to go ashore on any of the posted lands. The VDGIF has posted signs at public access areas recommending that you have written permission when fishing on private, posted land and oral permission before fishing in private areas where there are no signs.

With all the controversy and haggling over the Jackson tailwaters, you might be inclined to simply forget this stream and go fishing elsewhere. On the other hand, many anglers in the Old Dominion now consider the Jackson the state's premier tailwater trout fishery. In the first two years of stocking, 57,000 browns and 30,000 rainbow trout were released into the river. Another 53,000 trout of both species, including 5,000 Kamloops-strain rainbows, were planted in 1993. The Kamloops rainbows originated in southern British Columbia and are noted for attaining large size. Presently, brown trout in the 14- to 20-inch range are showing up regularly on the Jackson tailwater, as are 10- to 17-inch rainbows.

The VDGIF originally envisioned a trophy brown trout fishery developing in this tailwater, but that idea is being rethought. In fact, the rainbows are showing much better growth in the river than are their European cousins. This is attributed to the scarcity of forage fish. The carnivorous browns are having difficulty finding much to eat, while the very fertile aquatic insect habitat is providing plenty of food for the rainbows.

One side effect of the continuing controversy over access to the Jackson River is that the VDIGF has ended all trout stocking in the tailwater. Fortunately, that has not ended the fishing. Both rainbow and brown trout spawn in the river. Recent state surveys have shown that the populations of both species, which declined when stocking ceased, have now rebounded to levels comparable to when stocking occurred.

The entire 19-mile length of the Jackson tailwater from Moomaw Lake down to the town of Covington is open to fishing under special regulations. Any type of bait, lure, or fly is allowed, but only 4 fish per day may be kept and those must be over 12 inches in length.

The Jackson River is a very popular destination for fly-casters. As mentioned earlier, the insect population is excellent in the stream, which adds to its appeal with the long-rod anglers.

The portion of the river just below the dam at Moomaw is noted for producing large hatches of black flies, especially early in the year. These are very small bugs, requiring midge imitations in the size 22 range. Farther downstream, blue-winged olives, caddis, and true midges all appear on the water. In the fall, terrestrial patterns will attract some trout as well.

Although much of the Jackson is wadable during low water, float-fishing is the most popular method of tackling the stream. Five public access points are spaced at intervals to accommodate that activity. All of these are in the George Washington National Forest but, as mentioned in the summary of Virginia angling regulations, a national forest fishing permit is not required for fishing on the Jackson.

To reach Gathright Dam take US 220 north from the town of Covington. At the village of Clearwater Park, turn northwest onto County Road (CR) 687 (Jackson River Road). Next, turn west onto CR 638 (Natural Well Road) near the crossroads of Natural Well. A turn north onto CR 666 (East Morris Hill Road) is next; then, at ½ mile, head northeast on CR 605 (Cole Mountain Road). A ¾-mile paved spur road runs down to the foot of the dam at an intersection marked with a MAINTENANCE AREA & DOWNSTREAM FISHING sign.

This first access point is a Corps of Engineers area with a parking lot and rest rooms. There is roughly ¼ mile of access. The site is very popular with wading fly-casters.

The Johnson Springs Access is located about 2½ miles downstream of Gathright Dam, just off Natural Wells Road (CR 638) at 0.3 mile west of Jackson River Road. This site has a canoe landing and parking area, but is on a deep bend of the river that offers very limited wading access.

Farther downstream the Smith Bridge Access offers better wading conditions. It lies at the end of North Smith Bridge Road, 0.65 mile east of Jackson River Road. There is a wadable stretch of water just under the abandoned metal bridge over the river, as well as for a short distance downstream. Parking areas and a canoe launch are also available here.

The next public area to the south is at Indian Draft Access on Jackson River Road near its intersection with Indian Draft Road. Parking, a canoe launch, and limited, wadable shoals are found here.

Finally, at Petticoat Junction Access on Jackson River Road in the Clearwater Park community there is another canoe-launch facility, parking lot, and some wadable area under the highway bridge. The access point is situated on Mays Lane (gravel) just east of the Jackson River Road bridge.

The trout water on the Jackson ends in Covington at the WESTVACO pulp mill's low-head dam.

Water-release schedules for Gathright Dam are available by calling the Corps of Engineers' recorded message line at 540-965-4117.

## SMITH RIVER

### *DeLorme 26*

Not only is the Smith River Virginia's oldest tailwater trout fishery, but it can also support the claim of being the best wild brown trout stream east of the Mississippi. Upon first glance, however, it is hard to conceive of this river as

Jeff Goodwin, © The Countryman Press

a world-class trout stream. Much of its course is through a suburban-to-urban environment, it is filled with litter, and it flows sluggishly through the lowlands of Franklin and Henry Counties in south-central Virginia.

Yet the 45-degree waters released through Philpott Dam create ideal trout conditions for 20 miles downstream to the town of Martinsville. Along this stretch, brown trout have been thriving and reproducing since the 1970s. In fact, the VDGIF estimates that the Smith River comprises fully 60 percent of all the water in Virginia that contains naturally reproducing brown trout.

Recognition of the Smith as a haven for big bruiser brown trout came first in the summer of 1974, when the Virginia state record for the species was broken three different times on this tailwater. At the end of that summer the mark stood at 14 pounds, 6 ounces. After a 5-year pause, the Smith yielded a new record fish to Bill Nease of Martinsville, who landed an 18-pound, 11-ounce brown. Just to prove his catch was no fluke, within two months he had also caught a 17-pound, 12-ounce brown. Since those halcyon days, the Smith has continued to produce large numbers of brown trout weighing 10 pounds or more.

One unfortunate footnote concerning the Virginia brown trout record is that Nease's catch is now described as the "historical record" for the species. A number of years ago the VDGIF revamped its record book because of some older, questionable records. Though there was no controversy connected with the Nease fish, it got swept into the historical category anyway.

Soon after the impounding of Philpott Reservoir in the 1950s, the Smith River was stocked with large numbers of brook and rainbow trout. Those plantings soon switched over to strictly rainbow trout. Still, it was the browns that proved most at home in the river. Almost immediately they began spawning throughout the tailwater. Today there is some indication that the rainbows may also be spawning here, but the Smith is firmly established as a blue-ribbon brown trout stream.

While the Smith produces lots of browns of trophy size, it no longer gives up fish in the 14- to 18-pound range as it did in the 1970s. Several factors are suspected of contributing to this decline in monster fish. Early on in the operation of the powerhouse at Philpott Dam, large numbers of alewives were sucked through the turbines to float helplessly downstream. The brown trout gorged themselves on these drifting baitfish. Then, in the 1980s, the alewives quit coming through the dam for unknown reasons.

During the mid-1980s a couple of major floods struck the Smith, and these are thought to have washed some fish downstream. Finally, there can

*Several of the bridges over the Smith River between Philpott Dam and Fieldale offer convenient access to the water.*

be no doubt that the increased fishing pressure and the high level of expertise among spin-fishers have also dented the big-fish population in recent years.

Knowing that the Smith River tailwater contains quality trout, however, does not make the fishing easy. The Smith is a fairly wide stream, often spreading to 100 feet or more even during low water. Its course is a continuous string of riffles and pools, often so calm that they look as though there is no water movement at all. Almost all of the water is wadable, for even many of the deeper pools are edged by shallow, gravel shelves.

The long flat stretches of water make the fishing difficult. Under these conditions the trout are easy to spook. Even wading can be an ordeal because any waves you create travel far ahead of you to send the fish scurrying for cover.

When fishing the Smith, the rule of thumb is to cast to the middle of the stream for the freshly stocked trout, but to work the deeper holes along the shore—particularly those shaded by vegetation—for the larger fish. Do not overlook visible holding areas around logs, rocks, or even large items of trash, such as auto tires. They will often have a trout or two hiding close against them. On low water, flies need to be extremely small and spinners need to be fished very slowly to keep from spooking the trout.

The entire tailwater of the Smith River is open to year-round fishing, but anglers encounter three distinct sections on the stream. The first of these is composed of the initial 3 miles of water from Philpott Dam down to the mouth of Towne Creek (the VDGIF uses this spelling, but some maps use Town). Through here the water releases scour away much of the insect life in the stream, leaving trout forage in short supply. Thus, stocked rainbows make up the bulk of the fish encountered. Open under general state trout fishing rules, this part of the tailwater is stocked from November through mid-May each year.

Next, there is a 3-mile stretch downstream from Towne Creek to the CR 666 (Trent Hill Road) crossing at the village of Bassett that is open to fishing under special regulations. Through here only single-hooked artificial lures are allowed and the creel limit is 2 fish per day of a minimum size of 16 inches. The quality trout area receives no stockings. Decreased levels of scouring provide more food for fish in this part of the flow, so bigger brown trout begin to show up regularly. This is also the most aesthetically pleasing portion of the Smith, with wooded shorelines, rocky shoals, and shaded pools.

On the rest of the 14 miles of tailwater down to Martinsville, general Virginia trout regulations and creel limits again apply. This section is stocked with rainbow trout at higher levels than the upper river, with releases taking place from October through May. The heaviest plantings take place in March through May. This is also the area of the stream noted for producing most of the large brown trout today.

When the turbines begin to run at the Philpott Dam powerhouse, drawing water from 200 feet below the surface of the reservoir, the Smith River is transformed. The pastoral pools change suddenly to raging torrents. This is not a stream to wade during high water. Near the dam, a 3-foot wall of water will sweep down the river after the warning siren at the dam sounds. When power generation starts, keep above the high-water mark even when bank-fishing. It is possible to leapfrog ahead of the rising water to get in more fishing before the surge gets downstream. The rising water takes an hour to get to Towne Creek, 2 hours to North Bassett, 3 hours to South Bassett, and 5 hours to reach the village of Koehler.

The periods of falling water levels, just after the end of power generation, are the easiest times to fool the really lunker-sized trout on this tailwater. The water is slightly stained at these times, making the fish less wary. Casting Rapala-type minnow lures and bait-fishing with spring lizards or night crawlers are popular ways to target the big trout below the below the special regulation area at the dam. This action continues when the river level is falling. It generally takes the flow about 1½ hours to get back down to ideal low-water fishing levels.

Once the river is back at low levels, it is again the domain of fly-casters. The hatches on the Smith River are so massive in May and June that they have become legendary in the state. Kicking off with the appearance of Sulfur duns in the late-spring afternoons, other insects soon appear, including Light Cahills, Hendricksons, caddis, and olive midges. In each case, however, the Smith's brown trout are noted for being finicky about what they eat. They will target the predominant insect to the exclusion of any of different size and color. And the size is often quite small, requiring hooks in the 16 to 20 range. About the only fly noted for attracting much surface action when no active rises are visible is the Blue-Winged Olive in sizes 16 to 26.

Later in the year, beginning in September and October, terrestrial insects become important trout attractors on the Smith. The best imitations are beetles and ants. Cinnamon or black ant flies in sizes ranging down to 26 are deadly on the browns and rainbows.

There is access to both shores of the Smith at the foot of Philpott Dam. On the southern side of the river, a recreation area contains a parking lot and the Smith River Trail, which runs downstream for ½ mile. It is possible to walk along the trail and spot fish in the clear water at nongeneration times.

To reach this access, take CR 904 (Philpott Dam Road) for ¾ mile north off VA 57 (Fairy Stone Park Highway). Next, turn right onto CR 905 (Dam Spillway Road) and proceed ¾ mile to the parking area.

On the northern shore of the river, ½ mile of land is open to the public. Parking, canoe launches, and rest rooms are provided here. To reach this park, take CR 727 (Stoneybrook Drive) west from the CR 674 bridge over the Smith. At 2¼ miles the road changes from pavement to gravel. The last ½ mile of road is on power-company land, but before this point there are some roadside turnouts and access to the water along CR 727. After this point there are a number of bridges across the river down to Martinsville. Most of these offer limited parking and river access. The most accessible are on CR 674 at the crossroads of Philpott and in the town of Bassett at the VA 57 and CR 673 (Bullock Drive) bridges.

There are two other points of access near the US 220 crossing to the west of the town of Collinsville. Roughly ½ mile north of US 220, The Great Road (CR 683) runs east off VA 57A (Riverside Drive). Where the road loops behind a CPFilm plant, there is a stretch of suburban parkland with picnic tables along the river. Through here there are long stretches of wadable sand flats, broken by several mild shoals.

The other location is 0.9 mile south of the US 220 bridge and to the east of North River Road, on Shadyview Road. Near the dead end of Shadyview there are a couple of roadside turnouts that provide parking and access to the water. It is possible to wade upstream from this point through several good shoals that stretch all the way to the US 220 bridge.

Additionally, just upstream of the town of Fieldale, CR 682 (River Road) parallels the southwestern side of the river and has a number of roadside turnouts providing access to the water.

For information on water-release schedules at Philpott Dam, call the Corps of Engineers' 24-hour recorded message line at 276-629-2432.

# CHAPTER 12

# The Murky Crystal Ball

T t would be nice if the future of Dixie's tailwater trout fisheries were as crystal clear as the water flowing down many of those rivers. Unfortunately, guessing is not a very exact science.

It can, however, be surmised that the great age of dam building is over in the southeastern United States. Although there will probably be a few more large reservoirs created in coming decades, the environmental impact of losing our few remaining free-flowing rivers is becoming too high a price to pay for such projects. The trend in the U.S. is toward removing dams, rather than building more.

At the same time, the tailwater trout fisheries that we already have will obviously become more crowded with anglers. The Sun Belt states of the South are growing rapidly in population, and many of these new residents will become trout anglers looking for a place to wet a line. Wild mountain streams are a joy to fish, but they are also small, delicate, and difficult to reach. On the other hand, tailwaters are large, produce big fish, are relatively resilient, and are usually close to major population centers.

So it is a safe bet that our tailwater trout streams will become more popular in the future. This also means that more care will be needed to protect them. The downside of these rivers being near anglers is that they are also close to many potential points of runoff pollution. These flows are manmade trout fisheries, but they need to be protected from man-made problems as well.

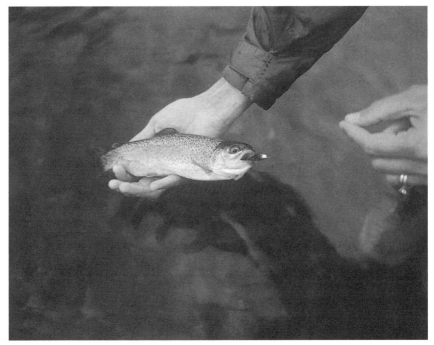

*Can anglers provide enough protection to Dixie's tailwater trout fisheries
to ensure that the resources will last?*

Another by-product of creating these great tailwater trout rivers is the appearance of the Trout Unlimited chapters and fly-fishing clubs in the metropolitan areas surrounding many of them. Getting involved with these groups is one way the average angler can ensure that the resources endure. These clubs and chapters are the local watchdogs that monitor and fight for the individual rivers and fisheries.

For more information on Trout Unlimited chapters in your area, write to Trout Unlimited, 1500 Wilson Boulevard, Suite 310, Arlington, VA 22209-2404, call 703-522-0200, or visit their web site at www.tu.org/. To find out about fly-fishing clubs in your vicinity, contact the Federation of Fly Fishers, P.O. Box 1595, Bozeman, MT 59771, call 406-585-7592, or visit them on-line at www.fedflyfishers.org/.

# Index

# C